Palgrave Gothic

Series Editor

Clive Bloom
English and American Studies
Middlesex University, UK

This series of gothic books is the first to treat the genre in its many inter-related, global and 'extended' cultural aspects to show how the taste for the medieval and the sublime gave rise to a perverse taste for terror and horror and how that taste became not only international (with a huge fan base in places such as South Korea and Japan) but also the sensibility of the modern age, changing our attitudes to such diverse areas as the nature of the artist, the meaning of drug abuse and the concept of the self. The series is accessible but scholarly, with referencing kept to a minimum and theory contextualised where possible. All the books are readable by an intelligent student or a knowledgeable general reader interested in the subject.

Editorial Advisory Board
Dr Ian Conrich, University of South Australia
Barry Forshaw, author/journalist, UK
Professor Gregg Kucich, University of Notre Dame, USA
Professor Gina Wisker, University of Brighton, UK
Dr Catherine Wynne, University of Hull, UK
Dr Alison Peirse, University of Yorkshire, UK

More information about this series at
http://www.springer.com/series/14698

Gina Wisker

Contemporary Women's Gothic Fiction

Carnival, Hauntings and Vampire Kisses

Gina Wisker
Centre for Learning & Teaching
University of Brighton
East Sussex, United Kingdom
University of South Africa
University of Southern Queensland

Palgrave Gothic
ISBN 978-1-349-67168-7   ISBN 978-1-137-30349-3 (eBook)
DOI 10.1057/978-1-137-30349-3

Library of Congress Control Number: 2016953848

© The Editor(s) (if applicable) and The Author(s) 2016
The author(s) has/have asserted their right(s) to be identified as the author(s) of this work in accordance with the Copyright, Designs and Patents Act 1988.
This work is subject to copyright. All rights are solely and exclusively licensed by the Publisher, whether the whole or part of the material is concerned, specifically the rights of translation, reprinting, reuse of illustrations, recitation, broadcasting, reproduction on microfilms or in any other physical way, and transmission or information storage and retrieval, electronic adaptation, computer software, or by similar or dissimilar methodology now known or hereafter developed.
The use of general descriptive names, registered names, trademarks, service marks, etc. in this publication does not imply, even in the absence of a specific statement, that such names are exempt from the relevant protective laws and regulations and therefore free for general use.
The publisher, the authors and the editors are safe to assume that the advice and information in this book are believed to be true and accurate at the date of publication. Neither the publisher nor the authors or the editors give a warranty, express or implied, with respect to the material contained herein or for any errors or omissions that may have been made.

Cover illustration: © Stuart Aylmer / Alamy Stock Photo

Printed on acid-free paper

This Palgrave Macmillan imprint is published by Springer Nature
The registered company is Macmillan Publishers Ltd.
The registered company address is: The Campus, 4 Crinan Street, London, N1 9XW, United Kingdom

Acknowledgements

It has been a really enjoyable experience writing this book and I thank colleagues at Palgrave Macmillan and Clive Bloom for their patience and support, and the hard work of Michelle Bernard, Alison Curry and Liam Wisker in various aspects of research and finessing. My Gothic literature students at the universities of Brighton, Anglia Ruskin and Cambridge have been wonderful in responding to early drafts of parts of the book as we've discussed the literature, and friends in the Contemporary Women's Writing Association, the International Association for the Fantastic in the Arts and the International Gothic Association have shared insights which have made this a better contribution to Gothic criticism. Finally, thanks to Roxy who sat through all of it just hoping for a walk.

Contents

1 Introduction   1

2 Angela Carter: Living in Gothic Times   33

3 Margaret Atwood and Canadian Women's Gothic—Spite, Lies, Split Selves and Self-Deception   63

4 Cultural Haunting: Toni Morrison and Tananarive Due   91

5 Postcolonial and Cultural Haunting Revenants—Letting the 'Right' Ones in   117

6 Testing the Fabric of Bluebeard's Castle: Postcolonial Reconfigurations, Demythologising, Re-Mythologising and Shape-Shifting   133

7 Vampire Bites   157

8 Vampire Kisses   187

9	Ghostings and Hauntings: Splintering the Fabric of Domestic Gothic	207
10	Opening the Gates to Darkness: Gothic Diversity	235

Bibliography 253

Index 261

CHAPTER 1

Introduction

Contemporary Gothic has made horror respectable. As a literary form studied in universities, enamoured of critics, when contemporary Gothic combines the edgy enlightenment of queer theory, and postcolonialism, with the multiple perspectives and angles of diversity of origin, sexuality and culture, this broad scope offers a disconcerting enrichment. Gothic is everywhere. Through its relentless questioning, it exposes dis-ease and discomfort, sometimes only to reinforce the complacencies it disrupts, but more thrillingly, very often leaving writers and readers more aware and less comfortable. As Marie Mulvey-Roberts comments, 'Gothic life, like that of a giant poisonous plant with far-reaching tendrils, has found its sustenance by feeding off the credulities of its reader. This hot-house hybrid is constantly mutating, making new growths out of old as in its propensity for parody and pastiche. What remains consistent, according to Angela Carter), is the retention of "a singular moral function—that of provoking unease"' (Mulvey-Roberts 1998, p. xvii).

So why do contemporary women write the Gothic? And what are the essential links between feminist perspectives and critiques, and the contemporary Gothic written by women?

I want this book to explore and celebrate contemporary women's literary Gothic, the contradictions and the richness of ways in which contemporary women writers, both established and new, conventional and radical, use the opportunities afforded by the Gothic to engage with culture, imagination and their arguments. The Gothic undercuts and destabilises single readings, as it does its own conventions, and in this spirit I will question how we read them, draw attention to an ongoing dialogue between the texts and indicate what readings are offered by a growing body of critics, popular and academic. We need to appreciate the diverse panoply of the Gothic which has been seen perversely as both ubiquitous and negligible in contemporary society and contemporary writing.

So why is the literary Gothic the focus of this book? It is because it has designs upon us. The Gothic, at least in its literary form, shakes up and problematises tired ways of perceiving and expressing normality by disrupting the everyday world of residual compliance. It disturbs, upsets, ironises and parodies our deeply held beliefs and our safe but constraining narratives of, among others, progress, identity, power, family, safety and love. Many of those issues have a particularly nuanced meaning for, and effect on, women, and contemporary women writers of the Gothic are particularly concerned with those bedazzling and constrictive narratives of security, safety and collusion which society peddles and which the Gothic undercuts and queries. Dis-ease and uncertainty are key coordinates in Gothic literature. Like bees and wasps fertilising the garden, its disturbance is, I argue, ultimately good for us because it shakes us out of blinkered complacencies and encourages questioning. Even the unpalatable insights the Gothic serves us can be fruitful. However, like wasps in particular, it can pack a cruel sting, since defamiliarisation, instability and contradiction are often uncomfortable. As such, the Gothic can be transformative, since the act of destabilising can trigger critical or even promote new radical thinking. Not surprisingly, it might not be welcome in certain repressive regimes. Owing to this critical edge, it causes us to rethink and reconsider the world around us. Much of its current popularity, even necessity in terms of literary study, derives precisely from that sting, that disturbance which leads to transformative thinking.

There are several voices in this book. One is my own, because much of what I am discussing is my own response to the texts and authors I have chosen and my response to developments in contemporary women's Gothic, based on my reading of texts and critics, and from discussions with students over the years. The word 'we' has been used to indicate how we are part of a readership with rights to comment on these texts, which facilitate our engagement with cultural and personal issues. I use 'we' too in recognition of the readers, critics and students who might find this book useful. An academic scholarly voice is focalised in the expectation that this book will be part of a useful, informed and ongoing critical discussion with other scholars in this rapidly growing field.

In discussing contemporary women's Gothic writing, I begin with some general thoughts regarding assumptions about the Gothic, its reception and sets of definitions. I am also arguing for the value of the Gothic as a contemporary mode of expression and exploration and its penchant for articulating concerns which really matter. First, there is an issue concerning the characteristics of contemporary women's Gothic writing, plus the nuances that women writers might bring to the Gothic, whether they are using it as a crucial, critical vehicle to explore issues which beset us, or just as a popular fictional mode of choice. The latter might suggest frivolity, which is not applicable to the works I am dealing with here, which engage with issues of particular concerns to women and men, for whom gender interacts with power, culture, society and the self, both with and through representation. While I mention and explore some writers who produce a rather conventional version of Gothic in their works, I am more concerned with women writers who engage with confusions, transformations, troublesome paradoxical experiences and challenges to their way of being. Through a set of general definitions, the continuities of the Gothic will emerge, alongside some of its new emanations. For this there will be an interaction between the familiar and that which undergoes change in terms of context, location, time and perspective.

After the general introductory discussion, the book continues by exploring the work of established figures who have received a great deal of critical attention, including Margaret Atwood, Angela Carter and Toni Morrison. It suggests ways in which these highly respected writers, who are cornerstones of contemporary women's writing of the twentieth and twenty-first centuries, use and develop forms and expressions provided by the literary Gothic in order to argue their points about power, identity, relationships, culture and history. At the same time, they offer a combination of established and new perspectives, new versions of reality and sometimes potential new futures. I also introduce some newer writers who are worthy of greater appreciation and who revive familiar Gothic forms often for different ends. Several are from postcolonial contexts, including Shani Mootoo, Nalo Hopkinson, Erna Brodber, Ana Lily Amirpour, Helen Oyeyemi and Beth Yahp. Some have developed that favourite genre for women writers, the ghost story, as do Susan Hill, Kate Mosse, Helen Dunmore and Catherine Lim. Others use the figures of the vampire or the werewolf to explore lesbian relationships, question definitions of normativity and undercut beliefs about mothering, along with other conventional behaviours for women.

Just a couple of weeks ago, a non-literature colleague asked me, 'What do you mean by the Gothic?' I remember asking myself, where does one begin, since Gothic is actually so many different things, crossing numerous disciplines, such as architecture, art and film, discourses and even lifestyle choices.

As Catherine Spooner puts it when considering fashion and music, 'Like a malevolent virus, Gothic narratives have escaped the confines of literature and spread across disciplinary boundaries to infect all kinds of media, from fashion and advertising to the way contemporary events are constructed in mass culture' (2006, p. 8). The rich variations of Gothic influence on culture, clothes, furniture and music are sometimes shown in fashion choice, or elsewhere in deliberate challenge to more prosaic conventional forms, and sometimes both of these together. These versions are also enacted through the exploration of Gothic subcodes of a broad range of alternative sexualities (particularly queer Gothic), and occasionally exploratory, celebratory, even dangerous sexual exchanges moving into and/or exposing sado-masochism and pornography. These include many of Angela Carter's short stories, and her *The Sadeian Woman* (1978), as well as some radical lesbian Gothic vampire tales, some heterosexual erotic vampire romance and so on. The Gothic has proved itself to be more than a reflection of social anxieties, though it does engage with our secret fears and 'provides a language and a lexicon through which anxieties both personal and collective can be narrativized' (Spooner 2006, p. 9). Undoubtedly, Gothic is engaged with the past, since it is so fascinated by revivals and revenants. This is equally true of the architecture, as with the figures in literature, so the eighteenth-century resurgence of Gothic architecture was followed by the Victorian Gothic revival. In literature and film, many Gothic monsters are revenants, which return from the dead, such as the vampire, ghost or zombie. Joanne Watkiss takes this notion of endless return into the textual, arguing that rewriting returns the 'chaotic creativity of intertextuality and uncanny repetition' (2012, p. 3).

Ubiquitous Contemporary Gothic

We live in Gothic times. (Carter 1974, p. 122)

Monstrosity shadows millennial change. (Botting 2014, p. 498)

The quotations above were written forty years apart. Each focuses on the contemporary Gothic, each emphasising the ways in which we experience and read our times as Gothic. However, not everyone has found the Gothic as contemporary and engaged as Botting and Carter. Arguing that reading and writing through the lens of the Gothic is replicating 'a boring and exhausted paradigm' (1991, p. 289), Fredric Jameson apparently mistook for a temporary fad a richly morphed way of understanding and depicting the concerns of our times. The Gothic is far from worn out, dissipated, merely popularist trimmings and trappings. It is now mainstreamed. Zombies and vampires are the figures of choice for some TV advertisements, motifs on children's clothing and tourist paraphernalia, as well as a consistent frame of reference from horror to dystopian fantasy, crime and romance films and fictions. Yet might this not trivialise its cutting comment on contemporary ways? Alternatively, should this be seen as part of a continuum, embracing lifestyle and media representation at one end and cultural critique at the other? In the hands of women writers, the contemporary Gothic often has a deliberately comic, parodic and popularist edge which does not undervalue its critique. Simultaneously, it has a radical aesthetically inventive edge which problematises ways in which women are represented, controlled and considered in contemporary society.

Critically, David Punter led the way in exploring how, following the French and American revolutions, the Gothic emerged as a radical response to Enlightenment discourses which undermined and marginalised the working class, cultural difference and the powers of the imagination (Punter 1996). Gothic expresses the contradictions and ironies of the contemporary worlds in which we live. Its history is one of revealing hidden, silenced and subordinated voices and subtexts. Now the exposure of and often celebration of contradiction, performance and the dangerous investment in everyday complacencies is more than a subversive subtext—it is the necessary experience of everyday life (Punter 1996). While Gothic has been seen initially as having a radical edge, not every critic agrees that its energies enable and maintain that edge. Teresa Goddu commented as early as 1997 that while it may seem rebellious and radical, often it maintains a comfortable relationship with official narrative, de-energising its powers of change so 'gothic may unveil the ideology of official discourse, but its transformative power can be limited' (1997, p. 11). Commenting on the often conservative, even racist energies of an imperial Gothic that characterises the Other as a creature of horror, Johun Hoglund notes that 'the gothic can be seen to simultaneously embrace and disturb modernity and empire' (Hoglund 2014, p. 7). What is intended as radical might be read as parodic or conformist; what was once used for critique can be used and seen as advertising trappings and little more than Disney entertainment. Even that essential Gothic characteristic of return, repeat and rediscovery can seem mere dull repetition. Intention, context, self-critique, self-awareness and reader or audience response are crucial in the mix. You can laugh, cry or scream at *The Duchess of Malfi* (Webster 1614), *Dracula* (Stoker 1897), *Dawn of the Dead* (2004) and *The Shining* (2008).

Something that is so ubiquitous and popular in the contemporary has antecedents now rediscovered and remade at every opportunity, particularly in film (*I Frankenstein*, 2014; TV Dracula, and a Dracula every two or three years) and novelistic mash-ups (Seth Grahame-Smith, *Pride and Prejudice and Zombies*, 2009, and *Abraham Lincoln Vampire Hunter*, 2010). The Gothic has a perpetually haunting presence; it exhibits a fascinatingly confusing desire to replay and reconfigure, to see anew and differently at every twist and turn. Familiar Gothic characters and the cultural and personal issues are constantly revisited through its mix of playful, performative and cutting critique and exposure of serious, ongoing concerns. These might include identity, wholeness of self, domestic security, a whole range of values, borderlines between good and bad, living and dead, as well as human and animal. The Gothic enables us to question what is taken for granted and is fundamental to what it is to be human, often through its engagement with the liminal.

Contemporary Women's Gothic: Convention and Haunting

It is important at this point to introduce arguments which run throughout the book concerning the use of Gothic tropes, such as ghostings and hauntings, and the familiar, morphing functions of vampires and werecreatures, whose presence troubles surface complacencies. As such, they open up debate about the satisfactory nature of the narratives with which we live our lives and offer continued critiques of and challenges to comfort, order and compliance. The Gothic, its settings, creatures, atmosphere, tropes and narratives are put to work by contemporary women Gothic writers, to expose the horror in the domestic, oppression in the everyday, as well as the cultural and imaginative constraints perpetuated in forms as broad as romantic fictions, folk and fairytales, popular fictions and grand meta-narratives.

A consideration of some of the key theorists is useful here. Women's Gothic writing deals with the domestic, with sex and sexuality, spaces, places, behaviours and norms which oppress women, the body as a site for reproduction, and terror, technological control and power relations. Ellen Moers (1976) developed the term 'female Gothic', arguing that 'women's concern with their physical appearance colludes with their self-denigration' (p. 90). Much women's Gothic shows an awareness that the female body is frequently represented as monstrous, as abject, for as Karen Stein puts it, 'it is precisely this male disgust with woman's sexuality, the male hatred and fear of woman's awful procreative power and her "otherness," which lies at the root of the Female Gothic' (1983, p. 125). Moers (1976) characterises female Gothic texts as 'a coded expression of women's fears of entrapment within the domestic and within the female body' (p. 000). Contemporary women's Gothic writing points to 'a space where the absent mother might be' (Wolstenholme 1993, p. 151), and Suzanne Becker (2012) talks of the ways in which Gothic texts by women haunt each other, both in concerns and forms, reminding and revisiting the more traditional Gothic texts which disturbed but offered conventional rewards such as marriage and money, and those which leave women's conventional roles and rewards in question. She comments on the 'writing and re-writing of female texts haunting one another: around the interrogative texture of romantic love and female desire, of gender construction between *le propre* and the monstrous-feminine, of the (contextualising) dynamics of domestic horror' (p. 68). Also, she makes a grand claim for significant influence on women's writing more broadly, 'Gothic form in this sense has anticipated the textual and ideological liberation of the new feminine texts' (p. 68).

In their special issue of *Gothic Studies*, Andrew Smith and Diana Wallace (2004) trace a critical history of women's Gothic, which provides a clear and substantial background to our understanding of ways in which contemporary women's Gothic continues, or challenges and undercuts, the values and expressions found in earlier works. Most of this special issue concentrates on work predating that considered in this book, but it is invaluable as a considered introduction to the critical history. According to Smith and Wallace, Moers characterised the Gothic as mainly dealing with fear, and her ideas of its focus on women's roles and bodies, particularly the maternal role, as constraint has been highly influential in studies of women's Gothic: 'Moers' analysis of Female Gothic texts as a coded expression of women's fears of entrapment within the domestic and within the female body, most terrifyingly experienced in childbirth, was extremely influential' (p. 1). Meanwhile, Robert Miles' work (1994) is seen as offering a 'state-of-the-art snapshot which indicated some of the most important directions in which criticism of the Female Gothic would move in the ensuing decade' (p. 1), largely because it reassesses the use of psychoanalysis, and essays in the collection use 'Male Gothic' to contextualise discussions. As Smith and Wallace point out, an important element is that the essays are also invited to challenge 'the concept of gender itself' (Miles 1994, p. 134), which we could see as opening the way, later, to the development of queer gothic in criticism and literature. I would argue that while Moers, along with Showalter (1977), whose focus is on women's writing more broadly speaking, is concentrating on establishing some of the bases of feminist criticism by rediscovering then re-reading a range of current and historical texts by women, Miles is foregrounding the destabilising of underpinning categories on which normativity is built. As we shall see in the chapter on more radical women's vampire writing (Chap. 7), there was a flurry of lesbian Gothic vampire and werewolf tales in the early 1990s (Pam Keesey 1993, 1995 and Victoria Brownworth 1996) while Paulina Palmer's *Lesbian Gothic* (1999) explored a range of texts, including the contemporary. I always hesitate to characterise elements of women's writing in contrast with men's writing as if one is the original and the other a derivation, nuance or challenge. However, the characterisation of the two kinds of plot lines in Gothic writing by men and women is useful as explored by both Milbank (1992) and Williams (1995), who offer rather different formulae for that identified as 'male' and 'female', so that plots of the 'persecuted heroine in flight from a villainous father and in pursuit of an absent mother' (p. 32) are typical 'Female Gothic' and 'masculine transgressions of social taboos' (p. 2) male Gothic. There are further complications. 'Feminine Gothic' and 'Masculine Gothic' may be more accurate terms, since some women such as Charlotte Dacre and Mary Shelley wrote in the style of Male Gothic. While Williams and others saw Female Gothic as subversive, Diane Long Hoeveler viewed it as establishing a victim feminism.

Smith and Wallace open up some of the issues on women's Gothic more generally and identify as an important conformity the reinforcement of constraining narratives, while some authors also engage in a radical undercutting of such narratives. They query Robert Miles' comment that female Gothic has 'hardened into a literary category' (1994, p. 131) and his claim that early feminist criticism has reached an 'impasse'. They argue that there is now women's Gothic, feminist Gothic, lesbian Gothic and Gothic feminism, a confusing array of somewhat contested terms. Their edition of *Gothic Studies* includes essays which revalue and challenge established historical readings of women's Gothic from its very inception.

The Gothic derives from and expresses the substance of the unconscious, of dreams, the repressed of society and social everyday normality. While conventional and historical Gothic tends to foreground anxieties about inheritance and purity, and male fears of female sexuality, much contemporary women's Gothic is more likely to expose gender-based terrors. These involve the deceptively reassuring and entrapping social and cultural narratives of domestic bliss, the family, security of home, law and country, and of eternal love. Chris Baldick (1993) characterises traditional Gothic thus:

> for the Gothic effect to be attained, a tale should combine a sense of a fearful inheritance in time with a claustrophobic sense of enclosure in space, these two dimensions reinforcing one another to produce an effect of sickening descent into disintegration. (Baldick 1993, pp. xii–xiv)

Furthermore, he points out that such texts are usurpers in the sense that 'Gothic writers have borrowed the fables and nightmares of a past age in order to repudiate their authority' (1993, p. xiv). Some contemporary women Gothic writers continue the Gothic romance genre of helpless victimised woman; strong lovers, who initially are a bit demonic; unspeakable repressions and histories; and an eternity of romance. Stephenie Meyer's *Twilight* (2005–2008) falls into this category. But this fictional pattern is by no means confined to the Gothic and extends to soft core porn, Young Adult (YA), or conventional romances flooding the internet sales sites. This book will look only briefly at *Twilight*, and not delve into other Gothic romances, even though they are indeed an indication of repetition and return, as a popular form. Contemporary women Gothic writers replay some of the concerns of the past but from a different gender-based vantage point. In their work, the location of horror or fear often resembles the reward in more traditional Gothic plot lines characterised by eternal, heterosexual love, comfortable consistencies, domesticity and the safety of home. What is seen as controlling, terrifying and disgusting is often the oppression of abusive relationships of power, the constructions, silencing and disempowerment of legitimised containment. Much contemporary women's Gothic critiques and undermines the assumptions underlying male sexualised terrors. Some conventionally oriented contemporary women's Gothic writing might collude and restore order; however, it could also trouble so deeply as to bring about changed perspectives and behaviour. In terms of Gothic literature as a taught subject in the academy, it triggers the troublesome, transformative effects of what are termed threshold concepts in the disciplines (Cousin 2006). Following awareness of how subjects/disciplines see the world, the ways we construct knowledge mean we can never operate superficially again in thinking, for example, that history is fact or literature is a representation of the real. So, by appreciating much contemporary women's Gothic, we cannot operate with naïve innocence in our awareness of cultural constructions and representations because literary Gothic refuses that simplicity. I love the Gothic because I believe it halts and troubles such naïveté, and yet it also allows for self-aware performative playfulness, a delight in the repetition and the haunting of the versions of the past, and the artifice, performance and the revelation and unpicking of these.

Pivotal Moments in Criticism

I just mentioned teaching the literary Gothic, how it can open up new ways of seeing the world, constructing knowledge, reading texts. There have been some pivotal moments in the rediscovery of the literary Gothic and its rebirth in contemporary women's Gothic fiction, in both literature and criticism.

Chief among the critical texts are Gilbert and Gubar's *The Madwoman in the Attic* (1979) and Barbara Creed's *The Monstrous Feminine* (1989). The year 1979 was a pivotal moment for Angela Carter, whose *The Bloody Chamber* was published, and for Gilbert and Gubar, whose *The Madwoman in the Attic* (1979) brought out revelations and a radical re-reading of texts we felt we understood. It was a truly momentous change in thinking, in which women writing from feminist perspectives and the Gothic became aligned. Gothic reading practices afforded new insights into what Diane Long Hoeveler (1998) has since identified as the victim position women were written into within traditional Gothic fictions of the eighteenth century. Frequently this involved terrified virginal heroines who were pursued by inappropriate men along dark corridors. Threats to their virtue abound in *The Monk* (Lewis 1796), *Mysteries of Udolpho* (Radcliffe 1794) and *Castle of Otranto* (Walpole 1764), right up to contemporary representations such as the vulnerable Bella in Meyer's *Twilight*

(2005–2008). What Gilbert and Gubar did was to open up a different reading of texts from the start of the Gothic, exposing the sources and causes of gendered inequalities, dispossession and the vulnerability of mind and body.

Some of the undercurrents then became a little darker. Barbara Creed works with Kristeva's notions of the abject, taking them into mother–child relationships and exposing how the 'maternal figure is constructed as the monstrous-feminine' (1989, p. 68) who prevents the child from becoming individual and having a distinct sexual identity. This derives from the relationships that have been constructed and explained by both Freud and Lacan, which lead to abjection, through which there is a demonising of women and the body. Basing her work on Kristeva, Creed explains the mixture of idealising and demonising of women in a wide range of Western narratives including film. Writers of contemporary Gothic variously repeat this abjection, or expose, challenge or change it.

Robert Miles' (1994) collection expresses relationships between women's writing, suggesting that the Gothic can be read from a re-scrutiny of materialistic and psychoanalytic focuses, and also 'challenging the concept of gender itself' (p. 134). In 1995 Anne Williams argues in *Art of Darkness: A Poetics of Gothic* (1995) that male and female formulae exist within different forms, producing divergent assumptions about the supernatural.

Interestingly, Long Hoeveler's *The Gothic Feminism and the Professionalisation of Gender from Charlotte Smith to the Brontës* (1998) argues for a passive-aggressive strength in the victim role for Gothic heroines, which might well feed into the ways in which contemporary women Gothic writers turn the tables on roles of caring mothers, vulnerable heroines, bringing about ultimate punishment for any kind of freedom or radical action. Avril Horner and Sue Zlosnik (1998) revived the appreciation of Daphne du Maurier as a Gothic writer and in so doing overturned the established version of female Gothic as offering resolutions and a happy ending, since this is rarely possible in a du Maurier novel or story. More radically, Paulina Palmer's work on *Lesbian Gothic* has aligned the position of the lesbian with that of Gothic, the Gothic's freedom of expression of transgressive behaviour and sexuality making it a creative, radical space for lesbian perspectives, and its questioning of what is 'normal', compliant, arguing that the abject highlights a constructedness and constraint against which lesbian lifestyles, perceptions and writing operate. In Palmer's view, the problematising of given expectations over domesticity, motherhood, heterosexual relationships and compliance fits well both with lesbian and feminist perspectives more broadly. Her work opened up perspectives on lesbian Gothic which enabled a celebration of the outsider, the lesbian, as a radical voice and Gothic champion.

Historical, traditional Gothic might disturb, but it was also a force for returning and restoring order. Radical challenge based on different perspectives and gender, from contemporary and postcolonial and lesbian women writers in particular, might change the culture, context and sexuality but still reinforce conventional endings of romance with its comforting resolution of conflict. However, traditional Gothic can sometimes offer radical alternatives to conventional formulae and closure. Not everyone restores order, and it is unlikely to be the same order based on the same values. Much critical work focuses on pre-1900 texts, while the work of Tania Modleski and Joanna Russ, who consider more current work, such as Mills and Boon, Harlequin Romance, specifically focuses on the traits of more modern Gothic romance exposing the limiting narratives which it peddles. In *Sweet Dreams* (Radstone 1988) and in my 'Weaving Our Own Web, De-Mythologising/Re-Mythologising and Imagining in the Work of Contemporary Women Writers' (1994) and 'If Looks Could Kill—Contemporary Women's Vampire Fictions' (1999), I use a range of Gothic texts to argue about the constraints of buying into popular and historical, conventional romance narratives, all prevalent in female Gothic.

Pivotal Moments: Fictional Texts: *Rebecca* (1938), *Wide Sargasso Sea* (1966) and *The Magic Toyshop* (1967)

As with definitions of contemporary women's writing on the Contemporary Women's Writing Association website, we could start looking at contemporary women's Gothic with work as early as the pivotal years 1966/1967. In 1966, Jean Rhys published *Wide Sargasso Sea*, arguably the first contemporary, postcolonial women's Gothic fiction, which writes back to Charlotte Brontë's Gothic *Jane Eyre* (1847), and in 1967 Angela Carter published *The Magic Toyshop* (discussed in Chap. 2). Both novels undercut conceptions prevalent and rewarded in traditional Gothic romance—love, wealth, inheritance, security—while also exposing the silencing and disempowerment of women under colonialism and imperialism, and in Carter's case, the entrapping gendered narratives of fairytale and myth. Both texts appeared early on in second-wave feminism (argued to have become articulate by the time of Betty Friedan's *The Feminine Mystique*, in

1963). On reflection, contemporary women's Gothic does not just appear suddenly in 1966/1967, nor does it spring from a vacuum. It grows from a latent or explicit unease with the certainties and complacencies which are expressed in earlier, more conventional Gothic romance and the narratives of normativity appertaining to the cultural, sexual and racial.

We need to dig a little deeper and recognise the revival of women's Gothic in earlier work, particularly that by Daphne du Maurier (*Rebecca*, 1938), which turns the conventional romantic Gothic on its head. Daphne du Maurier revitalised Gothic writing by women for the 1930s, most particularly with *Rebecca*, which offers a parallel text to the illusions of romantic fictions, hallmarked by the strong lover/husband, property, wealth, romance and happiness as a reward. In this text, all of those goals and achievement are undercut by decadence, repression, death and conflagration. The novel reconfigures Gothic romance, even turning the narrative trajectory around to do so, as the 'happily ever after' romantic reward is established in the first chapters, before being disturbed and undercut through the rest of the events in the novel. These events enact an unsatisfying and disturbing ghosting of the narratives of the past, through failed attempts at replay by the unnamed, second wife of Maxim de Winter, who is always in the shadow of Rebecca herself or rather a construction of her. Drawers hide notes, labyrinthine wings, corridors and alternative rooms obscure and cut off parts of the house, hide the history of a partying past. Elaborate clothing hides the pretensions and deceptions which Rebecca performed and which led to her infidelity and death. The catalytic moment explodes the performance in a night of partying, fireworks, storm, masquerade and confusion. The sea throws up long-hidden wreckage, and like a turbulent revenant, Rebecca's remains are also revealed. Hidden histories burst out. It is discovered that Rebecca was murdered by Max, a fact covered up by her husband and subsequently by the second Mrs de Winter. The remainder of the novel is about collusion, the dull deception of the married couple trapped in their shared lie, hiding their knowledge of Rebecca's death. However, the figure of Rebecca, errant, wayward, energetic, haunts women's contemporary Gothic as a reminder (and disturbing critique) of the punishment for sexual disobedience.

Narratives of romance, security, identity and home and of Britain's colonial success are similarly deeply disturbed in Jean Rhys' *Wide Sargasso Sea* (1966), which is a significant moment in the development of women's postcolonial Gothic. It exposes the misreadings, misunderstandings and condemning of difference, the theft of property and people, with reference to the slave-trade, and the silence surrounding this. Rochester's sour cynical marriage to Antoinette leads to her loss of identity, power and her home. First she is renamed Bertha; then, as a colonial subject, her wealth becomes his on their marriage. She is brought to dark, cold England and incarcerated in the prison of an English house. Her heritage is sold off. Bertha's psychological disturbance is a sign of the mis-presentation, oppression and theft that was (and is) misapplied colonial power. This is written through the body of the incarcerated and mixed-race, unwanted wife, the proverbial mad woman in the attic (although strictly speaking, in *Jane Eyre* she is not in fact incarcerated in the attic but on the third floor). Antoinette/Bertha represents an undercutting of romantic narrative and a local, imprisoned, silenced version of woman as Other, and in this case in particular, a colonial subject.

The silencing and incarceration, the living and the ghosting in these two texts, are the seeds for contemporary women's Gothic to follow. Versions creep down from our attics or up from our dungeons and cellars and speak out from our pasts to reveal alternative readings of history, identity and ways of seeing the world. In formal terms, this is expressed in the rewriting of culturally inflected narratives, enabled by creative splicing with and between popular fiction forms, a highly self-conscious exposure of the limitations of established tropes, and their new revitalised use.

Contemporary women Gothic writers are always dealing with ghosts and hauntings. The legacies of women's Gothic from Anne Radcliffe onwards appear replayed and questioned in contemporary texts, which often re-read scenarios of gender and power, exposing hidden histories and different perceptions. There are also noticeable roots of Gothic writing by both men and women in the current interests of rewriting history in historiographical meta-fiction, within neo-Victorianism, which replays and Gothicises the experiences and fiction of the Victorian era (Chap. 10).

Gothic Horror

A popular branch of the Gothic, Gothic horror, names and dramatises that which is otherwise unthinkable, unnamable, indefinable and repressed: split selves, false identities, erupting bodies and unsafe spaces. Liza Tuttle relates Gothic horror and women's writing with women's lives. She says, 'We all understand the language of fear, but men and women are raised speaking different dialects of that language' (Tuttle 1990, p. 5).

Freud's 'The Uncanny' (1919) is important in any consideration of the ways in which the Gothic works on our imaginations. This essay in particular influenced psychoanalytic readings of the fantastic, and of Gothic and horror literature, showing ways in which they engage with and enact the uncanny or *unheimlich*, the intrusion of the unfamiliar when the familiar is expected. The Gothic makes frequent use of 'the uncanny', destabilising fictional characters, spaces and readings, enacting confusion, dread and apprehension. It makes the homely frightening, the familiar unfamiliar, and the secure insecure, and this destabilisation produces both fear and potential new insights and understanding. The uncanny, as a tool of the Gothic, reveals what is concealed and unexpected: those alternative versions of self, of relationships, home and family, which relate to everyday 'reality'. It opens the way for energies that might burst out or intrude on and threaten everyday life. What results is a projection of something repressed, embodied in a demon spirit, ghost, monster or disruptive energies, hence those films of children possessed by demons (*The Exorcist*, 1973; *The Omen*, 1976) and houses that start to collapse or explode because they are built over desecrated graves (*Poltergeist*, 1982).

Mark Jancovich explores common perceptions that pleasures offered by Gothic horror are

> based on the process of narrative closure in which the horrifying or monstrous is destroyed or contained. The structure of horror narratives are said to set out from a situation of order, move through a period of disorder caused by the eruption of horrifying or monstrous forces, and finally reach a point of closure and completion in which disruptive, monstrous elements are contained or destroyed and the original order is re-established. (1992, p. 9)

Conventionally, Gothic also finally shuts down these disturbances and restores order. Comfortable dismissals of horror as mere entertainment that just consists of silly scary monsters avoid its well-established, politicised role as an exposer of social and cultural deceits and discomforts. Horror is a more physically disturbing and invasive, destructive relation than the Gothic from which it draws its impulse and much of its form. It acts as a vehicle for us to face up to and face down what we avoid, repress, ignore, or can see no escape from. The objects and subjects of horror are not always what they appear to be and are very often socially, politically and culturally transgressive and challenging.

Restoring order is not always the aim of the radical horror writer. This signals one of the problems of horror, which links it to the political and the horror comics scare of the 1950s (see Martin Barker's *A Haunt of Fears*, 1984). Challenges to the status quo, whether they be cultural, gendered, social, political or emotional, etc., destabilise, but sometimes this very instability is a vehicle for imaginative change, as in the bringing about of equality though the rewriting of forms and relations of power, and other reimaginings.

Horror shows that 'rationalist, consumerist socio-modernity produces alienation from the body and denial of desires and terrors. Usually, the remedies proposed are conservative, depending not on new attitudes towards the repressed or abject, but on violent confrontation, ritual cleansing, rediscovery of lost heroism and authenticity, and re-imposition of order'.

Women writing Gothic horror problematise what is considered normal, such as domestic settings, and enact what troubles us. Examples include the revelation of hidden family histories, the haunting of the past in the present in the fabric of the home, and inherited illnesses. Julia Kristeva's notions of abjection in *The Powers of Horror* (1982) enable a theorised critique of conventional representations of women in horror, besides other literary and artistic or media work, and offer a perspective clarifying how much feminist Gothic horror challenges and moves beyond such conventions, constraints, misrepresentations and even demonising. Kristeva identifies abjection as a stage in an infant's development when it rejects that which is not-self in order to begin to recognise and define the limits of self as opposed to Other. What is rejected includes faeces for, according to Kristeva, 'refuse and corpses *show me* what I permanently *thrust aside* in order to live' (Kristeva 1982, p. 12). The first Other a child encounters is the body of the mother, which is regarded as abject, a form of rejection with disgust. For her predecessors, Freud and Lacan, the male child is the primary focus. Kristeva argues that while growing up, the child can extend this negative reaction to the maternal body as a projection towards women in general. Fortunately, this is usually noticeable only in pathological versions of the response. In these pathological versions, while attraction and alignment might be the first responses to the body and self of the Other, disgust and fear at women's bodies, sexuality and women's power through sexuality rapidly follow, displacing attraction with rejection, and abjection. Conventional fears, which invariably are male, derived from abjection, range from disempowerment and rejection, to engulfment. Both ends of this continuum are based in terror, disgust at the alien Other, prompting a need to close it down, to refuse agency. Women, it seems, are the object, location and source of horror and disgust of the abject. Gothic horror builds on the notion of abjection as a rejection of what is not you. This Otherising may be described as offloading onto something or someone else that which cannot be faced, 'qualities, feelings, wishes or even "objects" which the subject refuses to recognize or rejects in himself are expelled from the self and located in another person or thing' (Laplanche and Pontalis 1973, p. 25). Women writers of the Gothic can choose to collude with this construction of women as abject, or to refute, expose or even ridicule it. Many rewrite collusive myths (Angela Carter, Margaret Atwood and Nalo Hopkinson) and histories which silenced, marginalised and hid or destroyed women (Sarah Waters and Toni Morrison), offering alternative culturally and gender-inflected versions which re-empower women. Some of the more radical women writers of lesbian vampire fiction (Chap. 7) completely turn the tables, celebrating what is elsewhere considered abject. Here we might find lesbian sexuality, the centrality and celebration of the outsider and the Other as radical energy and agency.

Gothic literary critics are often at pains to distinguish between the spatialised, whether it be castles, turrets, awe-inspiring landscapes or eighteenth and nineteenth-century buildings, some of which, like Walpole's Strawberry Hill, are delightfully, excessively, if artificially Gothic. Separating space and the literary might help unscramble some minds, but the locations remain important for Gothic literature: haunted houses; wild, abandoned, urban but decayed no-go areas, some as specific as Whitechapel, where the Ripper murders took place; spaceships in which the crew is confined and threatened by a deadly creature or virus. The places and spaces have changed over time, but they still resonate with cultural messages and interpretations, and continue to act as visual architectural forms through which fears are projected, which is an important feature of the Gothic. Some of the chief lasting characteristics of the Gothic are its spatialisation, its cultural connectedness. Lisa Tuttle also considers space and gender when she explores some of the issues around what might inform contemporary women's Gothic, when dealing with women's horror writing. She highlighted that men and women fear different spaces, for different reasons; women are more likely to worry about being alone in a car park late at night or walking home unaccompanied (Tuttle 1990, p. 5).

History Revisited

Re-scrutinising history is a Gothic favourite. Lucie Armitt (2007, 2011) focuses on the horrors of the two world wars, represented in a constant haunting for those in Europe, while those and other wars, such as in Vietnam, also haunt the United States and South East Asia. That most revisited European war, the First World War, produced Gothic short stories by Rudyard Kipling, and Pat Barker's *Regeneration* trilogy (1991–1995), particularly *The Ghost Road* (1995). Sarah Wasson's powerful book on Gothic texts (2010) of the Second World War looks at the Urban Gothic of wartime London, focusing on earlier work than this book deals with, by among others, Elizabeth Bowen. In such works, vans carry human blood, raids and air raid shelters produce terrifying claustrophobia and London is constructed 'as a hallucinatory, claustrophobic and labyrinthine realm, writing topical anxieties onto the wartime streets' (Wasson 2010, p. 2), all of which we find in a contemporary text, Sarah Waters' *The Night Watch* (2006). Here, some of this terror transforms into an alternative freedom for lesbian ambulance driver Kay, and her friends and lovers, for whom the altered geometries of the houses and streets in darkened London offer new freedoms.

Wars haunt us, and so does the colonial and imperial history which piled up European and US wealth. David Punter's revival of the Gothic first appeared in relation to terror and horror, then moved into exploring and exposing the haunted postcolonial spaces both 'at home' and 'abroad', since the conqueror and the conquered are bound together, differently infected by the greed, theft and poison of imperialism and colonialism.

This book will largely focus on haunted pasts and haunted spaces, threatened selves and complacencies—the domestic coupledom, the safety of the family, the security of a coherent identity—and it will focus on postcolonial recuperation, alternative readings of once colonised spaces and lives, such as the rewriting of Malaysian spaces haunted by importers and oppressors and liars (seen in Beth Yahp's *Crocodile Fury*, 1992). There are also ways in which those living in and moving on from postcolonial locations reinterpret and re-historicise the places and spaces into which they move, offering a Gothicising of diversity (as seen in the work of Helen Oyeyeme). The split selves of once colonised peoples and the locations saturated with histories of exploitation, silencing and marginalisation are their histories speaking out. Their interpretations of history, self and place provide alternatives, parallel worlds, places like male writer Tash

Aw's (2005) floating and disappearing islands, places which are idyllic one moment, hell the next and gone another. In the midst of the postcolonial recuperations of haunted pasts and reinterpretations of histories are lives and spaces which have silenced, enslaved peoples, whether in the homeland or the land to which they have moved, or the land which enslaved and hid the sources of wealth as another dirty secret, another haunting to return in the future. In this midst, there is a Gothic of travelling, sometimes a Gothic tourism, noted for defamiliarisation of different places, spaces and cultures. This travel and tourism Gothic links the postcolonial and the disturbances of self and security—two of the Gothic strands on which this book is built. I argue that late twentieth-/early twenty-first-century women's Gothic focuses on all the familiar themes and trends and uses the familiar strategies, signs and metaphors, but that it does so to deeply disturb certainties of self and identity (as does much late twentieth and twenty-first-century writing), of the domestic, and its cultural versions of the homeland. It emphasises haunted histories of war and the colonial through postcolonial Gothic writing, where Gothic travelling offers all this unease and confrontation with that representing a haunted past and the insecurities of self.

David Punter's second edition of *The New Companion to the Gothic* (2012) deals particularly well with the ways in which Gothic moments have produced different developments—seeing an overall agreement of the moments of the work of Walpole and Radcliffe as the agreed beginning of much of what we think of as historically traditional Gothic, with a revival at the end of the nineteenth century with Bram Stoker, Oscar Wilde, H. G. Wells and R. L. Stevenson, and Gothic texts in a large number of nineteenth-century writers, such as Charles Dickens, whose claustrophobic atmospheres and grotesque characters are certainly Gothic. Punter considers that modernists might be talking back to ghosts but perhaps now, when we read some of the writing of women literary modernists, we find the Gothic ever present in the haunted houses of Woolf, the vampire maternal domination of Mrs Ramsey in *To the Lighthouse* (1927), Charlotte Mew's colonial oppression and sacrifice in 'A White Night' (1903) and so on. We have rediscovered the Gothic because it was not the form of expression of choice but, like the tendencies it exposes, was running along underground, behind the wallpaper, as in Charlotte Perkins Gilman's *The Yellow Wallpaper* (1892), there but often misnamed, only occasionally emerging to grab your attention. Punter considers that cultural haunting and the contemporary recognition of the constant state of mutability might be elements of the Gothic which we have taken into the twenty-first century.

Traditional Gothic is a historical construction, a product of particular times, places and concerns, where issues of power, identity, religion, inheritance and heritage are bound up with the locations in castles and monasteries, prisons and wild landscapes. It is an intellectual and imaginative challenge to the ostensibly highly rational, ordered and restricted forms of thinking and expression which both preceded it and ran alongside it. Its attachment to and development from concerns with issues of freedom, equality and the human condition, then the radical, rebellious and the alternative (to conformity and obedience) have made the spirit of the Gothic coincident with much of what is also fascinating in Romanticism, while the darker side of the Gothic destabilises that which is taken for granted, and undercuts complacencies—about developments in science, the wholeness of identity, the match between outer charming comforts, developed self and an inner wilder self. Much of what we see in conventional or traditional Gothic fiction seems bound up with the Gothic locations: castles, convents, monasteries and wild nature. So what has this got to do with the Gothic revival of the late twentieth and early twenty-first centuries? With the vampire next door and the everyday use of Gothic tropes, settings, images and actors, to do with everything from selling perfume to exploring and explaining the contradiction in contemporary cities, where poverty and destitution, crime and sickness operate alongside almost a parallel city (*The City & the City*, Mieville 2009), to that of high finance, high buildings and high salaries and lifestyles?

The similarities for me are the ways in which traditional Gothic of both the eighteenth and nineteenth centuries also exposed the fragility of our certainties and social, personal and cultural naïveties and complicities. The religious impetus is less common now, although the spiritual dimensions of external creatures are much discussed (vampires retain that link with religion—blood, sacrifice, eternal life). While on the one hand the Gothic can seem now to be a cosmetic mode of choice to express any story and concern, on the other it retains its politically, culturally, socially and personally emotionally charged role, offering the opportunities to problematise, see things differently, undercut, undermine and construct forward. The latter is possible often through Gothic where it aligns with science fiction, the former more possible with horror, each politicised and making free use of the supernatural as well as of technology, the old and the new.

The current rise of critical work on the Gothic, of which this series is a significant part, helps us to clarify and confirm what many of us who love the Gothic and who love horror, as I do, have felt during the time of its staginess in Hammer Horror films, and its invisibility in the works of the modernists, as well as its popular fictional appeal throughout all of these moments. Talking about horror films, a branch of the Gothic, more visceral and violent than everything Gothic might need to or have to be, Forshaw points out that 'the iconoclastic forms which rejuvenated the horror genre both in this country and abroad, often achieved this status by taking radical new approaches to the genre, millennial horror has had a pervasive influence with an end of the century or end of time mind-set creating and feeding a fatalistic (often apocalyptic) strain' (2013, p. 165). He marks Romero's *Night of the Living Dead* (1969) as a film which built on Hitchcock's *The Birds* (1963) and turned the form of the horror film from the creaky artifice of the often risible Hammer Horror films to something more dangerously immediate perhaps, through (sometimes hidden) levels of seriousness (Forshaw 2013, p. 166). The horror film began, like the Gothic, to have designs upon our intellect, morality and sense of identity. Forshaw sees James Watkins' *The Woman in Black* (2012) film of Susan Hill's novel (1983) as evidence that however tired the horror genre and the Gothic film might seem to have been, they are back.

There is an earlier version of this film (1989), which for many is more terrifying than the remake, and more terrifying still is the ghost story upon which it is based. Susan Hill's revival of the gendered ghost story *The Woman in Black* (1983) was another turning point in gendered Gothic: haunting, repression, social stigma, women's silencing and absencing, domestic destruction, a Gothic version of the damned, bedraggled, fallen women who limp through Elizabeth Gaskell and the nineteenth-century novel. This fallen woman returns after her death to wreak vengeance on the very complacency and complicity which have denied her her rights, her child, his life, and any meaning for her own life: a true indictment of the nineteenth and twentieth centuries' gendered hypocrisy regarding women, families, self-worth and rights.

Angela Carter's baroque Gothic novels and stories, her critique of the constructions of femininity enshrined in cultural fairytales and myths and Susan Hill's ghost stories are works which have burst on our imaginations. Women Gothic writers returned with much to say about how women had been silenced, marginalised and misrepresented, and only recently through critical exploration (Gilbert and Gubar's *The Madwoman in the Attic*, 1979) have they been seen to be speaking. Often transgressive women have been locked up and considered mad (*Jane Eyre*, Brontë 1847; *The Woman in White*, Collins 1859; and *The Yellow Wallpaper*, Perkins-Gilman 1892) and exposed through the work of earlier Gothic women writers. The critical text was first, then Carter, then Hill, and then we backtracked and found the Gothic in the modernists. Revisiting, revival, re-reading: contemporary women's writing forces us back into the Gothic tracks of the past. Work of earlier women writers, even as it revisits the situations and constrained circumstances of which they wrote, also revives the energy of revelations and speaking out, turns that energy onto new revelations—of sisterly deception and spite, of potential apocalyptic dystopian futures where women's reproductive rights are denied (*The Handmaid's Tale*, Atwood 1985). The danger too is that they might foolishly only construct themselves as they are reconstructed, as romantic victims (*The Edible Woman*, Atwood 1969; *Lady Oracle*, Atwood 1976—most of Atwood). By contrast, the figure of the vampire points to a celebration of energetic alternative viewpoints and behaviours. Postcolonial perceptions and insights have led to totally rewriting spaces, places and colonial history through the vehicle of established fairytales, myths and Gothic figures, were-beasts (*Myal*, Brodber 1988), snow queens, Bluebeard, mermaids (*Skin Folk*, Hopkinson 1997 and *The New Moon's Arms*, Hopkinson 2007), and again vampires and ghosts (*Beloved*, Morrison 1987). Contemporary women's Gothic writers revisit the Gothic but have also revisited the past and shone a new light on it, even as they move forward into utterly new configurations and possibilities, when they combine their work, as do many postcolonial writers, with the power to imagine forward offered by speculative fiction.

What will we expect to find in Gothic by contemporary women's writers? Concerns about representation and self-worth, ageing, beauty, decay, the body as object, the reduction of self to commodity, cypher, object of desire or disgust. We might see the exposure of constraining myths, whether based on fairytales or more broadly cultural. Some of the issues which concern women perhaps more than men have been surprisingly resistant to change: identity, safety, incarceration, the worth of ownership, family, heredity, chastity, woman as a commodity of exchange, engulfment, invasions, disguise, deceit and performance. 'The Gothic was always a family affair, and the family it courted perpetually in decay', notes Lucie Armitt (2007, p. 16), but she goes on to locate an ascendance of the Gothic in the late twentieth century as a kind of confirmation of the expected, a way of defining the criticised experience of women as incarcerated and disempowered: 'second-wave feminism told us that Gothicism was inherent in women's lives under patriarchy, especially in relation to literature and the environment' (p. 16), so for the twenty-first century what might we expect? In the same essay, Armitt looks at four narratives, each of which replays and revives the Gothic in terms of exploring the brutalising of the female body: Nicole Ward-Jouve's compulsively gripping study of the Yorkshire Ripper, *The Street-Cleaner* (1986), *After You'd Gone* (2000) by Maggie O'Farrell, *Fingersmith* (2002) by Sarah Waters and *Case Histories* (2004) by Kate Atkinson. O'Farrell's work concerns the haunting of a young woman by her mother and lover, her attempts to get in touch with the ghost of her husband, while *Fingersmith* is a constant haunting of the Victorian era in the twentieth and twenty-first centuries, revived in neo-Victorian fictions, where London and the countryside are rewritten from the vantage point of two young women, each under the spell of the appropriately named Gentleman. *Fingersmith* emphasises the sexual and financial power, and status of men who can metamorphose, juggle and move between the two women: heiress and East End daughter of a woman hanged for murder (ostensibly). Gothic formulae operate: sleight of hand such as swapping at birth, incarcerations, deceptions, dressing up, all familiar Gothic traits, but the novel seeks to expose silencing, marginalisation, sexual predation embedded in conventional and legitimised relationships and the agency of lesbian love. The lesbian love affair between the women is a revelation of a different kind of history of the period, doubly Gothic.

There are many and various revelations in contemporary women's Gothic. In *Case Histories* (Atkinson 2004) an academic family in Cambridge is torn apart by the predatory, sexual behaviour of the coldly mathematical father, the back-ways and gated gardens of ostensibly upright families hiding a secret of paternal abuse which so ruined one daughter, Sylvia (just before she entered a convent) that her sense of order led her to believe her three-year-old sister Olivia was better off dead than to survive to become prey to the father. Armitt concludes that the contemporary novel and world are haunted by the Gothic—which is a nicely put explanation for the ways in which it can be used as shorthand for everything—hidden history, pretence, or everyday slip.

So 'none of these three novels could exist without feminism, but where Atkinson and O'Farrell could be called "postfeminist," Waters is clearly "third wave" in her outlook: she actively belongs to a feminist tradition of writing and hence affirms her place in what Gamble calls the "history of feminist struggle"' (2001b, p. 44). The future, then, lies in 'paying homage to the past—something at which the Gothic always excels' (p. 29).

Andrew Smith helps locate some of the changes to Gothic in the twentieth and twenty-first centuries by signalling its identification with 'horror', particularly in popular literature and film, while it grew because of the availability of both film and pulp fiction (so-called because of the poor quality of paper on which these cheap accessible books were printed—and they included other genres: fictions, romance, westerns, crime). Mentioning work by James Herbert, Stephen King and others, he comments that 'The popularity of novels should not detract from the fact that, in line with the gothic tradition, they still address cultural anxieties' (Smith 2007, p. 140). Though some of the anxieties remain favourites, such as identity, family and religion, there are new ones in the contemporary age: the destruction of family values, inner city decay and also the rash of Gothic fiction and films which focus on the end of days, on dystopian visions, apocalyptic moments, such as *The Road* (McCarthy 2006; film, 2009), mutations with creatures, alien invasions and eruptions (*Alien Trilogy*, 1979–1992), genetic engineering (*Transcendence*, 2014; *Never Let Me Go*, Ishiguro 2005; film, 2010), post-capitalist zombies apocalypse, and climate change. These are horror, science fiction and fantasy fiction scenarios, but now no genre remains unaffected by the Gothic. The Gothic locations of space ships, brutalist architecture, harsh metal suits, Pacific Rim monsters from the deep (*Pacific Rim*, 2013; *Godzilla*, 2014), contemporary threats of invasion, eruption (*The War of the Worlds*—films, 1953, 2005) all utilise Gothic characteristics and interests; focus on identity, troubling fixed beliefs, liminal spaces between safety and deadly danger, and hostile environments, including the home, which initially seemed safe. Twinning is represented in *Invasion of the Body Snatchers* (1956, 1978), building on *The Strange Case of Dr Jekyll and Mr Hyde* (Stevenson 1886), mad doctors, and perhaps more deeply than previously, a sense of undermining that which has been thought to be constant. There is nothing to be certain about, the contexts have changed, and now range from the streets of London to outer space, small town Iran to New England, hospitals, prisons, the postcolonial and postmodernist contexts of our reimagined neo-Victorian pasts, our current and future worlds. Contemporary texts use the Gothic to engage with recurring, reshaped and sometimes very different (undermined) certainties and challenges.

In much contemporary writing by women and men, the Gothic has become the genre of choice in which to explore and express anything from neighbourliness and hometown romance (Sookie Stackhouse novels, Harris, 2001–2013), to family values and the importance of the bonding of true eternal love (*Twilight*, Meyer 2005–2008), ways of dealing with post-traumatic stress and recuperating moments of history which have been lost (*Winter Ghosts*, Mosse 2010; *Labyrinth*, Mosse 2005), as well as offering a critique of racism, sexism, ageism and man's inhumanity to man. This latter is particularly found in the many postcolonial Gothic works which deal with haunted spaces and histories which must be enacted, embodied, faced and lived beyond (*Beloved*, Morrison 1987; *The Crocodile Fury*, Yahp 1992; work by Helen Oyeyeme). In another era, these themes would have been dealt with in realism, whether historically researched or gritty and contemporary, or they could appear in other popular fictional genres: crime, fantasy, romance, the western and sci-fi.

The Gothic enables a problematising of what is ostensibly normal, safe, taken for granted, widespread and incontrovertible, whether it be religious, historical, political or personal, and exposes these as narratives by which we live but which we take as incontrovertible truths at our peril. Historically, the Gothic used the fantastic and terror, horror, to expose complacencies and unearth the fears of the age—miscegenation; illegitimacy; disability hidden from view; oppression; slavery; the inhumane; the threat to lineage and security more generally; the very ambiguities and revelations that behaviours, relationships, scenarios and setting are more or less than they seem, less stable, more problematic. The critique and irony which are essential bases of the Gothic make it a well-suited genre with which to deal with an age which celebrates postmodernist performativity, the artificial alongside certainties of solidity. With its ambivalences and ability to hold contradictions in tension, contemporary women's Gothic enables us to look at our twenty-first century worlds with their echoes, artifices and need for performance and narrative, even while it explores, undercuts and critiques these in the world of politics, philosophy and personal relationships. It was oddly hidden from view for much of the twentieth century, to rise toward its later years, so now we even re-read modernists (Virginia Woolf, Katherine Mansfield, Edith Wharton, Charlotte Mew) for their Gothic. Contemporary writers who probably would be more comfortable writing realist romance, the traumas of the wars, or biographical narratives about postcolonial histories, choose the Gothic. It is mainstreamed, ubiquitous, no longer lurking in the juvenilia or the lesser known work of the greats, no longer a minority appeal or a strange intrusion on the canon.

The contemporary women's Gothic texts with which I deal in this book are neither watered down nor are all high Gothic. They deal with ongoing and vital issues: post-traumatic stress, hidden histories of abuse and neglect, the seemingly endless human potential for Otherising in terms of race, age, ability, identity, gender, potential, language, talent, geography or religion. Some might well have been written in another time and place without ostensible Gothic elements to vehicle their arguments; others might well have been the hidden fruits of someone's creativity about which their publishers and readers were surprised and which were themselves hidden because Gothic and not out in the open. Is Gothic out of the closet? The work is now blatantly Gothic and proud of it.

Aware of the performativity of identity and the constructed tenuousness of values, defamiliarisation is the norm, feeling secure rather naïve, and the ironic view offered by the Gothic enables us to hold the insecurities and instability in tension with human needs to try and invest, without falling into a state of nihilism. Gothic provides fantastic, horrific and often ironic scenarios, space and modes of being to help us deal with this liminality and troublesomeness. Andrew Smith comments, 'Whilst modernism focused on the fragmented nature of subjectivity (and so exploited the Gothic fascination with fractured selves), postmodernism represents a scepticism about the grand narratives (such as religion, for example), which once provided social and moral norms. In a contemporary postmodern age we can no longer believe incoherent, universal claims to truth which, so the argument goes, are replaced by moral relativism' (Smith 2007, p. 141).

Gothic in particular often includes elements of rebelling against or resistance to existing social norms. In this respect, although the reasons change with time and place, I like Julia Briggs' comment concerning ghost stories, an example of the Gothic, that while 'a taste for romance or a sensitivity to mood or atmosphere' contributes, as it does 'for the ghost story in particular, imaginative access to some kind of spiritual power', 'it's the slightly radical edge of the outsider which also appeals, the transition from a position of subordination and silence to one of a special kind of seeing and knowing, askance, richer' (Briggs 2012, p. 183). And while 'we tame horrors and make them manageable by writing about them' (p. 183) we can also query the established and complacent, undercut the dangerously comfortable and expose the fraudulently smug, through the Gothic.

Gothic writing by contemporary women sensitive to the effects of gender, whether feminist, postcolonial or lesbian, offers the opportunity to thoroughly reimagine place, identity and being, rather than just rebuilding 'massa's house'. As Canadian Trinidadian Nalo Hopkinson says: 'in my hands massa's tools don't dismantle massa's house—and in fact I don't want to destroy it so much as I want to undertake massive renovations—then build me a house of my own' (Hopkinson and Mehan 2004, pp. 7–8).

The subversive granddaughter of eighteenth-century Gothic fiction, contemporary women's Gothic mixes horror and fantasy, liberating latent denied desires and exposing the hidden histories, silences, the repressed or abusive, deadly, deceptive or banal past experiences of women and men. It is international, contextually and culturally inflected, often splicing the folk tales, myths and expressions of the contexts from which it springs with the traditional but morphed Gothic features of location, imagery, character and event.

Shape of the Book

This book starts to consider the range, variety, contradictions and the consistent interest of contemporary women's Gothic writing, in English, across some parts of the world. It has begun with a discussion of Gothic writing, its lasting fascination, its changes, and what forms and concerns are popular choices for women writers of the Gothic. We have considered some critical history and discussion of what could be called pivotal texts in changing the ways in which women's Gothic writing deals with themes popular in women's writing, including romance, the domestic, power, gender and identity. The main focus begins to emerge with second-wave feminism's challenge to the gendered status quo, considering the background and definitions of the Gothic and women's fictions of second-wave feminism, and so it links with theories of masquerade, duplicity and gender as performance.

There is so much good contemporary women's Gothic writing, but so little space. My choices here have been based on a desire to establish some trends, themes and concerns which will also be found in a wider range of women's Gothic writing, locally and internationally, so I hope the critical introduction leads to a richer exploration of the many other writers who readers will find for themselves, or find mentioned only in passing here.

I want to reintroduce and explore the more familiar, established writers, seeing and focusing on their work here where it is Gothic, so the three chapters following this introduction in the main provide some well-established and some new views on work by key contemporary women Gothic writers: Angela Carter (Chap. 2), Margaret Atwood (Chap. 3) and Toni Morrison (Chap. 4). Cultural haunting, a theme emerging in the Toni Morrison chapter, reappears in later chapters, which, among other issues, look at women's postcolonial Gothic. Chapter 5, 'Postcolonial and Cultural Haunting Revenants—Letting the "Right" Ones in', looks again at Jean Rhys' *Wide Sargasso Sea* (1966) and then moves on to consider postcolonial work by Atwood, with *Alias Grace* (1996), a tale of an immigrated Irish woman which problematises received histories and evidence in terms of colonial histories. It considers work by South East Asian writers Beth Yahp, Sandi Tan and Catherine Lim, whose haunted postcolonial spaces are Malaysia and Singapore. Chapter 6, 'Testing the Fabric of Bluebeard's Castle: Postcolonial Reconfigurations, Demythologizing, Re-Mythologizing and Shape-Shifting', focuses on the widespread Bluebeard fairytale to challenge patriarchal power and its expression in contexts under colonial or imperial rule. Here I explore work by Nalo Hopkinson, Erna Brodber, Shani Mootoo and Helen Oyeyemi. Chapters 7 and 8 both deal with the ever popular literary Gothic figure of the vampire, first looking at the critically engaged radical feminist and lesbian vampires of the 1980s and 1990s, then in Chap. 8 the more conservative conformist interpretation in YA fiction such as *Twilight*, but ending on a radical recovery with Moira Buffini's *A Vampire Story* (play, 2008) and *Byzantium* (film, 2013).

Women have always written ghost stories, and they offer a chance to recuperate, revisit and replay, so they are equally popular among contemporary women writers, particularly those who wish to open up the popular historical versions of women's lives in the more recent past. Ghost stories by Sarah Waters, Kate Mosse, Susan Hill and Helen Dunmore are discussed here (Chap. 9). Chapter 10 refuses to be a standard conclusions chapter. Instead, it does two things. It offers some tentative summarising thoughts to the main strands of contemporary women's Gothic writing which we have considered in the book overall. It also opens up in brief, as an introduction, a further range of writers, themes and texts in contemporary women's Gothic, giving a sense of the wealth of writing, to whet the reader's appetite for more.

Vital and relevant, contemporary women's Gothic undermines and problematises the grand narratives of gender equality, humanity and progress. We need its challenges and engagement.

For me, as for many others, Angela Carter's work was revolutionary, radical and revelatory in this respect and I will revisit her haunting presence in the next chapter.

Bibliography

Armitt, L. (2007) 'Dark Departures: Contemporary Women's Writing after the Gothic', in *Postfeminist Gothic: Critical Interventions in Contemporary Culture*, B. A. Brabon and S. Genz (eds.) (Basingstoke: Palgrave Macmillan).
Armitt, L. (2011) *Twentieth-Century Gothic* (Cardiff: University of Wales Press).
Atkinson, K. (2004) *Case Histories* (New York: Doubleday).
Atwood, M. (1969) *The Edible Woman* (Toronto: McClelland & Stewart).
Atwood, M. (1976) *Lady Oracle* (Toronto: McClelland & Stewart).
Atwood, M. (1985) *The Handmaid's Tale* (Toronto: Fawcett Crest).
Aw, T. (2005) *The Harmony Silk Factory* (London: Harper Perennial).
Baldick, C. (1993) 'Introduction', in *The Oxford Book of Gothic Tales* (Oxford: Oxford University Press).
Becker, S. (2012) *Gothic Forms of Feminine Fictions* (Manchester: Manchester University Press).
Botting, F. (2014) 'Post-Millennial Monsters: Monstrosity-No-More', in *The Gothic World*, G. Byron and D. Townshend (eds.) (London: Routledge).
Briggs, J. (2012) 'The Ghost Story', in *A New Companion to the Gothic*, D. Punter (ed.) (Oxford: Blackwell).
Brodber, E. (1988) *Myal* (London: New Beacon Books).
Brontë, E. (1847) *Wuthering Heights* (London: Thomas Cautley Newby).
Brownworth, V. A. (ed.) (1996) *Night Bites* (Washington: Seal Press).
Forshaw, B. (2013) *British Gothic Cinema* (Basingstoke: Palgrave Macmillan).
Höglund, J. (2014) *The American Imperial Gothic: Popular Culture, Empire, Violence* (Farnham: Ashgate Publishing).
Hopkinson, N. (1997) *Skin Folk* (New York: Warner Aspect).
Hopkinson, N. (2007) *The New Moon's Arms* (New York: Grand Central Publishing).
Hopkinson, N. and Mehan, U. (2004) *So Long Been Dreaming: Postcolonial Science Fiction & Fantasy* (Vancouver: Arsenal Pulp Press).
Horner, A. and Zlosnik, S. (1998) *Daphne du Maurier: Writing, Identity and the Gothic Imagination* (Basingstoke: Macmillan).
Ishiguro, K. (2005) *Never Let Me Go* (London: Faber and Faber).
Jancovich, M. (1992) *Horror* (London: Batsford).

Keesey, P. (1993) *Daughters of Darkness: Lesbian Vampire Stories* (San Francisco: Cleis Press).
Keesey, P. (1995) *Dark Angels: Lesbian Vampire Stories* (San Francisco: Cleis Press).
Kristeva, J. (1982) *The Powers of Horror: An Essay on Abjection*, L. Roudiez (trans.) (New York: Columbia University Press).
Laplanche, J. and Pontalis, J. B. (1973) *The Language of Psycho-Analysis* (London: Karnac Books).
Lewis, G. M. (1796) *The Monk* (London: J. Saunders).
Long Hoeveler, D. (1998) *Gothic Feminism: The Professionalisation of Gender from Charlotte Smith to the Brontës* (Liverpool: Liverpool University Press)
McCarthy, C. (2006) *The Road* (New York: Alfred A. Knopf).
Mieville, C. (2009) *The City & the City* (London: Macmillan).
Milbank, A. (1992) *Daughters of the House: Modes of the Gothic in Victorian Fiction* (Basingstoke: Macmillan).
Miles, R. (1994) 'Introduction, Women's Writing: The Elizabethan to Victorian Period', in *Special Number: Female Gothic Writing*, Vol. 1, No. 2.
Morrison, T. (1987) *Beloved* (New York: Alfred A. Knopf).
Mosse, K. (2005) *Labyrinth* (London: Orion).
Mosse, K. (2010) *The Winter Ghosts* (London: Orion).
Mulvey-Roberts, M. (ed.) (1998) *The Handbook to Gothic Literature* (Basingstoke: Macmillan).
Punter, D. (1996) *The Literature of Terror: Volume 2: The Modern Gothic* (London: Longman).
Radcliffe, A. (1794) *The Mysteries of Udolpho* (London: G. G. and J. Robinson).
Radstone, S. (ed.) (1988) *Sweet Dreams: Sexuality, Gender and Popular Fiction* (London: Lawrence & Wishart).
Showalter, E. (1977) *A Literature of Their Own: British Women Novelists from Bronte to Lessing* (Princeton, NJ: Princeton University Press).
Smith, A. (2007) *Gothic Literature: Edinburgh Critical Guides* (Edinburgh: Edinburgh University Press).
Spooner, C. (2006) *Contemporary Gothic* (London: Reaktion Books).
Stevenson, R. L. [1886] (2004) *The Strange Case of Dr Jekyll and Mr Hyde* (Harmondsworth: Penguin Books).
Stoker, B. [1897] (1979) *Dracula* (London: Penguin Books).
Tuttle, L. (1990) *Skin of the Soul* (London: Women's Press).
Walpole, H. (1764) *The Castle of Otranto* (London: William Bathoe and Thomas Lownds).
Wasson, S. (2010) *Urban Gothic of the Second World War: Dark London* (Basingstoke: Palgrave Macmillan).

Webster, J. [1614] (1927) *The Duchess of Malfi*, in *The Complete Works of John Webster*, F. L. Lucas (ed.), 4 vols. (London: Chatto & Windus).
Williams, A. (1995) *Art of Darkness: A Poetics of Gothic* (Chicago and London: University of Chicago Press).
Wolstenholme, S. (1993) *Gothic (Re)visions: Writing Women as Readers* (Albany: State University of New York Press).
Yahp, B. (1992) *Crocodile Fury* (Sydney: Angus & Robertson).

CHAPTER 2

Angela Carter: Living in Gothic Times

I wanted to begin the exploration of contemporary women's Gothic with Angela Carter because, for me, she is the one who brought it back into focus and popularity, almost slipping it under our noses at a time when other women were writing polemically about the inequalities of gendered lives, during second-wave feminism, a time of contradictions, challenges and opportunities. As Angela Carter comments: 'We live in Gothic times …' (Carter, *Fireworks*, 1974). She then goes on to expose the gendered constraints of dominant narratives, fairytale and myth:

> I believe that all myths are products of the human mind and reflect only aspects of material human practice. I'm in the demythologising business … How that social fiction of my 'femininity' was created by means outside my control, and palmed off on me as the real thing … This investigation of the social fictions that regulate our lives—what Blake called the 'mind-forged manacles'—is what I've concerned myself with consciously since that time. (Carter 1983, pp. 70, 71)

Carter was perhaps not quite the first revivalist, although she was the most thoroughgoing and influential. Daphne du Maurier disinterred and revitalised elements of Gothic writing by women in the 1930s–1950s, particularly with *Rebecca* (1938), referencing nineteenth-century and popular fictional Gothic romances (see *Jane Eyre*, Charlotte Brontë 1847; *Wuthering Heights*, Emily Brontë 1847) and non-Gothic romances (*Pride *and Prejudice*, Austen 1813; and pulp romantic fictions). Jean Rhys constructed a new postcolonial Gothic in her re-reading of *Jane Eyre* in *Wide Sargasso Sea* (1966). What we find with Angela Carter's work is more than a revival; it also builds on the new twists in du Maurier and Rhys, undercutting romantic endings, offering a postcolonial perspective, emptying out the narratives of power, identity and belonging which traditional Gothic often ultimately reinforces.

Carter explodes constricting narratives about romance, commodification, domestic bliss, family harmony and gender balances. She also breaks down the binary divisions of good/bad, right/wrong, black/white, male/female, safe/unsafe. This is done by her issuing fresh sometimes almost unrecognisable, vital versions of familiar types and genres: crime, science fiction, romantic fiction, the western. The Gothic, the mother of them all, in its ability to hold polarities in tension and inevitably expose performativity while celebrating potential and excess, is malleable in her hands. The baroque, embellished language and imagery of her later works, particularly the high Gothic *Nights at the Circus* (1987), grew from her cruelly, precisely, brittle, fine-tuned early work. Her scrutiny of now more obvious constraining narratives by which we lead our lives was revolutionary when she started rewriting fairytales and constructing new narratives in the 1960s. The myths, fairytales and urban narratives, the tales of the Hollywood screen about true love, honesty, honour, and the certainties of the forms with which she dealt, their catalysts, climaxes and seductive, calm conclusions are blown open throughout Angela Carter's work. She was influenced by the performativity and artifice of the Hollywood movies and the movie palaces which she and her father frequented. This delicious artifice is clearly smoke and mirrors and a blatant embellishment over what is tawdry and tarnished. Carter's play with performativity is influenced by feminist scholarship, such as Judith Butler (1990) and Joan Riviere (1929), along with postmodernist layering and eclecticism. By pointing out contradictions, Carter explores myths and constraints, the prison house of beliefs and stories by which we undercut our lives. The new wine in the old bottles of narratives and forms which Carter brings, explodes, then entertains and enables us to critically wonder while we celebrate and enjoy. It is Gothic because of its essential irony and exposure of limiting, formulaic narratives, but also because of its social designs upon us.

However, were Carter still alive and writing critically, I suspect she would be amused by the way the Gothic has spread like ivy, overwhelming all other imagery in advertisements, T-shirts, TV shows, its ubiquitous presence watering down remnants of a critical message. I expect she would have hated Stephenie Meyer's *Twilight* saga (2005–2008) as retrograde. Even though Bella becomes a strong vampire and saves her family and community, the saga replays the worst elements of the worst conventional Gothic work, ultimately only reinforcing the values of romance, family cohesion and dependency which, internalised, lock us into a blinkered vulnerable state. However, I suspect the parody and kitsch, Cthulhu fridge magnets and werewolf slippers might be appreciated, as might the conference papers engaging with politicised comment through zombies, ghosts, vampires and werewolves. Carter's work often uses the strategies of the literary Gothic against itself. Where the Gothic is used to destabilise complacencies but ultimately reinforce obedience and conformity, Carter reinvigorates its characteristics and refuses comfortable endings, leaving readers and characters with a mix of wariness and agency, even if only potentially. The locations and the metaphors are similar, the underlying message quite different. Several stories in *The Bloody Chamber* (1979), the ending of *The Magic Toyshop* (1967) and much of *Nights at the Circus* (1987) come to mind in this respect. In each she out-Gothicises the Gothic paraphernalia, imagery, setting and the trajectory of events and delivers alternative endings. In *The Bloody Chamber*, particularly 'The Company of Wolves', the threat of violence to curtail emerging sexuality is exposed at the core of versions of 'Little Red Riding Hood'. Should she stray, the vulnerable innocent girl will be rescued from being devoured by a wolf by a strong man, but in Carter's version she seizes her own freedom, sexuality and power and freely chooses the wolf. For Melanie in *The Magic Toyshop*, freedom from patriarchal manipulation and tyranny seems to lead to potential true love romance, as she and Finn face each other in the London version of the Garden of Eden, but the irony of this, with its intertextual references and absurd claims about the survival of the good, undermines its security as a conventional ending. In *Nights at the Circus*, Fevvers, an overly self-confident yet vulnerable woman (in being winged, she is already a spoof combination of patriarchy's binaries, the angel and the whore) just escapes being overwhelmed and predated upon by rich, powerful, older men.

Devouring, rape, conflagration and bodily harm are threats in the scenarios for all these texts. In more traditional Gothic, order is recognised and restored, true love wins, comfort (and its partner, complacency), however threatened and tenuous, is reinstated, but not in Carter's work. Carter's putting of old wine in new bottles (Gamble 1994, p. 4) applies to her use of the Gothic, as it does to her replay of constraining narratives and orthodoxies more generally. It leads to explosion, a rich ambiguity, the energy of carnival and creative chaos. Rebecca Munford explores the often contradictory nature of Carter's challenge to both patriarchal continuities and forms of writing, and the newer orthodoxies established by second-wave feminism. Carter gives a 'fervent critique of the mystification of female virtue and victimhood within certain strands of second wave feminist discourse' (Munford 2006, p. 4), and her exploration of the potential for a 'moral pornography' seen in *The Sadeian Woman: An Exercise in Cultural History* (1979) worried many feminist critics and readers. I wonder whether some of the lesbian vampire sadomasochistic activities which appeared in the 1990s are not fuelled by a similar radical questioning of the negotiations of sexuality and sexual practices. Carter's work also operates in a different space to the explorations of traditional Gothic and the exposure of the marginalisation of women and their voices, at the heart of Gilbert and Gubar's *The Madwoman in the Attic* (1979), which so powerfully unveiled the gendered texts and subtexts of nineteenth-century Gothic fictions, as mentioned in Chap. 1. My argument is that Carter shows us that the actually quite straightforward constructions and representations of women as victims of patriarchy in Gothic texts, while a necessary first revelation and excursion into re-reading those texts, somehow misses the sexual energies, the collusion, the radical and the deviant. She moves further, and baulks against replacing one form of dominant belief with another, this time based on the claims at the heart of second-wave feminism. These we might find in arguments widespread in the 1970s and 1980s, apparently worked through in some women's fantasy and science fiction, e.g. that women would never cause or approve of wars; and women-based communities would be harmonious and eco-sensitive. Munford quotes Lorna Sage, who astutely recognises that Carter's work is neither straightforward nor really an enactment of or reaction to the arguments at the core of Gilbert and Gubar's work, which as she explains, 'unravels the romance of exclusion. And this means it is in an oblique and sometimes mocking relation to the kind of model of female fantasy deployed by Gilbert and Gubar in *The Madwoman in the Attic*—where fantasy is a matter of writing against the patriarchal grain' (Sage 1992, p. 168).

In effect, Angela Carter has it both ways. In her Gothic-infused work, she tackles the narratives and myths supported by Western patriarchy. She revels in the explosions this causes, mixes realism with fantasy and splices in influential literary infusions, but she never offers a straightforward alternative. This is a performance with most serious issues at its core, a balancing act without a safety net, an aerialiste's leap from a trapeze when neither safety harness nor wings are assured.

Carter's early life was marked by stability and yet there were elements of disruption. We can see in her work the influence of a household of women, as well as that of a father who took her to the cinema and instilled in her a delight for artifice and performance. Born in Eastbourne, Sussex, in 1940, Angela Carter had one brother and spent the war in Yorkshire with her maternal grandmother, in a home dominated by women. Moving to Balham in lower middle-class South London in the 1950s, she became a junior reporter on the *Croydon Advertiser*, read English at Bristol University, 1962–1965, and then, following a failed marriage, lived in Japan from 1969–1972. This brief history gives some idea of her influences and the variety of her work: the realistic detail of journalism, the ideas, language and forms of the literary greats, who were then seen as predominantly male, the defamiliarisation of Japan and its ways, a land in which she felt herself to be a giant, and the performance, artifice and carnival of the cinema.

She is not easily pigeonholed as a feminist writer. However, several of her statements celebrate the sense of challenge and newness which second-wave feminism promised:

> truly it felt like Year One that all that was holy was in the process of being profaned and we were attempting to grapple with the real relations between human beings ... I can date to that time and to some of those debates and to that sense of heightened awareness of the society around me in the summer of 1968, my own questioning of the nature of my reality as a woman. How that social fiction of my 'femininity' was created, by means outside my control and palmed off on me as the real thing. (Carter 1968, p. 37)

Her notion of performative, everyday femininity as an artifice or fiction lies at the heart of her energetic exposure of the constrained narratives, the imprisoning roles underpinned by the falsities of romantic fictions into which women buy, at a cost. This is seen in the potential victimhood of the bride in 'The Bloody Chamber' (1979), and in the roles played by Tristessa in *The Passion of New Eve* (1977), the latter self-constructed from Hollywood film versions of the necessarily tragic condition of women, static and beautiful, existing only as performers and victims. Dipping more deeply, the corollary, the flipside of the entrapping artifice of a form of femininity is the sadistic patriarchal power of Uncle Philip in *The Magic Toyshop*, and Christian Rosencreutz's desire to idolise only to then sacrifice Fevvers, the winged woman, goddess, mythic being and potential victim in *Nights at the Circus*.

Carter won several awards, the John Llewellyn Rhys prize for *The Magic Toyshop*, the Somerset Maugham award for *Several Perceptions* (1968), and the James Tait Black memorial prize for *Nights at the Circus*. Influenced by Shakespeare, Yeats and Dickens, her fascination with Hollywood and with the US was also affected by reading the horror writer Edgar Allan Poe, H. P. Lovecraft, many modernist and nineteenth-century writers, seeing popular Hollywood films, pantomimes and fairytales, and immersing herself in the writings of the Marquis de Sade.

Interestingly, by writing in the Gothic mode, Carter was ahead of her time. 'Carter tended to think ahead of the culture in which she found herself writing' say Joseph Bristow and Trev Lynn Broughton in an earlier critical work on Carter (1997, p. 4), and for this they quote Lorna Sage's focused comment on her insightful outsider status and her ability to forge something new in the face of a feminist enterprise that favoured the realist. This links her back to Poe, Hoffman and Lovecraft, spliced with Butler, and with a wry, insightful view of second-wave feminism. Carter is never easily pigeonholed. Her single-handed revival of the Gothic in the 1970s is astonishing, since the mode was totally out of sync with the times, and yet her work exploded myths and repressive representations both for the mainstream and for the acceptable forms of feminist writing. In addition, she also set the pace or paved the way with her unique sensibility and uncompromising, catalytic force for the revival of popular genres interwoven with high art references and complex cultural contexts. Carter's work is influenced by romantic fictions, horror, science fiction (*The Passion of New Eve*), mythology and fairytale (*The Bloody Chamber*), pornography (*The Sadeian Woman*; *Fireworks*, 1974; *American Ghosts and Old World Wonders*, 1993), film, and text. Shakespeare, Yeats and Dickens are intermixed and updated with popular culture. Her modes of seeing and writing are eclectic and in this she also produces a postmodern Gothic, at once baroque and embellished. It harks back to the traditional forms and concerns of the Gothic, both replaying yet upsetting them, exploring and exposing women's entrapment, deceits, haunted histories, with layers of reference to those Gothic horror writers who have influenced her: e.g. Poe, Stoker and Le Fanu. Her work queries their resolutions, as it does those of second-wave feminist work, offering something completely new, a self-awareness, a repetition and return, a rewriting and exposure, flamboyance as well as darkness.

Lorna Sage noted this when she said in a profile of Carter in the *New Review*, 1977, that her 'fictions prowl around the fringes of the proper English novel like dream monsters—nasty, exotic, brilliant creatures that feed off cultural crisis', and Sage identified Carter's popular culture thefts and embellishments—ever in tune with the time and its wild portrayals of life and its contradictions. 'She has taken over the sub-genres (romance, spies, porn, crime, gothic, science fiction) and turned their grubby stereotypes into sophisticated mythology' (Sage 1977, p. 51). So perhaps we do indeed have Carter to thank for the rejuvenation of the 'grubby', out-of-favour Gothic. She embraced it and her work produced a loophole through which it could again be seen as the morphing, essential, pastiche (and postmodernist) form which can expose, explode, ironise, critique and then move beyond the contradictions of the twentieth and twenty-first centuries, and of more traditional Gothic itself.

Angela Carter revisited, recast and rewrote the Gothic for the late twentieth century, taking a relatively neglected perspective and mode of writing, and turning its tropes inside out, upside down. She undercuts and exposes the constraining myths and cautionary tales behind the familiar Gothic, reappropriating its spaces, tones and tensions from a simultaneously wise and wicked feminist perspective, and utilising an agenda of exposure, explosion of nonsense, and agency. In so doing she revitalises the power of the Gothic to highlight constraining narratives by which we live our lives and express hopes, desires and fears in fictions and film, art and popular culture. Her predatory Dracula in 'The Lady of the House of Love' (1979) is a woman spliced with the Sleeping Beauty, who dies once she has been awoken by a merely transitory love. In 'The Loves of Lady Purple' (1974), a marionette, constructed to play out whorish male fantasies transferred onto her by her puppeteer and audience, becomes animate, exposes the sources of these fantasies and takes revenge, seizing her own powerful violent future.

In traditional Gothic, young women are pursued by rapacious men of power (see *Mysteries of Udolpho*, Radcliffe 1794; *Castle of Otranto*, Walpole 1764; and *The Monk*, Lewis, 1796). They are rescued by rightful lovers and swept into the oblivion of eternal love, while these rescuers and society try to constrict and pin them down with an outdated ritualised male gaze. It is a process of collection, shrinkage and ownership.

The women collude with this rescue into family, male power and marriage. In an ostensibly similar scenario, Carter's Fevvers, who has her eye on the economics, manages to morph, fly, escape and reconstruct herself in *Nights at the Circus*. Carter's work began with the brittle critique of bohemian British city life in Bristol and London. This includes the so-called Bristol trilogy: *Shadow Dance*, 1966; *Several Perceptions*, 1968; and *Love*, 1971. She moved on to the myth and Gothic tale table-turning of the earlier short stories, *Fireworks*, then to the magnificent *The Bloody Chamber*, through the middle period to the late works. In the middle, she really got her teeth into the debunking of conventional myths which restrained and silenced women. Examples of this are Aunt Margaret and Melanie in *The Magic Toyshop*, and the philosophical, political Gothic of *The Infernal Desires of Dr Hoffman* (1972). In the sci-fi dystopian Gothic of *The Passion of New Eve*, gendered bodies are the location for control and reassignment, reconstruction, exposing the manipulative myths which inform their construction (as performance and artifice) and destruction. Fevvers takes off where Melanie was left stranded, the world all before her in a rewrite of Genesis and *Great Expectations* (Dickens 1860), in a garden with a burning house of patriarchy, leaving seedy twentieth-century Victorian oppression behind her. And with the metaphors of flight offering possibilities of freedom, agency, new constructions, ways of being and telling your own tale, Carter's Gothic combines with her feminism. Cranking up the momentum, her left-wing political embrace of freedom in action and speech ridicules and points out the results of 'mind forged manacles' (Blake, quoted by Carter 1983, pp. 70, 71). Her high Gothic is combined with her full-blown, wide-ranging, carnivalesque in Fevvers, an aerialiste, larger than life, a cockney showgirl with a heart that sought gold, and who embodies the contradictions which refuse a straightforward feminist Gothic. Hélène Cixous (1975) in 'Laugh of the Medusa' undermines and refuses limiting worldviews based on binaries of good/bad, black/white, male/female, and Angela Carter translates her philosophical feminist critique into fiction. Carter's is a form of Gothic which dissolves binaries and will not just replace patriarchy with feminism, seeing both as constraining, and, instead, in the figure of Fevvers, mixing angel and whore, fact and fiction.

The later period of *Wise Children* (1991) tempers the Gothic of the earlier work, laced with irony and reversals, tragic and comic together, moving into a more Shakespearian phase. In an interview with John Haffenden, Angela Carter expresses her surprise that her work has suddenly been seen as going in a new direction when she saw it as of a piece. Noting her response to a review by Robert Nye, Bristow and Broughton comment:

> Carter, who was always sure to reflect on her reputation, felt that Nye failed to grasp how *Nights at the Circus* did not mark a resolute break with her previous work, but extended a project she had been pursuing for many years. (1997, p. 5)

At that point, Carter's work was being aligned with the younger writer and her great friend, Salman Rushdie, and being described as magic realist, which Bristow and Broughton recognise 'might have irked her', not merely because it was seen as newly developed in the work of others, but because it had been always been a mode of hers, and possibly because in itself it is both enabling and limiting. Furthermore, Carter disliked being labelled. Magic realism, grown from the work of Latin American writer Gabriel Garcia Marquez, and before him Jorge Luis Borges, was able to mix the supernatural and the magical with left-wing critiques of power, to unlock a political and philosophical power. In Carter's hands, magic realism encompasses all of these things and gendered power besides, as well as the power of traditional narratives to constrain thought and behaviour. In a literary critical world which largely favours realism as a mode of such engagement, Carter was unusual in her choices of non-realist writing, which includes the Gothic, Gothic horror and magic realism, which she had been refining and exploding since the Bristol trilogy. In an interview with John Haffenden, Carter emphasises how she remained more or less alone in exploring anti-realist speculative writing until, that is, the more general trends in literary fiction changed in the early 1980s. She says:

> Nye's review in the *Guardian* was very nice ... but grudging, I think he seemed rather reluctant to concede that there had been anything more than a lot of high-faluting bluster in my earlier work. But this is bound to happen. I haven't had a novel out for a long time (i.e. seven years). And also everybody is doing it now. I am older than Salman Rushdie and have been around longer, but memories are short. (Bristow and Broughton 1997, p. 5)

Carter identifies her own version of magic realism, spliced with horror, moving into a new mix of the Gothic. Her forebears range from American westerns to Poe.

> I'd always been fond of Poe, and Hoffman [sic]—Gothic tales, cruel tales, tales of wonder, tales of terror, fabulous narratives that deal directly with the imagery of the unconscious—mirrors; the externalized self; forsaken castles; haunted forests; forbidden sexual objects. (1974, pp. 132–133)

These are the trappings and setting of the Gothic, and here she also acknowledges the influences of horror on her work, but the sense of an interest in undercutting the victim role, such as the role of sexual innocent, is also clear here, and worked out in the two tales I discuss in the next section.

'THE LADY OF THE HOUSE OF LOVE' (1979) AND 'THE LOVES OF LADY PURPLE' (1974): TURNING THE TABLES ON WOMEN OF THE GOTHIC

In another work I noted:

> Carter has ... been seen critically as part of the new wave of contemporary women writers of the Gothic for her use of paradox, irony, myth, fairy tale and horror tropes to critique the contemporary world. One of her favourite subjects for Gothic and horror writing is the gendered construction and representations of power which render women as automata, puppets and femmes fatale. Carter's rewriting of certain fairy tales and horror scenarios, including the female vampire and the werewolf, celebrate sexuality ... or critique family tyrannies and patriarchal power. (Wisker 2003b, p. 18)

In these tales we have a vampire and a deadly puppet. Dracula's descendant, Angela Carter's title character in 'The Lady of the House of Love' (1979), sits in her Transylvanian castle trapped by her heritage and her history and by the routine which nightly prevents her from escaping. She is a kind of sleeping beauty, in a fairytale complete with a turreted castle in a world of fable and myth. The Countess is condemned to the nature which she has inherited. She is a vampire drinking the blood of whoever crosses her threshold, whoever comes into her house, and her life is a lingering death trapped in that fable and history, so not even romance it seems can rescue her. In this static languid condition, she resembles contemporary women aware of the constraints of past and current reconstructions of their femininity, built upon directives and narratives relying on a necessity to please, looking beautiful, being languid, supported and nurtured, and to take a back seat. The heroine occupies the back seat of the historical Gothic tale, *Dracula* (Stoker 1897), because she is an anomaly, a vampire woman in a castle unable to travel afar and seek her own prey. She is equally unable to cast off the spell of her inherited history and role, both of the vampire and that of the female Bluebeard's castle. The young, bicycling soldier on the brink of his own future, which is likely to be death in the First World War, has crossed lands, borders and as yet unbloodied space and stumbles across her and her hospitality. Ironically she is not empowered; she is only a sacrifice to the awakening romantic love which he initiates in her. He leaves; she leaves a bloodied blood-red rose: her heart is broken and freed. Always only the predator, trapping others, she is also now a victim of the romantic trap. She dies upon his kiss.

Carter's Gothic tale reveals the position of women as predatory, vulnerable, trapped, silenced and marginalised, victim of their situation, including what they take as love. The Countess is Sleeping Beauty, in a tale which is reversed. Woken by a kiss, she will have neither eternal life nor love followed by domestic bliss. She will only be mortal and die. Carter's revelatory story does not have a happy ending for Dracula's descendant, but it does expose the ways in which conventional, traditional Gothic constructs women as vulnerable victims, who are both predatory and dangerous. The wandering soldier is totally unaware of what he has done. Like Orpheus, he has woken her up and then condemned her but also himself. He bikes off into his own unknown, fighting future, in the war to end all wars, which did nothing of the kind. This scenario is set in a liminal moment, the turn of the twentieth century, where it rewrites women's position but offers no way forward beyond that of the dead *femme fatale*.

Helen Simpson lets Carter point out the potential entrapment:

> The heroines of these stories are struggling out of the straitjackets of history and ideology and biological essentialism. 'There is a story in *The Bloody Chamber* called "The Lady of the House of Love"', said Carter, 'part of which derives from a movie version that I saw of a story by Dostoevsky. And in the movie ... the woman, who is a very passive person and is very much in distress, asks herself the questions, "can a bird sing only the song it knows, or can it learn a new song?" Have we got the capacity at all of singing new songs? It's very important that if we haven't, we might as well stop now.' (Simpson 2006)

The second short story which fascinated me after 'The Lady of the House of Love' is from *Fireworks*, also collected in *Wayward Girls and Wicked Women* (1985), and often overlooked but essential reading because so very raw. 'The Loves of Lady Purple' (1974) is a great Gothic critique of the ways in which women's agency is undermined by mythology and constructions of their femininity. Here a female Pinocchio repays vengeance on both her maker/master, and on the audience.

Carter's representation of the vengeful, whorish puppet in 'The Loves of Lady Purple' exposes male collusion in female subjection and objectification. The Asiatic professor uses his esoteric knowledge to bring to life a puppet of his own making, nightly playing out his obsessions, scenes of the degradation of others and her own degradation and destruction. He constructs the ideal woman, manipulates her and enables others to see his and their dream animated, their violence and lasciviousness enacted. Then he insists upon the ultimate control, putting the sexualised woman back in the box. He hangs her up, showing he has the power. The tale embodies Kristeva's notions of the ways in which the male mind in development constructs what it desires, idealises, fears and loathes, then offloads fear and disgust onto a version of woman, which is destroyed. This is the material of serial killers, of *Psycho* (1960) and of Jack the Ripper, who demonise women and manipulate and despise the female body. Lady Purple is the stuff of hidden fantasies and fears, written on the constructed body of woman. She is an icon of desired and hated woman, an embodiment of men's longings and fears, the 'petrification of a universal whore', both a 'nameless essence of the idea of woman' and yet, once involved in her performance, 'the image of irresistible evil'. She is also controllable, and static, an ageless marionette, whose body parts are hung up nightly after the show like a painted, false coquette. An archetypal figure of the monstrous female, she embodies all her audience's desire and fear and yet can be conveniently tidied away out of sight for future use. Until, of course, she seizes the moment. Carter's vampire marionette wreaks vengeance for being cast in the mould of *femme fatale*. Manipulated by the strings of male pornographic adulation, this she dramatises in her every move. Lady Purple, the embodiment and repository of the punters' horror, *cannot* be packed away. This monster of their own making can neither lie down nor be hung up:

> she could not escape the tautological paradox in which she was trapped; had the marionette all the time parodied the living or was she, now living, to

parody her own performance as a marionette? Although she was now manifestly a woman, young and beautiful, the leprous whiteness of her face gave her the appearance of a corpse animated solely by demonic will. (1974c, p. 39)

In Carter's story, Lady Purple turns from manipulated object into vampire, acting out fears the professor did not even consider. Carter's Lady Purple is an even more animated version of male dreams and nightmares than the Asiatic professor has imagined. His creation comes to life, a Trilby (in the novel by Gerald du Maurier (1895), Trilby is a singer manipulated by the magician Svengali) and *My Fair Lady* (1964) with a vengeance. She drains him, and walks off to carry out vengeance as a whore in the village brothels. Nevertheless, her achievement is flawed. She escapes the role of living doll but is somehow now still trapped in someone's script as a deadly whore. She freed herself but the scenarios she goes off to enact based on her own decisions are still only those constructed for her by a social mindset that has limited versions available to women.

The Magic Toyshop (1967)

It is not until Carter explores the sources of these versions of women as victims to manipulation, constructs of limited perspectives controlling them, and vulnerable to the internalising of popular narratives of subservience and victimhood, romance and domesticity, in the Dickens-influenced *The Magic Toyshop* that she evidences the influences on such internalised representations and constraints, replaying the narratives to move beyond them. The novel foregrounds performativity and enforced puppetry. Here a young woman is a victim and puppet, representing woman as object, while the novel's ending replays another controlling myth, a kind of deceptively false dawn of promise based on romantic coupledom. Here, Carter exposes ways in which not merely fairytales, but also nineteenth-century literature and contemporary cultural mythology have embedded constructions and representations of women that are difficult for anyone to escape. When in her 'normal' middle-class home prior to the deaths of her parents, Melanie tries on the role of bride destined for her, by putting on her mother's wedding dress. It overwhelms her, she feels she is drowning in ice water, and when she climbs out of her window into the freedom of the night-time garden, the incarcerating dress, representing her future wedded role, traps her in the apple tree. Melanie only partially escapes, despite her energetic refusal to fit the wedding dress offered her, get in and out of her house, and avoid the clutches of the domineering arch patriarch puppeteer, Uncle Philip.

From her reading of de Sade, Foucault, the Brothers Grimm, Charles Perrault and Poe, Carter exposes the mixed terror and desire to disempower and objectify others which underlies the manipulation of Melanie as human puppet, both on stage and in life. Latterly this impulse reappears in the dark disempowerment and dehumanisation at the core of Madame Schreck's high class brothel in *Nights at the Circus*, a living death denying humanity and agency. Melanie escapes evolution into the middle-class mould offered by her decidedly stereotypical mother, who is only ever portrayed in her wedding dress, clutching a bouquet hinting at pregnancy and gazing sweetly up at her distracted husband (p. 11). Taken in by her dour, manipulative Uncle Philip, a Dickensian figure, a toymaker who turns his wife, the dumb Aunt Margaret, her brothers and now Melanie and her siblings into silenced, bullied, obedient puppets, she faces a worse entrapment, as a human puppet in his cellar shows. As an orphaned adolescent with two dependent siblings, Melanie nearly falls victim to toymaker Uncle Philip's designs to turn her into a puppet and control her sexuality. He forces her to play onstage the role of Leda in a parodic but very real version of 'Leda and the Swan'. She is costumed, manipulated and partnered with a grotesque phallic polystyrene and wooden swan, the mythic, puppet product of Philip's (and to some extent Melanie's) wild sexual imaginings. This is not just a control game in a basement, since the rape of Leda by Zeus/Jove is a familiar choice of both Renaissance painters and later poets, including W. B. Yeats. Historically, these male artists have been fascinated by the tale which casts mortal women as willing receptacles of rape by the immortal king of the gods, who descends to them in a variety of guises: to Europa as a bull, Danae as a shower of gold, and Leda as a swan, inseminating each. They then give birth to a mortal/god, which acts out a patriarchal fantasy, but they are also victims of social mores and are each cast out of their homes as whores. In her role as demythologiser—'I'm in the demythologising business' ('Notes from the Front Line', 1983, p. 71), Carter engages with, exposes and parodies such culturally embedded and replayed myths, highlighting their tendency to establish and reinforce beliefs and behaviours which demonise, disempower and victimise women. In *The Magic Toyshop* Melanie is rescued from loss of self by the refusal of the Irish brothers Finn and Francie to continue to cooperate with their tyrannical step-father, and by us as readers, by Carter's debunking of the pompous, patriarchal control of the event through highlighting the ridiculous movements of the swan. Farce and horror are played out in equal measure:

> Well I must lie down, she thought, and kicking aside shells, went down on her knees. Like fate or the clock, on came the swan, its feet going splat, splat, splat ... all her laughter was snuffed out. She was hallucinated. She felt herself not herself, wrenched from her own personality ... and in this staged fantasy anything was possible. Even that the swan, the mocked up swan, might assume reality itself and rape this girl in a blizzard of white feathers. (p. 142)

This is rape by proxy. The farce undercuts the terror but the description of the swan's mechanical movements emphasises Philip's power, both physical and economic, which is somehow licensed by Jove himself, as another rapist. Melanie is both reified and disempowered, as she is forced into compliance through the context of the narrative and the controlling hands of Uncle Philip. Losing control of self and reality, 'She felt herself not herself', disempowered, until Finn and Francie refuse to collude further. Carter offers a simultaneously dual reading, a terrifying swan and a terrified girl who experiences the scenario as very real. The power we have as readers to undermine this controlling narrative shows it to be a fantasy, a mere performance. Though significantly, the power to refuse this debilitating narrative lies in the moment of the actual realisation that it is just a narrative. While this makes the swan no less terrifying, it does empower the reader by showing how pompous Philip is. Now his power can be seen to be illegitimate and the swan ridiculous, thus undercutting patriarchal power's hold on the imagination.

The Magic Toyshop is a narrative of domestic incarceration and forced performance. It is a reworking of Gothic horror, Poe, Dickens, and the cultural myths embedded in the mechanics of Uncle Philip's pornographic script. Through these, Carter rediscovers and reveals the potentially terrible consequences of domestic incarceration, family tyrannies and sexual abuse. Critiquing 'happy families', Carter looks here at how a domineering patriarch turns adolescent girls into puppets of his and their own perverse fantasies in a gritty, realistic post-war world of newspaper for toilet paper, and postcolonial oppression. Carter does not merely entertain; she causes us to think carefully about the oppression of colonial others such as the Irish Jowle family and the disempowerment of women. This is symbolised by Aunt Margaret's choker and the expectations of her sexual obedience to Uncle Philip; the attempted reification and control of Melanie; and the mind-set of generations of families in small houses. So we can take the microcosm of a finely drawn incident as a fairy story retold or a family drama held up to expose its own narrative influences, and see the macrocosm: colonial and imperial myths. The fungal enslimed statue of Queen Victoria, along with Albert, in a London park is an image which undercuts the predominant historical narrative of monarchical greatness. Severed hands appear in kitchen drawers as signs of disempowerment and rebellion. In *The Magic Toyshop*, Carter explodes family and national myths in front of us. Rewriting Dickens, especially *Great Expectations* (1860) and Yeats' 'The Circus Animal's Desertion' (1939), she offers these larger narratives in the post-war, mid-century period, using the Gothic to expose the contradictions and the ambiguities, the ironies and the perversities in the everyday. It is performance, a self-aware story, not just feminist and not just socialist, but both these things and more. She presents the toyshop of post-war Britain, its model and working-class values and its oppressions and meannesses, its artifices and constraints, and its potential to destructively explode, like the old wine in new bottles. But with the conflagration at the end of the novel the innocent escape the fire; Finn and Melanie face each other like Pip and Estella in *Great Expectations*, with a potential new start. Simultaneously we have the self-aware artifice of such narrative endings. This clearly demonstrates how the Gothic tale replays and undercuts at the same time.

Carter, in rewriting fairytales, gives us Gothic castles, werewolves, vampires, marionettes coming to life, transvestites and transsexuals, deep forests, incest, twinning, mirroring and doppelgangers. The settings, tropes and images of the Gothic pack her work; they are the tools she uses to both explode and re-energise the Gothic. It is the ideal, always excessive, self-aware, ironic vehicle of choice. Her version of the Gothic, self-critical and tending towards carnivalesque excess, does not merely explode and critique, but offers rich imagery and potential.

One of Carter's major contributions to contemporary revisions of Gothic uses fantasy and humour to critique sexualised power relations and stereotypical representations of women and men. For example, in her transformations of fairytales such as that of 'Bluebeard', and her use of werewolves and vampires, she re-reads myths of monsters and beautiful heroines, refusing the often conservative meanings implicit in the tales and exposing their subtexts of social and sexual power relations.

DE SADE AND 'THE BLOODY CHAMBER' (1979)

Part of Carter's repertoire is to unpick the controlling mind-set of male power and female subservience. She exposes the victim position invariably implicit in pornography and then turns it inside out, celebrating the sexuality and power of her female characters, sometimes to the confusion of readers, as in *The Sadeian Woman*.

From at least 1972 onwards (see Gamble 2001b, p. 112), references to pornography may be found in Carter's work. When asked in an interview with Helen Cagney Watts if she was influenced by Foucault, she identified the Marquis de Sade as her primary influence, admitting: 'my reading of Foucault has possibly influenced me to some extent [...] really, though, it had been my reading of the Marquis de Sade that has probably had more impact; it is *the* text on sexuality and power' (p. 170; emphasis in original). In his study of Carter, Linden Peach (1998) argues that *The Infernal Desire Machines of Doctor Hoffman*, published in 1972, is the first of her books to show the influence of de Sade, since she references both pornographic scenarios and a *style* attributable to a Sadeian influence. He sees her as parodying panoptical traditions, getting inside the mind of the male pornographer and oppressor through using a male narrator.

> Carter as a female author is appropriating a male consciousness to expose how women are trapped, like the woman reader of this novel, in a male imaginary. [...] the narrative technique of ventriloquism, a female author speaking in a male voice, is employed not just to create pornography but an essentially sadistic version of it. (1998, p. 111)

In this novel, Desiderio's narrative positions the male reader as voyeur but does not actually offer him an enjoyable pornographic spectacle. Again, Carter is turning the tables by exposing and parodying the particularly violent and oppressive aspects of a socially legitimated pornography which relegates women to victim status. As Vandermeer (2001) comments:

> Her characters are forever escaping, socially, mentally or physically, the traps laid by men. If she deals with established stereotypes in 'The Bloody Chamber' rather than fully fleshed out characters, then this is because fairy tales clothe themselves in stereotypes and archetypes. (Vandermeer 2001)

Since the time in which she wrote her collection of short stories, *The Bloody Chamber*, Carter, like other radical contemporary women Gothic writers since, refuses to reaffirm a status quo which reduces women to stereotypes, objects, puppets and even terrified dependants. She exposes women's own collusion in those 'traps laid by men', her feisty women increasingly making their own choices.

Lucie Armitt notes that Carter's are more Gothic tales than fairytales, since they revisit their often crueller originals, rather than the relatively tame fairytale versions:

> Perhaps we either need to accept that these stories are not fairy tales at all, or radically re-think what a fairy tale is. After all, while Carter's two 'Virago Book(s) of Fairy Tales' (1991 + 1993) are self-evidently collections of revisionary fairy stories, can the same so easily be said of a collection called 'The Bloody Chamber'? Quite clearly, rather than being fairy tales which contain a few Gothic elements, these are actually Gothic tales that prey upon the restrictive enclosures of fairy-tale formulae in a manner that threatens to become 'masochistically' self-destructive. (Armitt 2001, p. 89)

In her rewritten Gothic fairytales such as Little Red Riding Hood, as in 'The Company of Wolves', and Bluebeard's Castle, which is the title story of her collection, 'The Bloody Chamber', Carter exposes the latent sadism and the blatant, patriarchally derived enforced warnings to women to conform. This might involve denying them any active sexual excitement and choice and discouraging them to ask questions or challenge laws and rules. That she also celebrates sexual agency positions her beyond mere rewriting towards a revisioning of these tales as vehicles to recognise and celebrate women's sexuality, released from controlling narratives.

THE BLOODY CHAMBER (1979)

Baldick reminds us that 'The imprisoning house of Gothic fiction has from the very beginning been that of patriarchy', and notes the terror of 'the confinements of a family house closing in upon itself' (1993, p. 35). In 'The Bloody Chamber', Carter rewrites the Bluebeard tale and critiques romantic fiction, using Gothic spatialised horror, entrapment and reification. It is a favourite, archetypal male control fantasy, which Carter exposes as constructing the wife as commodity, an ornament and feast for the eyes, to be disposed of when she starts to question and query male control of power and knowledge. Here, a wealthy, sadistic 'Bluebeard' Marquis purchases his new, beautiful wife, removing her from genteel poverty. Her sexual awakening is empowering for her but for him it is one of his usual plots to control her, engulf and devour her innocence, and this he does through perversion. 'The strong meatify the weak' (*The Sadeian Woman*) says Carter, exposing the animal in us all. Her language emphasises the context of torture and sex. The tale aligns power and sexual activity, showing how latent cannibalism informs relationships ruled by economics disguised as sexual equality. Threats of violence attract as they repel the new bride. The Marquis views his young, lower middle-class wife salaciously and cannibalistically, as a butcher would a prime cut:

> I saw him watching me in the gilded mirrors with the assessing eye of a connoisseur inspecting horseflesh, or even of a housewife in the market, inspecting cuts on the slab. (p. 15)

The young bride sees her husband inspecting her like so much meat on a slab, but she is overwhelmed by his attention and the undying love offered. She is a Jane Eyre, second Mrs de Winter figure, poor and grateful for his attention and wealth. He is a man of plush furnishings, hidden rooms, turrets, fine cigars and power. They are cut off, rather like a dream holiday location, but this turns out to be actually dangerous for her: the romantic 'fairy solitude' of the castle is interrupted by hints of torture. Its seclusion has the sinister connotations of embalming fluid:

> And, ah! his castle. The faery solitude of the place; with its turrets of misty blue, its courtyard, its spiked gate, his castle that lay on the very bosom of the sea with seabirds mewing about its attics, the casements opening on to the green and purple, evanescent departures of the ocean. (p. 13)

In order to educate his most recent bride, the Marquis leaves open books of pornography. He is a voyeur of his own sexual acts and her awakening so replays it all in a series of mirrors. She is an object of desire, control and consumption, wearing only an expensive choker, which again expresses her imprisonment, with the lure of materialism for her. She is controlled as Uncle Philip controlled Melanie and his own choker-adorned wife in *The Magic Toyshop*. The Marquis is self-absorbed in his patriarchal power fuelled by previous successes, wealth and solitude:

> Rapt, he intoned: 'Of her apparel she retains/only her sonorous jewellery.'
> A dozen husbands impaled a dozen brides while the mewing gulls swung on invisible trapezes in the empty air outside. (p. 17)

'[I]n the viscera of the castle' (p. 27), the palpable heaving heart of the torturous place, there are smells of tobacco, leather, aftershave—male power. This Bluebeard's favourite poet supports his equation of sexual acts with torture and suffering, saying 'There is a striking resemblance between the act of love and the ministrations of a torturer' (p. 27). His ultimate control, as in all Bluebeard tales, is that of torture and death, the iron maiden, the rack. In most versions the young girl is rescued by a male saviour, such as a brother, but in Carter's tale, the girl uses her wits, allies with a blind piano tuner and is rescued in the end by her warrior mother who, after all, has won battles with pirates.

Carter's women are sexually aware rather than innocent victims. Like Margaret Atwood, she deliberately unpicks familiar fairytales and rejects the underlying message to women on how to behave, exhorting them to be silent, be still, and to be victims. Carter rewrites 'Little Red Riding Hood' in 'The Company of Wolves' in *The Bloody Chamber*, using the figure of the werewolf to express hidden and socially unacknowledged passions which empower the young girl to celebrate her sexuality, the 'beast' in herself. This is a powerful reversal of the conventional werewolf myth in which women are often the victim, while the abject, the animal, is killed off.

Rosaleen chooses to turn into a wolf. Neither she nor the wife in 'The Bloody Chamber' need a woodsman or brother to save them, and Carter suggests these would only be fulfilling other stereotypical roles in which men are the rescuers rather than the predators. Instead, Carter's young women find other strengths. Her strong women have no need for such narratives of victimhood. However, in making their own choices, they reject neither sexuality nor men.

At the end of this rewritten Gothic tale, 'The Company of Wolves', the girl and wolf unite. Discarding and burning her clothes, she refuses to be a victim and gets into bed with the wolf in a celebration of her sexuality:

> Every wolf in the world now howled a prothalamium outside the window as she freely gave him the kiss she owed him. (1979b, p. 118)

The motif of recognising the beast in ourselves and uniting like-with-like emerges again in 'Wolf Alice' (1979e), a werewolf tale published alongside 'The Company of Wolves'. Here a feral werewolf girl, Alice, moves through the mirror stage of self-recognition into loneliness. An abject creature, she has found shelter in the castle of another abject creature, the cannibal Duke, whose nocturnal habits of grave robbing and corpse eating equate him with the vampire. And like the vampire he casts no reflection. Wolf Alice recognises her own mirror image, and in nurturing the wounded Duke, two forms of the abjected support one another, like and like come together. She licks him until he is whole and once transformed is able to produce a reflection. This is a Gothic horror tale containing werewolves, vampires, cannibals, social exclusion and punishment, marginalisation, victimisation, mystery and superstition. It is also a tale which refuses to restore conventional order, pack away the horrors, but instead offers ways of living with them, as ourselves. It is a tale uniting the motifs Carter uses of recognising the animal within as our own self, and, using twinning motifs, showing us that the Other is ourself, to be brought into the open and nurtured rather than abjected or hidden away in ignorance and violence.

The binarism which underpins conventional Gothic horror is hierarchical and destructive. It is refused by the fracturing of boundaries between the abject and the self, the passive and active, male and female, as enacted in Carter's tales and in her language, which yokes opposites and combines carnival with horror. In this she embodies and dramatises Kristeva's arguments. Insistence upon boundaries, differences and hierarchies leads to dominance, and war—between nations—man against woman, black against white, and so on (Meaney 2000, p. 219). Kristeva locates 'at the doors of the feminine, at the doors of abjection … the drive foundations of fascism' (Kristeva 1982, p. 154).

By recognising the Other and the abject as part of ourselves, refusing that borderline and opposition, we can, Carter argues, overcome the need to find victims, scapegoats and enemies. Kristeva's *Strangers to Ourselves* (1988) provides a political exploration of the way the West treats foreigners based on an examination of racism in France. Here she links the need to expose the boundaries, rejections and repressions of Western patriarchal-based horror with the need for equality, both racial and political:

> Our disturbing otherness, for that indeed is what bursts in to confront the 'demons', or the threat that apprehension generated by the protective apparition of the other at the heart of what we persist in maintaining as a proper, solid 'us'. By recognising *our* uncanny strangeness we shall neither

suffer from it nor enjoy it from the outside. The foreigner is within me, hence we are all foreigners. If I am a foreigner, then there are no foreigners. (Kristeva 1988, p. 192)

Carter challenges what is conceived of as the stuff of Gothic horror. One the one hand, she explores the domestic as a space for legitimated violence and repression, exposing the horror in the normalised destruction of animals, Otherising and rejecting what is different, as well as through the operation of hypocritical, terrorising laws. On the other hand, she rejects what is conventionally seen as horror—the Other—and the conventional closure of horror—a restoration of a disempowering, rather blinkered status quo. Her language embodies these exposures and refusals, cutting to the heart of cultural paradox and hypocrisy, of which conventional horror is a servant. Her writing interweaves the fairytale and the everyday real, the domestic and the bizarre, using the oxymoron figures of twinning self and Other/self to refuse the polarisation which lies at the heart of conventional horror.

Nights at the Circus (1987)

Carter sets her masterpiece *Nights at the Circus* at a Gothic moment, the turn of the century, a gap in possibilities, a moment of change for women in Europe in particular. It is a novel of liminality and of threshold crossings, of troublesome contestation between what seems real or possible and what is fantastic. In this liminal moment, the repetitive chiming of midnight, a magic space (see *Tom's Midnight Garden*, 1958) and the transition from the nineteenth to twentieth century, anything is possible. It is a moment of potential and thus, like the narrative of the novel, is an example of Gothic twinning, the real with the fantastic, the imagined. The novel opens with Walser, a young American journalist, interviewing Fevvers, legendary aerialiste, on the cusp of the century, in her dressing room, in France, and they talk of performance, artifice, truth and the parallel worlds of reality and the circus. As a high Gothic text, *Nights at the Circus* constantly splices the fantastic with the historically sound and realistic. It offers parallel readings and refuses a closed version of Fevvers as winged woman (or not). As is noted of Fevvers, a larger than life, cockney Venus straight from a billboard advertisement, 'in a secular age, an authentic miracle must purport to be a hoax, in order to gain credit in the world' (p. 17). In the moment between centuries, truth and fiction are intermixed, confused. This mix also reveals how the internalisation of a specific projected life narrative could lock you up forever in a limited state. Fevvers as a teenager realises this when she comments that life is not just about waiting for a prince to release her. She plays the role of a mascot in Ma Nelson's brothel by standing in an alcove, holding her ornamental dagger. Her youth and the sisterly qualities of the establishment keep her safe. Fevvers watches the artifice of brothel relationships mimicking managed fairytale romance. These reveal its tawdry underside in economic exchange and sexual power games. This novel plays a great deal with Gothic spaces of limitation, incarceration and freedom, and Fevvers' time at the brothel takes place in an enclosed, protected space in which there is an interaction of power and freedom among the women, who each learn other trades by day and earn their keep by playing sexual roles by night. Fevvers, ever the performer, knows a fake when she sees one:

> Sealed in this artificial egg, this sarcophagus of beauty, I waited, I waited … although I could not have told you for what it was I waited. Except, I assure you, I did not await the kiss of a magic prince sir! With my two eyes I nightly saw how such a kiss would seal me up in my appearance forever. (p. 39)

What is empowering is that the very representation of liminality, the Gothic, holds a tension between imposed narrative and alternatives, the fantastic and the real. So the difference between life at Ma Nelson's, the motherly brothel owner, and at Madame Schreck's, the petrifier of female objects, is clear. At the brothel, candles and shut, dark curtains and the maintenance of a relatively safe space, both the whores and their clients are voluntarily bought into relationships, a relatively nurturing way of being. In the cold light of day after Ma Nelson's death, the revelation of a moth-eaten decaying artifice not only jeopardises their security but also the veracity of the narrative into which they had willingly bought. Each exits with the self-development skills they had acquired, since no one is a victim, despite their poverty. At Madame Schreck's, on the other hand, the women are forced into paralysis and stasis and are totally controlled. Melanie in *The Magic Toyshop* is a puppet who rebels, but these women are silenced into a deep sleep, unable to move and constructed as objects and in economic terms, who physically and mentally are unable to break free from this lived imprisonment. They have neither physical nor imaginative freedom and, therefore, no agency. Carter consistently offers the polarities of constraint, imprisonment and freedom: freedom to imagine, expressed through the winged woman with the freedom to fly and to construct herself as a performance, which she finds satisfying as well as lucrative.

Fevvers is a down-to-earth miracle. In a familiar Gothic trajectory, the novel replays various scenarios which oscillate between imprisonment and freedom. Fevvers' freedom and the freedom to think other than in a constrained narrative are shown, for example, in the circus segments of the novel, in the broken mirrors in which the tigers are trapped, and in the relationship between Mignon and the bullying strongman. Fevvers is not merely flying in the face of patriarchal dominance, as I would have observed years ago, but she is also constructing her own narratives in escape mode. She knows when she is fooling herself and the reader, as well as Walser, the smitten American journalist. She is not trapped in her appearance, like someone else's version of her, and so she is an expression of liberated thinking, flexible, inexplicable, self-empowered. Hers is a Gothic tale not just because of the circus trappings and the darkness of the threats, but because as a woman with wings she troubles complacencies and fixed categories.

The tales she tells are of predatory male behaviour, constructions of self as artifice, disempowerment, and a sense of agency, parallel tales, realistic and fantastic. There are Gothic horror scenarios of disempowerment and near dismemberment, incarcerating contexts of castles, and potential transformation into a clockwork performer in a Fabergé egg (at the Grand Duke's, one of those who try to imprison and own her). Carter's Gothic demonstrates that women's constructions and perceptions are artifice, objects of interest to be manipulated. Her work problematises the difference between the real and the fantastic, the historical and the magical, consistently interrelating that with the women's real worth. In terms of the relationship of women to power, the novel focuses on the ways in which a series of powerful men try to capture, disable and ultimately restructure, commodify and objectify Fevvers, turning her into a possession, an icon of life. Fevvers is constructed as Azrael, the angel, for the fanatic Christian Rosencreutz, who wishes his own immortality through controlling her, and as a static, shrunken performative bird on a golden bough for the Grand Duke.

His is a Gothic castle. Its cold halls are medieval, yet modern, as are its technology of ice sculptures of swans and Fabergé eggs with miniature controlled orchestras, trains and small worlds. Its location is one of entrapment, artifice, a house which is a 'realm of minerals, of metals of vitrification of gold, marble and crystal; of pale halls and endless mirrors' (p. 184).

Reification is familiar in Gothic horror, where people become objects and objects come alive in a terrifying and strange reversal. The Grand Duke has designs to turn a woman into an object of control, to place a shrunken Fevvers as a golden bird in a golden cage.

> The cage was empty. No bird stood on that perch, yet. Fevvers did not shrink, but was at once aware of the hideous possibility that she might do so. (p. 192)

Controlling the Duke's sexual activity, she escapes as the ice sculpture table decoration of herself as a swan melts into free-flowing water.

In the high Gothic *Nights at the Circus,* the new Victorianism of Fevvers, the brothel and the circus troupe enable Carter to delve into a Europe deep in its nineteenth-century power struggles and differences. Escaping the clutches of the Grand Duke, Fevvers lands at the last minute on the Trans-Siberian railway, exiting a Fabergé egg, then continues her journey with the circus. Fevvers is able to cross boundaries in the safe guise and space of the circus, which has its own internal strife and perverse struggles and oppression. This is not the idealised circus of Dickens' *Hard Times* (1854), on which it is based, but instead it can cut straight through the geographies of historical Europe, from France to Russia and back, as it also cuts through time and space.

Each tableau is a product of particular, personal formulae for controlling life. Fevvers resists and shifts away from the restraining visions of Madame Schreck and her underground chamber of torment populated by static women for the purposes of feeding bizarre sexual fantasies, Christian Rosencreutz and his religious fanaticism based on a need to control the education, economic situation and power of women, the Grand Duke and his desire to reduce Fevvers to an ornament and performative object, and the American Colonel who owns the travelling circus. Each has designs on Fevvers, which reflect the exploitation of women throughout history and within wider society. Her escape is the triumph of her energy and alternative power, in other words—her agency. Carter's Gothic text finally has Fevvers having the last laugh, retaining her knowledge about her own status as a winged woman, and/or 'intacta', in a reference to the virginity she has managed to retain. She is an aerialiste. She represents refusal of gravity and logic, and she wins. And as the last laugh, the fast-talking, slow-flying aerialiste Fevvers defies others' controls, constructions and representations. She acts her way out of the role into which she is placed by others, tricking, shrinking, flying or whatever is appropriate. Carter takes conventional Gothic stories of constructions of women, fairytales and popular culture and turns them inside out. Historical reality, magic, the fantastic, Gothic darkness and its imaginative possibilities dominate the novel. Fevvers' controlling power enables her to manage the story and its resolution. Carter's Gothic exposes culturally and gender-enforced relationships of power, and enables Fevvers to fly free from these. Fevvers, the larger-than-life billboard pantomime trapezist, is the performative virgin whore of historical construction, but she is also her own self. She escapes, she tricks everyone and she is the ultimate female carnivalesque celebration.

Domestic horror is a favourite of Carter's, and Gothic horror and the work of H. P. Lovecraft and Edgar Allan Poe are frequent sources of inspiration, atmosphere, imagery and tropes. She visited Providence, Rhode Island and explored Lovecraft's influences, defining his horror as often based in repulsion from sexuality, as well as miscegenation. In a television interview with Les Bedford in 1977 she shows how Poe is a kind of family descendent.

> I have a kind of familial attachment to Poe. I've used him a lot decoratively, but never structurally. I don't know if that makes sense. [...] I've used a lot of the imagery from Poe. I say I've used it, I've used it as a starting point for imagery of my own.

Carter updates and places into the twentieth century some of the concerns we find in Poe's work: duplicity, hypocrisy, deceit and performance, since nightly he saw his mother on the stage be constructed and destroyed in a series of Shakespearian heroines. Chief among these was Ophelia. Poe's own family life is reimagined in Carter's short story 'The Cabinet of Edgar Allan Poe' (1985), with its echo of E. T. A. Hoffman's (1920) *The Cabinet of Dr Caligari*.

Carter replays and deconstructs representation of the lives of women. With murderous brothers and incestuous relationships, she stretches back to the Jacobean revenge tragedy of poison, swordplay and death, and then on to Poe and beyond to Hammer Studios and the Hollywood films which she enjoyed watching with her father in the over-painted artifice of London cinemas. Carter enacts and deconstructs the sexualised Gothic of the past masters, and moves on with her own addition of carnivalesque. She is well aware of the potency in mixing these influences together and exposing the performance, complicity and concealment of oppressive behaviours. Myths and their perpetuation in fairytale and popular culture are her focus and her tools. In 'Notes from the Front Line' she admits, 'I am all for putting new wine in old bottles, especially if the pressure of the new wine makes the old bottles explode' (1983, p. 69).

Carter's take on the Gothic unites the realistic with the symbolic and excess. In another work, I noted that she uses:

> the oxymoron to expose as fallacious assertions that behaviours, such as relationships of power and hierarchies, are based, in fact, in a shared reality. Postmodern Carter reveals 'realities' as versions, constructions, as does nineteenth-century Poe, but his work can ignore the pressures of everyday social and cultural institutions, while Carter, both earthy and symbolic, deals with them. (Wisker 2006a, p. 133)

On a high wire above the rest of those who rewrote fairytales and pointed out oppressive scenarios for women, Carter's swings both crucially enact those contradictions and their results. Using the carnivalesque, that deliberate temporary artifice of explosion and new potential, she creates new worlds and offers new imaginative opportunities. Her Gothic is dark. *The Sadeian Woman* and the bullying strongman of *Nights at the Circus*, Uncle Philip, the father and death in the short stories 'John Ford's 'Tis Pity She's a Whore' (1994) and 'The Executioner's Beautiful Daughter' (1974) shirk neither incest nor death. And her work also rises above the darkness once it has truly exposed its origins. While Poe leaves us walled up or entombed alive, Carter laughs. Her burlesque and the symbol of the trapeze offer imaginative alternatives, but they are also true Gothic. The contradictions are always in tension. The reader will find neither final answers nor morals or homilies. They will have to work it out for themselves, never forgetting the importance of irony and ambiguity in Carter's work.

Using the accoutrements of the dark Gothic, exposures of Poe and others before her, Carter moves towards the comic, the absurd. She is like Shakespeare in her ability to present both together, and so the fine tension and ironies of the message and the metaphors, the exposures, are also those of the potential to renew, make the bottles explode, create something else.

Celebratory excess moves beyond even carnival: 'the noise of negotiation and dialogue' (Donald 1989, p. 17), a radical refusal of the politics and power games which keep difference and the energies of the subordinated poor (and women) under control. Carter's use of the carnivalesque, that subversive, energetic exploration of opposites, emphasises the comic, liberating alternative to established values and meanings. As such, it enables dialogue between beliefs and behaviours rather than insisting on one right way. However, Carter moves beyond the time-limited radicalism of carnival. There is no need to put the circus away at the end of the show. Everything changes.

Conclusions: Angela Carter and the Literary Gothic

With a Gothic turn, Carter's favourite figure, the oxymoron, builds upon the paradox and twinning of double selves, opposites, self/Other, good/evil and so on, refusing to privilege one reading, one version of self or events. In her work, the yoking of opposites in language, techniques and descriptions, mixing the historically realistic and the metaphorical, fantastic and imaginative, the Gothic and the carnivalesque, enacts the attraction and terror of what could otherwise seem comfortably relegated to nightmare and myth, on the one hand, and fantasy dreams on the other.

In the Afterword to *Fireworks* (1974) Angela Carter made some famous, often quoted comments about her fascination with the Gothic:

> 'The Gothic tradition in which Poe writes grandly ignores the value systems of our institutions; it deals entirely with the profane. Its great themes are incest and cannibalism. Character and events are exaggerated beyond reality, to become symbols, ideas, passions. Its style will tend to be ornate, unnatural - and thus operate against the perennial human desire to believe the word as fact. Its only humour is black humour. It retains a singular moral function - that of provoking unease. (Carter, 1974 collected in 1995, p. 459)

And Fred Botting also celebrates her work:

> In her late twentieth century fiction, Carter powerfully, and often critically, demonstrates the reversal of values and identifications that occurs via the Gothic Genre. Otherness takes centre stage: sexual transgression, dark desire, and fantastic deviance wonderfully subvert the restrictive orders or reason, utility and paternal morality ... In Gothic times margins may become the norm and occupy a more central cultural place. (Botting 2002, p. 286)

Carter uses the literary Gothic to critique oppressive relationships of gender and power, to expose artifice and to explore representations and their power over us, to explore performance of roles—the performativity of being human. She uses it to critique social contradictions and explore/embody/dramatise what we are most afraid of. She also uses magic realism, a mixture of realistic detail and the imaginative, imagery, metaphor and symbol to represent a credible gritty world of South London poverty, post-Holocaust USA etc., *and* the world of the imagination, which is not less real but shows us people's inner feelings and constructions—making sense of the world, desires and fears which rule us. Her Gothic narratives destabilise our certainties, showing that what seems respectable and secure—values of love, marriage, relationships, identity, heritage, inheritance, property ownership, and professions—are constructions and artifices, pretences and performances. Uniquely at that time, she splices the Gothic with the carnivalesque and comic power to suggest people might be and behave otherwise.

Carter's work is socially, politically and sexually subversive, as well as entertaining and disquieting: Gothic, magic realism with a healthy dose of sexual politics. She offers us the werewolf in the kitchen, the living doll in the bedroom, the female icon, fevered construction of a brain determined to control women's minds and bodies, freed into a woman with her own wings and freedom, a celebratory figure for a potential new future. Recognising her powers of gendered, politicised Gothic, Lorna Sage called her 'a witch or wise woman' (1994, p. 1) and she is, of course, both.

Bibliography

Armitt, A. (2001) 'The Fragile Frames of the Bloody Chamber', in *The Fiction of Angela Carter: A Reader's Guide to Essential Criticism*, S. Gamble (ed.) (Basingstoke: Palgrave Macmillan).
Austen, J. (1813) *Pride and Prejudice* (London: T. Egerton).
Botting, F. (2002) 'Aftergothic: Consumption Machines and Black Holes', in *The Cambridge Companion to Gothic Fiction*, J. E. Hogle (ed.) (Cambridge: Cambridge University Press).
Bristow, J. and Broughton, T. (1997) *The Infernal Desires of Angela Carter* (London: Longman).
Brontë, E. (1847) *Wuthering Heights* (London: Thomas Cautley Newby).
Butler, J. (1990) *Gender Trouble: Feminism and the Subversion of Identity* (New York: Routledge).
Carter, A. (1968) *Several Perceptions* (London: Heinemann).
Carter, A. (1983) 'Notes from the Front Line', in *On Gender and Writing*, M. Wandor (ed.) (London: Pandora).

Carter, A. (1995 [1974]) *Afterword to Fireworks, Nine Profane Pieces* in *Burning Your Boats: The Collected Short Stories* (London: Chatto and Windus).
Cixous, H. [1975] (1976a) 'The Laugh of the Medusa', in *The Signs Reader: Women, Gender, and Scholarship*, E. Abel and E. K. Abel (eds.) (Chicago: University of Chicago Press).
Dickens, C. (1860) *Great Expectations* (London: Chapman and Hall).
Donald, J. (1989) 'The Fantastic, the Sublime and the Popular: Or, What's at Stake in Vampire Films?', in *Fantasy and the Cinema*, J. Donald (ed.) (London: British Film Institute).
Du Maurier, G. (1895) *Trilby* (London: Osgood and McIlvaine & Co.).
Frayling, C. (2006) 'Introduction', in *The Gothic Reader: A Critical Anthology*, M. Myrone and C. Frayling (eds.) (London: Tate Publishing).
Gamble, S. (1994) *Angela Carter: Writing from the Front Line* (Edinburgh: Edinburgh University Press).
Gamble, S. (ed.) (2001b) *The Fiction of Angela Carter: A Reader's Guide to Essential Criticism* (Basingstoke: Palgrave Macmillan).
Kristeva, J. (1982) *The Powers of Horror: An Essay on Abjection*, L. Roudiez (trans.) (New York: Columbia University Press).
Kristeva, J. (1988)*Strangers to Ourselves* (New York: Columbia University Press).
Lewis, G. M. (1796) *The Monk* (London: J. Saunders).
Meaney, G. (2000) 'History and Women's Time: Heroes and Villains', in *Angela Carter: Contemporary Critical Essays*, A. Easton (ed.) (Basingstoke: Macmillan).
Munford, R. (2006) *Revisiting Angela Carter: Texts, Contexts, Intertexts* (London: AIAA).
Peach, L. (1998) *Angela Carter* (Basingstoke: Macmillan).
Radcliffe, A. (1794) *The Mysteries of Udolpho*(London: G. G. and J. Robinson).
Riviere, J. (1929) 'Womanliness as a Masquerade', *The International Journal of Psychoanalysis*, Vol. 10.
Sage, L. (1977) 'The Savage Sideshow: A Profile of Angela Carter', *New Review* Vol. 39/40.
Sage, L. (1992) *Women in the House of Fiction: Post-War Women Novelists* (London: Macmillan).
Simpson, H. (2006) Review of *The Bloody Chamber*, *The Guardian*, 24 June.
Stoker, B. [1897] (1979) *Dracula* (London: Penguin Books).
Vandermeer, J. (2001) 'Angela Carter', *The Scriptorium*, http://www.themodernword.com/scriptorium/carter.html
Walpole, H. (1764) *The Castle of Otranto* (London: William Bathoe and Thomas Lownds).
Wisker, G. (2003b) *Angela Carter, A Beginner's Guide* (London: Hodder & Stoughton).
Wisker, G. (2006a) 'Behind Locked Doors: Angela Carter, Horror and the Influence of Edgar Allan Poe', in *Revisiting Angela Carter: Texts, Contexts, Intertext*, R. Munford (ed.) (Basingstoke: Palgrave Macmillan).

CHAPTER 3

Margaret Atwood and Canadian Women's Gothic—Spite, Lies, Split Selves and Self-Deception

This chapter looks in the main at the work of Margaret Atwood, arguably the leading living Canadian writer, whose work can be recognised (among other things) as Gothic and ecofeminist (though she resists such limiting labels). I begin by looking at Atwood's work in the context of Canadian Gothic more generally, with some mention of other great Canadian women writers, particularly Alice Munro.

Devendra Varma identifies hauntings and the supernatural in many Canadian fictions, suggesting these 'emanate from the darkness and cold', as do the context of their writing, and that 'Canadian literature, therefore, is kindred to the spirit of magic and the supernatural, a fertile ground for the exploration of the unknown and beyond' (Varma 1986, pp. 31–43). Atwood both ironises and revitalises the shaping narratives of Canadian culture, critiquing yet revaluing survivalist narratives, and those of small town, small tale constraints, so expressing a particular take on the cultural identity of many Canadians, with a universal appeal. Atwood deals in the main with two dominating narratives, one of adventurousness, another of entrapment. There is an idealism, attraction, promise, therapy and stupidity to the narrative of the adventurous explorers (the tales of Lord Franklin's doomed expedition, lost on the ice, mentioned several times in Atwood's work, for example, in *Survival,* 1972, and again in *Moral Disorder* 2006). This is countered by warnings about the death of the planet resulting from a blind investment in capitalism, consumerism and selfishness. What is offered is a celebration of wilderness which revitalises the ecosystem. Atwood's other favourite constraining narrative relates perhaps to all women, but is seen as particularly widespread in Canada. This is the leitmotif of Rapunzel, the Lady of Shallot in her tower, awaiting rescue from her present into a future defined by a fairytale prince. Atwood reveals this to be a flawed and dangerous fiction. Our own internalisation of constraining narratives is disempowering. Emphasising the constructedness of all narratives, the deception of storytellers, including herself, Atwood has one of her characters, the probable murderer Grace Marks, comment: 'Perhaps I will tell you lies' (*Alias Grace*, 1996, p. 41). For Shannon Hengen, a familiar Atwood landscape is 'littered with the wasted bodies of damaged women and the menacing shadows of the men who wounded them either by their distance or their presence' (Hengen 1994). Threats, alternatives and possibilities are expressed in Gothic terms, exposing contradictions, complacencies and blinkered narratives and offering hope through the speculative fictional Gothic, a mode of expression also found in postcolonial speculative fiction Gothic writers such as Nalo Hopkinson (Chap. 6). Alice Munro's work is equally rich with deceits, dead ends and self-delusional narratives of love and happiness.

Canadian Gothic and Alice Munro

Canadian Gothic is a cultural and geographical version of the Gothic, translating the threats to body and soul, the incarceration and the terrors born of gender and power into a cold, inhospitable, immigrated, wilderness context. It is often seen as produced by the harsh winters, and the relentless oppression of isolation and wilderness, the revived myths which threaten from the endless frosts and snows, which produce that wild mythic creature, the Wendigo. A necessary hardiness enables some to begin to understand and manage their surroundings, seek self-protection in refusing relationships and developing a tough survivalism. In talking of 'Canadian Gothic', Rebecca LeDrew identifies characteristics that 'include the concept of "North," or "Northernness," the binary opposition of wilderness/civilization, monstrous histories, post-colonial hauntings, and a permeating sense of spatial and cultural disorientation' (2012, p. 1). Faye Hammill (2013) defines the characteristics of modern Canadian Gothic texts as regional. 'Prairie Gothic' begins in the 1920s with Martha Ostenso's *Wild Geese* (1925), followed by episodes in the work of Margaret Laurence. In such tales of small towns marooned in vast open spaces, there is a sense of both isolation and incarceration, a result as much of the location as of the limited mind-sets which threaten women in particular, given their dependency on men. The regionalised 'Southern Ontario Gothic' is a term Margaret Atwood and Graeme Gibson coined for 'a subgenre marked by a focus on the repressions and claustrophobic terrors of small towns surrounded by bleak landscapes' (Hammill 2013), comparable with Southern American Gothic. In developing this term Atwood was thinking of, among others, the Nobel Prize winning Alice Munro (2013a), whose short stories combine both the domestic and the uncanny, emphasising life's emptiness, loss, misinterpretations, and, for women, a kind of entrapment in social roles going nowhere. Munro's women live in small towns, their location exacerbating restricted lives and minds in a bleak terrain, cut off by the cold and distance. The Gothic qualities of Munro's work sit side-by-side with the everyday, undercutting its comforts. They include split selves, an inability to read social signals, and imprisonment in mind-sets which often offer a fantasy view of situations ultimately unrewarded, refused. This is especially so when related to potential relationships, or investing in the creative futures of oneself or others. Alice Munro's collection *Dance of the Happy Shades* (1968) is a good example of her finely observed tales of obsessions and frustrated passions in which her characters hope to get away from the bleak isolation and small-mindedness of rural and small town life, but partners move on, families enclose them, and they wind up ageing, stuck and disillusioned. Munro's 'accessible, moving stories explore human relationships through ordinary, everyday events' (British Council Arts website). These stories are also examples of a stifling colonial legacy, exhibiting inherited versions of parochial Englishness, with outdated colonial mores, manners and tea parties, repressive domestic values and claustrophobic relationships, violence and oppression. In *Lives of Girls and Women* (1971) and *Who Do You Think You Are?* (1978) she mixes outdated, settler beliefs with tales of growing up and reducing one's aspirations. Lives indoors are claustrophobic, tautly managed, filled with ultimately curtailed aspirations, while outside the strange and threatening encroach. The tea party guests listen to children playing the piano indoors, preserving an outdated set of colonial aspirations and untruths, whilst outside the Canadian Wendigo haunts the vast forests, and parents make pacts with wild people in coming-of-age tales, sometimes replaying adult versions of fairy stories. In 'Images' (1968), for example, a young girl and her father meet an axe-wielding recluse in the woods. Threats, promises and the strange are all around and such tales warn that progress, happiness and cosiness are mere constructs of human existence.

Alice Munro won the Nobel Prize for Literature in 2013, simultaneously with the publication of her most recent collection *Dear Life* (2013), and won the Man Booker International Prize in 2009. In many ways, *Dear Life* typifies her use of characteristics of the Gothic to explore stalled, contained and imprisoned relationships in small towns, in periods where male power dominates, and where women are cowed, performing and managing to fulfil some imagined, implied or forced version of their husband's view of life, trapped in the house. Initially at least, Munro's trapped women characters are usually utterly without any desire to challenge or move on from this constrained existence, supported as it was by the beliefs of the 1950s, prior to the onset of second-wave feminism. Maternal, domestic and married constraints predominate. Romance is lacking, or just a sham or let-down. There are deaths, drownings, deceits and losses. However, there is frequently a female protagonist who questions these constraints and presents a challenge to the status quo by such adventurous activities as riding a bike, travelling or reading and writing books. But the dominant male who brings in the main wage usually silences and undermines her position, and she learns to keep quiet. When women take risks, their imagined escapes are no more exciting than another romantic liaison, another version of the relationship they have lost, become bored with, or been sidelined by.

I am reminded of Adrienne Rich's powerful poem, 'Aunt Jennifer's Tigers' (1951), in which, in the face of her husband's noise and power, Aunt Jennifer can only express her challenge and energy covertly and artistically, through her stitch-work of tigers. In the periods of which Munro, Rich and Sylvia Plath write, women were often silenced, marginalised and in service to the domestic and the marital. The insights of these two poets and Munro recall a period of general conformity, even though a quiet revolution was taking place among articulate women. As with Sylvia Plath's work (see Wisker 2004), Munro exposes emptiness, constraint and meanness. Conformity does not lead to happiness; rather it leads to silence and vacuum. In 'Amundsen' (2012), a young teacher finds her life taken over by the doctor running the sanatorium in which she works, and he plans their wedding, only to renege on this at the last minute, putting her back on a train to Toronto. In 'Gravel' (2011), the young girls in a family are hemmed in and threatened by the behaviour of their parents, and also by the potential danger of the gravel pit near where they live. The gravel pit claims the life of younger sister, Caro, who seeks attention while her mother conducts an affair. She constructs a story about rescuing the dog, Blitzee, but no one takes any notice of her own cry for help, and Caro drowns in the flooded pit. Both minds and lives are constrained in these ironic tales, so the arts are frequently the object of loathing, seen as pointless, as is socialising with the neighbours, indeed anything that upsets reinforced regimes. In the ironically named 'Haven' (2012), small moments of semi-rebellious questioning are quashed. The story focuses on a young girl, living with her aunt and uncle while her parents are in Africa, who senses the utter compliance demanded in the regime which the uncle operates in his own home. Everything is neat, tidy, cleaned, silenced and hemmed in. One evening, the cowed aunt is forced to return hospitality to the new neighbours, something her husband would never allow. She has a brainwave, and in the absence of her husband, she secretly invites the neighbours over and coincides their visit with that of Mona, her husband's estranged, musical sister, who is touring with her classical music ensemble. The ensemble perform, the evening goes well, but at the entrance of Jasper, the husband, the mood turns. He exerts his dominance by continuing with his routines despite the guests and the evening collapses. Although even Jasper is briefly somewhat stuck, on show, at Mona's funeral, Aunt Dawn's conditioning is terminal, she has neither the imagination nor the energy to think beyond an existence presented by the narrator as exhausting, disempowering and paralysed. Uncle Jasper rules, Aunt Dawn complies and the girl gets used to the regime and the beliefs underpinning it, beginning to think that 'Devotion to anything, if you were female, could make you ridiculous' (p. 128). Munro's Gothic is domestic, focusing on the terrifying, debilitating power of domineering behaviour, small-minded beliefs, and the constraining narratives of everyday normality in average households.

'To Reach Japan' (2013), the first tale of the *Dear Life* collection, offers some kind of escape but through a scenario which emphasises liminality, dangerous transitions, transient escapes and imagined resolutions based on fantasies. Although the tale does not concern Japan, the name suggests otherness, foreignness, displacement and, to some extent, it moves beyond Gothic locations, constrained places and domestic incarceration. The protagonist, Greta, is unable to really celebrate her identity as a poet in the 1950s, because she feels she is an outsider and odd, so she restrains her views, both about reading and the news, because her husband, Peter, deliberately holds no views. Her visit to a writer's party on the other side of Vancouver is daring and unusual but she is both ill at ease and reckless in her actions. Her awkwardness is emphasised through her uncomfortable clothes, her lack of acceptance on entering the strange, defamiliarised space where she is a stranger, outside the conversation, a little drunk, isolating herself physically. The shared discourses and understanding exclude and destabilise her as 'Nobody spoke to her or noticed her' (p. 8), and 'Everybody but Greta was equipped with friends, jokes, half-secrets' (p. 9). She realises 'Here nobody was safe' (p. 10). The mundane awkwardness yet terrible alienation of a social occasion into which one cannot fit is identified in Gothic terms of hidden communications, awkward entrapping spaces and isolation. Greta is the marginalised Other and when she accepts a lift home her disorientation and defamiliarisation place her in a vulnerable position. Although the initial danger is only that the stranger who gives her the lift decides not to kiss her, the actual upset of this evening has a much greater reach beyond the party and the lift home. The evening, the potential adventure of it, shakes her out of her everyday existence so that she obsesses endlessly about this man, Harris, as a form of escape, and she writes to him when she realises she will spend the summer in Toronto, where he lives. Greta takes the long train journey with her small daughter Katy through hundreds of miles of changing landscape. The vistas and large open spaces, the liminal space of the lengthy rail journey from Vancouver to Toronto and the new people she interacts with also disturb her, forcing her out of her equilibrium. Two young actors/teachers, Greg and Laurie, get on board and entertain the children, and the newness and destabilisation suggested by their embrace of performance and the ending of their relationship, indicate the transitionality of everything. On this long journey people get on and off, develop intense relationships, then disappear forever into a crowd. All this is perceived by Greta as extraordinary, dangerous and exciting, both disorientating and liberating. In the train speeding through the Rockies and the prairies a new space emerges, unsafe, unusual, creative, and this stimulates Greta's uncharacteristic behaviour and her brief liaison with Greg. However, such freedom is represented as risky and reckless. Katy leaves the small bed space and ends up in the metal link between two carriages, a dangerous liminal space on a speeding train. She could have been stolen or killed. Finally, Greta and Katy arrive in Toronto, where suddenly they are taken over by Harris, who presumably offers a new life. But like Greta, the reader is left hovering between potential excitement and numbness. In the end her lack of agency is emphasised: 'She didn't try to escape, she just stood waiting for whatever had to come next' (p. 30).

Joyce Carol Oates comments on Alice Munro's work that 'the evocation of emotions, ranging from bitter hatred to love, from bewilderment and resentment to awe ... [in] an effortless, almost conversational tone' evidences that 'we are in the presence of an art that works to conceal itself, in order to celebrate its subject' (2014). Hers is a quiet, cruel, insightful Gothic, a small town Gothic, of domestic, incarcerated silences, opportunities which lead to emptiness, dangers, absences and death. Romance is rarely rewarded, so her tales undercut traditional Gothic. Mostly, the women are left stranded. Her work is subtle, self-effacing, like so many of her female characters, but insidious, relentless in its undercutting of the fictions with which we might (dangerously, falsely) reassure ourselves.

Like Munro, Margaret Atwood upsets the myth and fairytale, and as is so often the case in Munro's work, the result is often another form of incarceration or emptiness. However, while moving through intense, desolate spaces and constrained relationships, Atwood often also empowers her characters in their challenge to conventional romantic narratives and sometimes offers new freedoms and agency alongside their new self-awareness.

Margaret Atwood

Margaret Atwood's poem 'Speeches for Dr Frankenstein' (1968) revisits the foundational women's Gothic text, Mary Shelley's *Frankenstein* (1818), depicting the self-absorbed scientist 'I, the performer' who would be God as Gothic performer, under the moon, his wrist a scalpel, 'unmasked' destroying and constructing from an image in his own mind, figuring his own version of something he needs, loves and fears, translated into the object of contradiction, desire and intended destruction.

Pinning it down, wrapping it up, it is a 'reflection, which steals every joy and hope from its maker', which then accuses her/him. The setting is wintry, 'this vacant winter/plain', where she scratches 'a message / on the solid snow'. The intent is a self-delusional construction of a version of self onto which to load dreams and fears, and which, as it turns on its maker, exudes self-awareness and a dangerous agency. Such Gothic images of splitting, mirroring, violence, construction and destruction; the self projected onto a hated and loved, feared other; and the performative nature of the self in this narrative in which the doctor is trapped recall Sylvia Plath's poetry, and are essential characteristics playing out in Atwood's Gothic.

Margaret Atwood is known as a leading practitioner of Canadian Gothic, a prolific writer, speaker, dealer in genres and insightful critic of the stories we tell ourselves, whether of the longevity of the planet, or the fulfilment of romance. Barbara Hill Rigney (1987) suggests that the Canadian literary tradition is victim-oriented, because of Canada's political status as a colony and so, necessarily Gothic, exploited, isolated. Hill Rigney sees Atwood reflecting the bigger picture of the country onto the characters of the novels, portraying Canadians and particularly women as an oppressed minority, and says that: 'Although defined by several critics as pessimist and negative—Atwood herself sees herself as a realist' (Hill Rigney 1987, p. 132).

Atwood is a feminist who refuses that amongst all other labels, and she is a writer of dystopian, science fiction who, until quite recently, also refused that term, characterising it as suggesting the unlikely and the unreal. In so doing, she was somewhat misrepresenting her own tendency to write to the same ends, project forward from the current mistakes and false narratives into logical dysfunctional futures, then begin to suggest speculative alternatives. Atwood parodies the Gothic while widely using its formulae to problematise internalised self-deceiving myths and narratives, expose the deceit, spite and meanness underlying ostensible female friendships, and fundamentally undercutting and terminally troubling the certainties of any record, report or representation. Atwood's Gothic work also specifically focuses on exploring and exposing romantic fictions, using popular fictional genres and forms to relate to contemporary and ongoing issues. She does so, offering a spotlight on the stories we tell ourselves, the constructions and representations which constrain our visions, the impossibility of reaching 'the truth'. Her engagement with the irony and constructedness of versions of everyday life is a familiar focus of the Gothic, vehicled by Gothic locations, characters, language and scenarios. In her work, she unpicks the tales we tell ourselves, exposes their stranglehold, and through critique and the speculative, offers a liminal space for agency and the construction of new stories. In this way, she builds on conventional Gothic, using its characteristics of landscape and buildings, human mind-sets, imagination, the haunting of the past in the present, and offers imaginative ways forward into a less constrained space and narrative. Her work always avoids idealisation and final solutions, since, as an ironic Gothic writer, she knows there can be none, only preferable constructions. I do not read her work as negatively as Hengen, above, since the speculative element of Atwood's Gothic, as well as its irony and intellectual play, enable the construction of ways forward, whether by the characters themselves or by the reader as a result of working through that liminality, the rich opportunities offered by moving beyond contradictions and constraints. Some of this liberating vision is due in part to her refusal to adopt stereotypes, her cutting through even the new feminist stereotype of sisterhood (*The Robber Bride*, 1993; *Cat's Eye*, 1998) and the flawed dream of positive eco-solutions to dystopian destruction (*The Year of the Flood*, 2009; *Madd Addam*, 2013), where 'God's Gardeners' also receive irony and criticism.

Atwood constructs a form of wilderness Gothic in *Surfacing* (1972) and *Survival* (1972). The first of these develops the kind of ecological focus which later re-emerges in the *Madd Addam* trilogy, and her investment in the importance of not merely survival in, but an ecological care for, equality with the planet and living things, informed by her interest in indigenous beliefs and practices from the Canadian North, and Aboriginal people in Australia. However, what she lauds, she can also parody, and expose. Her theme of false endeavours circles through the tales she repeats, of the failed Lord Franklin exploration to the snowy, isolated, deadly North, one of several entrapping tales people tell themselves, of finding the Northwest Passage, out-surviving the harshest occurrences, and, in this case, the intolerable blinding, overwhelming winter of the Arctic. She exposes the false narratives, and emphasises the danger, delusion, self-deception and deadly outcomes, features of the Gothic wilderness. Simultaneously she exposes the sense of entrapment in narrative, also a major feature of the Gothic. Atwood parodied these hopes, delusions and disasters, as she does to some extent in repeating the tale, reminding of it in *Strange Things* (1995), as well as *Wilderness Tips* (1991). The parodic edge of some of Atwood's own Gothic fictions is echoed in her critical writings, in *Strange Things* and in replaying versions of her father's worldview in *Stone Mattress* (2014) and the novel *Moral Disorder* (2006).

Her most popular and well-known text, and her most studied novel, *The Handmaid's Tale* (1985), is a dystopian feminist fiction but probably less clearly a Gothic fiction. It has none of the trappings of vampiric characters and enclosed dungeons and castles, but instead the entrapment of women in their roles defined by childbearing capabilities, and their silencing and masking, cloaked in the handmaid's religious garb. These are a Gothic set of curtailments which reconfigure the locked attics or dungeons, the dank corridors and entombment in castle walls as a late twentieth-century incarceration in roles, clothes and behaviours based on religious fundamentalism, on political mind-games translated into legal and social bondage.

In *The Handmaid's Tale*, Gothic, as a vehicle for critique, emerges through the silencing, the surrogacy of women in the face of infertility, and the deadly working of a regime whose power is both hypocritical and absolute. Following a global disaster, much of what is left of the world is toxic, a wasteland, with strict hierarchies among its remaining population, and a desperate problem for the survival of humankind: infertility. The novel focuses on North America, home to consumer capitalism and frequent target of Atwood's criticism. She sets Gilead in Cambridge, Massachusetts, and the wall where demonstrators are hung is one of the walls of Harvard University, an ironic comment on the liberating and egalitarian nature of intellectual pursuits. In Gilead, people are strictly divided according to their use, and for women, their fertility. The Maryanns do the housework, the wives perform and entertain, and the Handmaids produce children, if they can. Each has been schooled by the violence of the Aunts who, like excessively controlling convent nuns, force them to learn to be humble and behave. All comply, except a few, including Offred's friend Moira, who escapes and finds a role in a brothel. Each woman is named for the man they serve. Offred (of Fred), a fertile woman, has to join the Handmaids, and wear a wimple, walk in silence, befriend no one, love no one and perform sex to requirements to produce children in this barren land. Language operates against her and friendship is dangerous but she rebels in her own way and seeks to escape, leaving us her legacy as a testimony of the riot, traces, like ghostly sounds, on tape, to enable those who come after her to uncover the secrets of a time about which they have only been told various lies. This Gothic silencing and disempowering, renaming and historical tracing has a gendered political intent, pointing out the dangers of ecological disasters grown from human antagonisms, collusion with a materialist state, and pointing out the delicate balance of equality for women and the socially subordinate, since any equality in this notionally civilised world is only temporarily tolerated rather than genuine. The Gothic has designs upon us, and this tale, though not often discussed as an Atwood Gothic, uses Gothic tropes, motifs, characters and settings in a future dystopia, to point out the dangers of complacency and of taking false comfort in appearances. Women are always on the edge of being silenced and disempowered.

The Handmaid's Tale is also worryingly realistic, too close to current contexts for comfort. Atwood was influenced by a visit to Iran, and here describes women similarly shrouded, silenced and disempowered like those she saw behind shutters, or on the streets. The novel exposes the conditions of contemporary US and Western society which believes it cannot fall so far in terms of individual freedoms, health and prosperity, and which believes that equality, security, comfort and international power can enable everyone to live in some kind of harmony and balance, even when a holocaust removes their fertility and future. In *The Handmaid's Tale*, in one gesture, women lose their bank accounts and freedom to make choices, move around or own property. They are disempowered, disenfranchised and silenced, and if they cannot produce the children the regime needs for human survival, they are killed off by the regime, or sent to the toxic wasteland to work and die. The novel shows how easy it is to fall into a situation of inhuman, cant-based disempowerment and constraint. It is a prison society, where role play and silencing predominate; hypocrisy and horror are an everyday occurrence. Terrifyingly topical, the Handmaids of Atwood's dysfunctional future US-set world remind us, all too painfully, of the march of religious fundamentalism, which now (2016 at the time of writing), in much of the Middle East, demands that women return to or are forced for the first time into a medieval, barbaric, silenced subordinate condition, their sexuality controlled by powerful men.

The novel's defamiliarisation has become shockingly familiar on our TV screens, more frightening than any sudden onslaught or attack. What is so alarming is that for some years this Gothic scenario of silencing, torture and social entombment, incarceration, homes without privileges, roles without rights, seemed only a sci-fi feminist dystopia, some ironic malfunction of a brave new world, a 1984 from which, realising its horrific potential, we could use our insights and powers to escape. However, arguably, women's rights are more in danger than they have been for decades.

Atwood's Gothic is political and ecological and focuses on the narratives by which we entrap, fool and delude ourselves, exposing these narratives as dangerous constraints. *The Handmaid's Tale* is a dysfunctional near future Gothic. Later in *Oryx and Crake* (2003) and the whole *Madd Addam* trilogy (2013), the ecological elements of the nightmare continue. Perhaps the ironies, parodies and exposés of the Gothic might only be safely possible as representations when we have some of the intellectual freedoms to construct and express alternative visions and versions.

ROMANTIC GOTHIC UNCLOAKED: *LADY ORACLE* (1976), *ALIAS GRACE* (1996), *CAT'S EYE* (1988), *THE ROBBER BRIDE* (1993)

In Atwood's Gothic, the main focus of delusions which entrap are the romantic narratives women tell themselves, the constraining myths and narratives which delude and limit women's worldviews. This trope reappears throughout her work, particularly with the motif of Rapunzel. In the original tale, Rapunzel was imprisoned in a tower by a witch, an example of female spite. In a traditional female manner she lets down her long hair for her rescuing prince to climb up and claim her, showing her desire for escape into a traditional marriage. In Atwood's version, this is no more than a repetitive delusion. Like the Canadian tale of Franklin, the tragic adventurous explorer, the Gothic story of Rapunzel, originally from the Brothers Grimm, emphasises self-delusion, parallel worlds of the everyday and the internalised narrative of an ideal existence and escape which, in the case of Rapunzel, leads to a victim position. Canadian women construct their own towers of myth and isolation, depending on a prince who can somehow climb up their hair and release them from the spell of a wicked witch who, Atwood points out, is a construct they have themselves invested in. They are prisoners of their own restrictive narrative. 'Canadian literature shows women as icy, stony Rapunzels who are their own tower' (McCombs 1988, p. 28). The Gothic image of a woman trapped in her own tower, her own narrative, is also challenged by Jeanette Winterson in *Sexing the Cherry* (1989), where her Rapunzel falls in love with the witch, their relationship rendering valueless any need for the rescue by a male prince. *Lady Oracle*, the short stories, *Alias Grace* and *Cat's Eye* all reference Rapunzel stuck in her own tower. The Canadian Rapunzel is a victim. None of the princes offer anything but a façade of rescue or support.

Alfred Lord Tennyson's poem *The Lady of Shalott* (1842) is another reference point. This is a version of the Rapunzel tale which has no prince, only death, itself undercutting the Gothic romance. In this poem, a beautiful nameless woman is trapped in a tower. Because of a deadly curse, she can only look in the mirror at Camelot and Sir Lancelot. If she joins in life by leaving the tower, she dies. She chooses to leave; she chooses life and freedom over incarceration and so, she also chooses death. But the only version of life she chooses is a romantic fantasy, a longing for Lancelot. She seeks escape from her role, but in seeking such an escape, there is nowhere to go; she cannot imagine beyond a forbidden romance. Lifeless, she drifts down river in a boat, scarcely causing the knight and his friends to notice anything except her lovely face. An entrapped figure, sacrificial, static, the Lady of Shalott, Rapunzel and Canadian women (Atwood suggests) buy into the myth of rescue through love and a strong man.

In *Surfacing* Atwood discusses the refusal to be a victim, and this challenge to succumbing to destructive forces through inner collusion and self-destruction, to internalised negative narratives runs throughout her Gothic work, whether it is wilderness Gothic (*Surfacing*), dystopian sci-fi Gothic (*Oryx and Crake*, *The Handmaid's Tale*), romantic Gothic (*Lady Oracle*, *The Edible Woman*, 1969), historical (*Alias Grace*), or new urban Gothic (*The Robber Bride*). Delusion and self-delusion also run throughout the novels and short stories, in the tales Grace Marks tells (*Alias Grace*) and in how Iris withholds and misleads (*The Blind Assassin*, 2000). The stories Zenia (*The Robber Bride*) develops from the painful fears of her female victims, as she intrudes herself on their lives, are only successful if the women themselves agree to be their victims, to believe the constraints of vision the stories offer. Agency enables Grace Marks to fool her listeners, but it also enables Iris to restore the history of her sister Laura, and in Atwood's greatest Gothic tale, *The Robber Bride*, it enables the three women abused in their own personal histories to finally rid themselves of Zenia and the corrosive power of self-destructive narratives.

Scenes of hard-edged realism mix with narrative excitement as Margaret Atwood exposes the inherited familiarities of conventional Gothic roles for women: hapless heroine, entrapped victim, domestic constraint and split selves, exploring these as the natural everyday ways in which we live and treat each other in the twentieth and twenty-first-century world. This revives and exposes the traditional scenarios of more conventional Gothic romances, showing these scenarios to be constraints which women have ironically, or paradoxically, actually taken on board as versions of their future lives. So in *Lady Oracle* there is initially no escape from being a duped heroine in a work of romantic fiction, even while writing such fictions.

Atwood gets inside the behaviour of women and shows their toxicity, exposing split selves and sisterly, seemingly friendly destroyers. Traditional Gothic usually has male persecutors, but not in work by Atwood; the self, the mother and female friend are the brutal assassins. She exposes the ways in which women internalise gendered narratives which infantilise, disempower and caricature, and exposes the need to fit, look right, behave correctly, and marry Mr Right, as myths which ask far too much of everyone, and leave women stranded and emptied out. *The Edible Woman* shows Marion reliant on love and marriage, feeling consumed and finally offering up herself as a cake, to represent a way of refusing this consumption; *Lady Oracle* replays romantic fictions; *The Handmaid's Tale* traps women in their own bodies' reproductive technologies, disempowerment and silencing. Labelling it specifically Canadian Gothic, Atwood uses the fairytale of Rapunzel to explore and deconstruct entrapment in constraining myths and to debunk romantic fictions. She does this in *The Edible Woman* and *Lady Oracle*, and her short stories, particularly those in *Bluebeard's Egg* (1983). Her consistent treatment of fictionalising and narratives in *Alias Grace*, *Lady Oracle* and *The Blind Assassin* exposes ways in which women lie to construct acceptable versions of their behaviours, reliant on social norms to complete the stories they weave, quilt and script. Gothic characteristics are duplicity, twinning, acting, turning yourself into someone else (*Lady Oracle*). Atwood's Gothic enclosed spaces are domestic houses, constricting narratives. With these tales and in these ways she undercuts myths of sisterhood and exposes both deluding romantic myths, and women's spite. First we look at the romantic legacy embedded in *Lady Oracle*, then move to *The Robber Bride*, a tale of vampiric 'friendships', false investments, insights and agency.

A major theme running throughout Atwood's work is that of exposing and coming to terms with dangerous, delusion-based narratives and with split selves, with the ways in which women in particular, for these are usually her focus, have versions of what they should or could be palmed off on them as if they were the one and only truth. Historically, in traditional Gothic, tamed maidens are caught—in the locations and confined spaces of castles, corridors, dungeons, prisons and homes. They are also caught within systems which construct them in limiting ways and in prison-house versions of self which they internalise. Ways out of these varied confinements and constraints are often no more than fairytales of rescue. Powerlessly awaiting that prince, half asleep, in an entrapping, disempowering and internalised story about their own limitations, these

Rapunzels and ladies of Shalott are cursed by confinement in a virtual tower: the story of themselves as dependent and vulnerable, longing and waiting for someone else to manage their lives. Rapunzel is finally rescued into romantic love, but the Lady of Shalott, pursuing her own romantic dream, is punished for her only act of agency, ignoring the curse, leaving the tower, and seeking out Sir Lancelot, the knight whose reflected image she fell in love with, a knight to whom her life or death is meaningless. Interestingly, Tennyson's version of the lies of the love trap emphasises both the danger of challenging expected norms, leaving the tower, and the casual negligence of those on whom desire is projected—Lancelot, in this tale.

Atwood's exposure of the constraints of romantic-oriented Gothic is most clearly seen in *Lady Oracle*, which also reveals the deceits and stupidity of romantic narratives which offer idealistic relationship solutions, a kind of post-Second World War blitz of bliss. Internalising a divided, entrapped, destructive, paralysing version of self in a period of the late twentieth century when questions concerning split subjectivities are rife (for example, popularised by the work of R. D. Laing and Thomas Szasz), Atwood's Gothic explores and shows how it could be otherwise. It dramatises the dangers of internal fracture and entrapment in a socially and culturally woven set of myths, showing that potential is actually curbed by both context and self-delusion.

LADY ORACLE (1976)

Lady Oracle, Atwood's parody Gothic novel about a writer of Gothic novels whose life resembles a Gothic novel, is a fully fledged example of her critique of the entrapping stories we tell ourselves. Conventional, traditional, late eighteenth- and early nineteenth-century Gothic gave us figures of heroines endangered, invaded, chased down corridors for their lives, their chastity threatened. They were certainly vulnerable. Atwood's novel plays out these patterns through the life of Joan Foster, which resembles a Gothic tale of deceit, performance, disguise and ghostly visitings, and attempts to construct and reconstruct the performative self: all Gothic motifs, and formulae. It also emphasises their constructedness in Joan's own fictional bodice-ripper Gothic romances, which she writes alongside her famous poems.

Joan, overweight, is oppressed by her mother, who later returns as a ghostly figure, and ridicules her. As a child she was expected to perform, and dance in a ballet (ridiculously, as a Mothball), and she always felt ungainly. In her adolescent years, Joan's first encounter with a man sets a pattern of threat and promise, desire, deceit and distaste, which accompanies the rest of her relationships. Coming out of the cinema into the foyer, she experienced a dubious semi-sexual encounter with the 'daffodil man', who offered her a flower. This undeveloped exchange clearly verges on abuse, but lingers in her mind as alluring, an offer of sorts. During her adult life, Joan performs a series of roles with various lovers, and tries to escape herself, her life and her body when she fakes drowning in Lake Ontario. So many aspects of her childhood are also tinged with the Gothic: watching her mother put on her face/her makeup, everything being covered up, her father growing spider plants, suggesting the tendrils engulfing Joan's life, spread from her mother, and then his job as an anaesthetist bringing (often reluctant) people back from the dead. Joan has little chance to tell the real from the fantastic, the safe from the threatening, grisly, dangerous and insidious. She always lives in a made-up version of herself, a liminal space between how people see her and how she sees herself: a construction and a performance.

In *Lady Oracle*, Atwood responds to traditional Gothic romances. The culturally entrapping self/selves Joan plays out track through the parallel lives she leads. Joan is stuck in a variety of limiting scenarios, colluding with others' manipulation, first that of her dominant mother, with her spiteful, critical response to Joan as an ungainly, plump teen, then haunting her after Joan believes she has escaped; the initially predatory, ineffectual lovers and husband; and her many disguised and changing body shapes (from fat to slim, wigs, etc.), pursuits and escapes, dyeing her hair, faking her own death. These show her simultaneously playing while criticising a role in her own lived Gothic romance. Her descriptions are Gothic, emphasising the haunting intent of previous lives, roles and clothing. For example, referencing space and time she says, 'Below me, in the foundations of the house, I could hear the clothes I'd buried there growing themselves a body' (p. 321). She tries to move on but the past actively refuses: 'I wanted to forget the past, but it refused to forget me; it waited for sleep, then cornered me' (p. 216). This highlights the performativity of Gothic roles and women's adoption of them as ultimately constraining life stories. Joan internalises versions of what women 'should' be and 'should' want, and becomes victim to these, to the extent of choosing the ultimate performance of faking death in order to escape their lived constraints. She is not very successfully reconstructed in Italy, a popular setting of the Gothic novel.

In Joan's own Gothic fictions young women are sought by wealthy rakes and lured into hedged or walled gardens. This all resembles her own life, with its series of inappropriate relationships. She is a victim who writes her own collusive tale. First is the 'daffodil man' from the cinema, and though we realise his dubious intentions towards the young Joan, she later misremembers and idealises him. The 'daffodil man', the older Polish Count, and the activist husband, Arthur, are each like figures from a traditional Gothic tale, each an escape for her because of their versions of her, which she internalises and enacts. Each man is exposed as inauthentic, limited, playing games. 'Love was merely a tool, smiles were another tool, they were both just tools for accomplishing certain ends. No magic, merely chemicals. I felt I'd never really loved anyone, not Paul, not Chuck the Royal Porcupine, not even Arthur. I'd polished them with my love and expected them to shine, brightly enough to return my own reflection, enhanced and sparkling' (p. 345). Buying into the stories, the romances, is Joan's main problem.

Brooks Bouson (1993, p. 219) sees *Lady Oracle* as a complex, oppositional text, in dialogue with the promises of romance and marriage made by popular culture, so, 'dialogically contesting the official voices of culture, Joan insists that the basis of heterosexual romance is not openness and honesty but secrecy and lies'. And when Joan produces poetry through automatic writing, it is seen as Gothic by McCombs (1988, p. 77): 'a high-brow upside-down spirit-dictated mythic Gothic'.

Atwood's undercutting and rewriting of myths, fairytales and culturally based constricting narratives builds on conventional Gothic but particularly favours both the tale of Rapunzel and also that of Bluebeard. While Joan writes Gothic romantic fiction in *Lady Oracle*, her own life as a series of performances and relationships consistently mimics Gothic romance plots and undermines their promise, exposing it as dangerous nonsense. A major influence on Joan's fascination with women's roles, entrapment and escape is Tennyson's *The Lady of Shalott*, since it offers both a rebellious refusal of enforced roles, but an escape into nothing more than emptiness, and death, punishment for such daring. Women trap themselves in their own fantasies, waiting to be released by a love that either never arrives, or if it does just turns out disappointing, destructively negative. Trapped by their fantasies, they lack energy, imagination and agency. *Lady Oracle* is parodic Gothic but the warning is just as acute nonetheless.

Margaret Atwood uses the Gothic as a means to undercut narratives of repetition, from which there is no imaginable escape. Such narratives are perpetuated by history, family and popular culture, and whether of romance, equality, a sustainable world, or a secure future, each is seen as a dangerously undermined investment. In *The Robber Bride*, she exposes the complicity of selling oneself a narrative of family and relationship security. Such narratives might seem to ward off evil experience but actually they ultimately still render the woman a victim to delusions, self-deceit and trickery. Unusually in the period of the tail end of second-wave feminism, Atwood uses the Gothic to undercut feminist myths of sisterhood, as she also does in *Cat's Eye* (1998).

The Robber Bride (1993): Ghost Tale—Return from the Dead

The Robber Bride begins as a Gothic, magical tale of a return from the dead. In the Toxique Restaurant, three women, Roz, Charis and Tony, gather for a meal following the death and burial of Zenia, their nemesis, their ostensible friend, their construct, when suddenly they catch sight of Zenia herself, alive, in the mirror. Her return provokes each woman to recount her own history. Zenia is the hub for these three women's suffering, self-denigration and finally exorcism and agency, the rewriting of their own tales.

The Gothic enables a revivification and re-scrutiny of seemingly fixed moments of time, and in postcolonial Gothic, place is also reimagined, interpreted from different perspectives. In this novel the defamiliarisation which it introduces troubles every fixed certainty, narrative and complacency of worldview, culture, national, family and personal history. Coral Anne Howells sees *The Robber Bride* as a product of a particular moment in Canadian self-definition and history, and also a ghost story of the past version of alternatives.

> *The Robber Bride* is a ghost story or rather a story about exorcising ghosts, in an attempt at a realistic reappraisal of Canadianness in the 1990s and a more honest recognition of the differences concealed within constructions of personal and national identity. (Howells 2003, p. 89)

In 'Bewitched, Bothered and Bewildered' (1993) Peter Kemp sees it as a witch fable with its, flickering imitations of vampires, doppelgangers, macabre mixings, the fatal inviting of an evil spirit over the threshold are shown as events sharply located in everyday actuality as Atwood extends a vast web of conflicts: sex antagonisms, domestic infighting, warring aspects of the self, battles from medieval bloodbaths, hi tech hostilities in the Gulf. (p. 44)

Sherrill Grace's 'Atwood's Postmodern Fairytale' (1994) compares *The Robber Bride* to Atwood's earlier *Good Bones* (1992) and *Wilderness Tips*. She sees the work as fairytales for grown-ups with inchoate fears and powerful desires. The mundane comfort zones of life are prowled round by fears like wolves, and Atwood lets them in.

Mirroring, twinning and Gothic figures of delusion and destruction run alongside historically credible facts and locations. Atwood Gothicises women's lives and emphasises the disguises and deceits which we seem to deliberately perpetuate. Tony, Charis and Roz in *The Robber Bride* suffer from self-delusions and self-imposed limitations, but through their unity, reflection and planning finally free themselves from Zenia's evil grip (their own victim position). In *Cat's Eye*, Elaine Ridley also frees herself from the grip of her past when she revisits her childhood and adolescence following her return to her retro-introspective Toronto, and escapes from the turreted tower of narratives of longing, incarceration, paralysis and lack of self-worth, into agency.

In *The Robber Bride* there is no escape from falling victim to masquerades of friendship leading to invasion and temporary lack of self-worth. Atwood rewrites the Brothers Grimm tale of the robber bridegroom, who dismembers three wives, as a tale of female spite and destruction, leading to enforced self-awareness and agency. In so doing, she constructs and exposes the robber bride, Zenia, a vampiric, intrusive and destructive figure who encourages three women: Roz, Charis and Tony, to self-sacrifice, turn themselves into victims. But her intrusive disruption is also a wakeup call. Her invasion and destruction acts as a catalyst for their own rebuilding of a less delusional self. Atwood's Gothic exposes, upsets, threatens and destroys, then moves beyond conventional endings. The novel splits in the middle with two parallel halves, each of three narratives, one for each woman. The first part recalls disruption and loss. Her women characters are seen to be adopting and enacting their own narratives of constraint, performance and destruction, but in the second twinned half of the novel, they learn to move away from this impasse and gradually develop agency. *The Robber Bride* is constructed as a series of ghostly returns, with twinned lives, and a twinned shape, with histories revisited and finally understood. It has Gothic undertones and reconstructed messages, the vampiric metamorphosing Zenia at its centre, and a triad of harmed and deluded women. Part of its narrative power is the replaying of traditional fairytales concerning women's self-imprisonment ('Rapunzel') and victimhood ('The Three Little Pigs'). But it is also a Gothic tale of agency in which these three women finally weave their own web, exorcise constricting narratives by exorcising Zenia, telling their own versions of their tales.

Twinning self and the written fictional selves is both the Gothic motif which reveals performance and entrapment and a mode which might enable self-scrutiny and escape, elucidated by consideration of Julia Kristeva's theories, including those of abjection (1982). Kristeva's theories inform discussion about split selves and identity, within a feminist psychoanalytical critical frame, since she discusses the textual subject as split, fragmented, conscious and unconscious, characterising its signification process. Kristeva's theory of language suggests a subject in crisis and multiple selves in dialogue. Bringing her theories to bear on Atwood's work identifies those works as polyphonic, many voiced. Kristeva's view of the modern subject seems aligned to that which we find in Atwood's fiction: one of ambivalence, split selves, daydreams and the doubt of any wholeness, all characteristics enacted and played out. Psychoanalytic concepts can help explore the thoughts and actions of Atwood's protagonists, so they express and we see debate and diversity, not just the entrapment and disempowerment, but agency through carnivalesque moments. This is particularly so in *The Robber Bride*, a polyphonic novel which expresses many voices, many views, offers many perspectives. In *The Robber Bride*, Zenia, the fourth member of a set of female college graduates, systematically undermines and exposes the tenuous fictions in which each of the others invests, including social fictions of happy partnerships, happy families, and of wholeness and security of self.

Atwood comments on the novel's own deliberate artifice through the figure of Zenia who, like the novelist herself, makes up stories to gain power over people. She even compares herself to Zenia, 'because of course I'm Zenia-like. She's a liar, and what do novelists do? They lie.' So the very art of lying is Gothic, and the novel is also distinctly Gothic, dominated by Zenia's self-aware, self-reflective artifice, abstraction, a twin to whatever reality and truth might be thought to be. In the fabric of *The Robber Bride*, the stories Charis, Tony and Roz tell themselves, their versions of themselves and their own limitations and dark paralysing secrets predominate and are then exposed and re-written.

Shannon Hengen, referencing Leslie Fiedler's (1917–2003) *Love and Death in the American Novel* (1960) definition of the Gothic as a 'series of genre clichés exaggerated to grotesqueness', characterises *The Robber Bride* as clearly female American Gothic filled with lost mothers, abusive fathers, damaged children, vicious upbringings, double characters and overlapping contradictions. Twinning, deception, performance of self, enclosed domestic spaces and damaged life narratives entrap the three women characters, Roz, Tony and Charis, who each call up a version of the predatory, charismatic, metamorphosing Zenia, described in terms which usually connote a vampire, such as being invited over the threshold or blowing in on a wind. As Marina Warner says of her, she is 'the novel's hollow core, the incubus with implants for breasts who, like a weasel kills not to eat but for the pleasure of it, or, like a fox, always digs back doors and makes havoc at the feast these have provided' (Warner 1994).

In Warner's view, the basic causes of such destruction are the failure of family, of luck and the damage done by weak men. She pins down social and personal issues as the sources of the vulnerability which lets Zenia into the women's lives, so that such insecurities become real events.

At the opening of the novel, Roz, Tony and Charis believe Zenia dead, so her return initially triggers their memories, which reinstates her power over them. But within the novel, her role is to disturb, and as Atwood notes, to provide energy and interest, since malevolent, active characters cause things to happen and are more interesting to readers. Through this notion of disturbance, the catalyst, the interest of upset, she aligns the role of Zenia in the women's lives both with that of her own as a novelist, and the catalytic power of character and event in a novel, a role of manipulation, applied to engage interest, in this case, concerning power, gender, identity and agency. Stephanie McKinnon notes in 'In Search of Evil Women' that 'Atwood emphasises that we know from real life that women are not programmed like a robot to be good.' Really 'good' people might be quite dull, she suggests, and in narratives without the more feisty and wicked there would be no real plot or interest. She says, 'I think the key is complexity and if all you can be is good you can't be complex' (1994).

If *Lady Oracle* is Atwood's deliberate reproduction or/and ironising of the Gothic romance tale, *The Robber Bride* is an ironic comment on the stories we tell ourselves, and in which we become entrapped, and the novelist's role in this falsity. This storytelling is a self-constructed web, dungeon, attic or tower of our own making, and each of the women invites vampiric Zenia over the threshold to bleed herself dry, and show herself her own worst faults and fears come true.

> [Y]our attraction to the Zenias of this world is that they are pure forms of all kinds of things that we unitarily suppress. And there was something attractive about a kind of outlaw figure. (Atwood in Ritchie 1993)

This is contemporary feminist Gothic in contemporary Toronto, real yet altered, a revelatory looking glass enabled by the Gothic. The women are 'casualties of the second world war and a variety of abusive domestic scenarios, child abuse, child beating' (*Robber Bride*, p. 39). They are each recovering in their own way from damage done by non-nurturing childhoods. Tony's mother walked out, her father was distant; Charis' mother gave her to her grandmother and she was abused; Roz is driven at work and has a cheating husband, Mitch. Each seeks love to round themselves out, give life some meaning. However, each is very insecure, and so vulnerable. Zenia's evil wind blows her into their lives but she is really constructed by their fears and tenuously held sense of wholeness of self. Tony, Charis and Roz each hide behind a constructed twinned self and Zenia lays bare the decisions, desires and fears of each, paring away their front of coping and success in their chosen lifestyles. Tony loses West; Roz, Mitch; Charis, Billy. Zenia steals their men, but this reveals a truth to each of them, and to us as readers. They have misled themselves in investing in a myth, a grand romantic, domestic narrative which leaves them empty and bereft until they can reconstruct a new version of themselves. Zenia also threatens each differently in alignment with their nightmares and fears: 'she makes me sick of myself', says Charis. 'What is she doing here on this side of the mirror?' (*Robber Bride*, p. 35). For Tony, Zenia's influence is destructive, a war image. She is the evil twin to each, but her invading, predatory presence ultimately enables them to move through collapse and crisis to some form of new clarity and agency. Twinning and otherising are significant motifs throughout. Charis' repressed Other, the more violent, abused Karen, returns when Charis is destabilised. Tony reverses words and Roz's twins, Erin and Paula, tell different versions of fairytales and construct life differently. Each defines Zenia in relation to their different natures: 'inspirational' (Tony), 'peaceful' (Charis) and 'kaput' (Roz). Zenia, their mirror image/opposite, threatens each. Making Charis sick of herself, she appears as an existent on the other side of the mirror, and re-embodies the destructiveness of war for Tony, her influence suggesting menace, chaos, cities, flames, towers crashing down, and the anarchy of deep water. The women are each damaged by her, then believe her dead. Her return causes them to relive and retell their stories, and by doing so they have to find a new narrative which will help them escape her influence, which is their own embodiment of victimhood and negativity.

Twinning for each woman is also a safety construct. Tony is a historian of war and uses reversal of words as a spell to ward off the harmful, destructive real. Her control of versions of history is a way of managing the past, the taught past and her own history. Abandoned by her suicidal mother and her alcoholic father she took refuge in the centre of academic behaviour, in teaching, reconstructing history and particularly battles, even playing them out with coloured beans in her kitchen. As Zenia removes West from her (a name she reversed from 'Stew' to make him more interesting) she manages the harsh histories and any current deviations through word reversal, her own personal widdershins language, to give her power as words might in some magical incantation.

Charis, divided from her hard suffering past through her name change from Karen, is a gentle soul caught up in New Age beliefs and behaviour, living on her own on an island, islanded in her own construction of alternative beliefs about healing powers. She's a self-tricker. Her prince charming is the draft-dodging, unemployed Billy, who also happily follows Zenia out, off and across the bay in a boat. Charis cuts herself off from her more destructive version of self, her abused past, by her name change, but she's caught in the victim role with the loss of Billy. Her weaving of New Age tales and behaviours is no protection against the destruction brought by investment in a story in which she's the nurturer of damaged others, Billy, and Zenia, because each of these takes her for what they can get, then leaves. These are stories with which women constrain themselves, growing from the Gothic romance, as does *Lady Oracle*, and harsher fairytales: Rapunzel. Each woman is invested, stuck and vulnerable in her own invented, tower version of a safe self. Zenia's invasion of their constrained, honeycombed, cotton wool self-protective stories first shatters then enables them to toughen up.

Roz, the tough contemporary businesswoman with the historically Jewish worries about weight, self-image, success, family and food, in her sharp suits with her well-managed house and her twin daughters and son, is trapped in a myth of the successful family, with Mitch, the macho husband at its core. Her own involvement in the myths of contemporary women and family are exposed by the twin daughters, who want to retell the fairytales with more powerful, less victimised roles for the oppressed and devoured. In the hands of Erin and Paula, the tale of the three little pigs and the wolf is exposed and rewritten. The wolf in this tale and the bridegroom in 'the robber bridegroom' are male, but Atwood replaces the male villain. The wolf in sheep's clothing is Zenia. Engagement with her, while very damaging at first, ultimately re-empowers the victims through their own energetic selves. They rewrite the tale of their victimhood, as Paula and Erin rewrite 'the three little pigs'. This is a feminist fairytale Gothic, as Alice Palumbo notes, seeing the novel as filled with typical Atwood elements:

> the use of Toronto and menacing urban settings, the constant reworking of Gothic and fairytale elements, and reflections on female friendship ... A macabre, sentimental and naive romance ... An overgrown Gothic. (1994, pp. 40–41)

Atwood has argued that while the fairytales we grew up with feature handsome princes, there are others with violent, different roles for men and women. She comments on storytelling, constructedness and how we can never find any final truth, only versions of it. As a meta-fictional, Gothic fantasy, the novel investigates versions of sexuality, gender roles, male/female relationships and female/female relationships. It plays with and comments on the power of language, of memory and history. The stories the women tell themselves preserve them from harsh truth but also make them vulnerable to Zenia's invented tales from her own life (forced to be a prostitute, turned out by her mother, abandoned, a refugee). Each story is only another construction, her shape-shifting a response to the weaknesses of the other women, and no doubt the men she steals from them.

Zenia is a vampire; she drains women of their relationships and security. However, as Atwood warns, like vampires, 'People like Zenia can never step through your doorway, can never enter and entangle themselves in your life, unless you invite them in. There has to be a recognition, an offer of hospitality, a word of greeting' (*Robber Bride*, p. 114). She is a construct of their own making. They let her destroy what they have and that destruction needs to happen twice, once in events and once in recall, in the twin halves of the novel, before they have the power to move on. The first destruction left them confused victims, and the return, with which the book opens, begins their reflections, talking of their own sufferings, observations of the past. As they share and begin to understand their stories, they develop a new, initially very tenuous sense of empowerment. If you sit up a tower waiting to be freed, you can also be cut off, the tower can be collapsed, the one who frees you can also leave you, trap you, harm you. Following the final dismemberment of Zenia, and of their own pasts, each woman begins to recognise their position and to re-story their lives, avoiding simplistic fairytales.

Alice Palumbo (1994) sees this as 'one long act of exorcism', as each woman tries to exorcise her own past by way of her relationship with Zenia, so that Tony sees her life and interactions with Zenia using the rhetoric of history, Charis sees through New Age prophecy, and Roz through the language of mystery novels and fairytales. Marina Warner identifies the novel as recognisably Gothic, having the usual onset of villains from fairytale in the tales Zenia tells and the evil she invites into the lives of these women, and comments on the bad mother, wicked queen and the three little pigs, as well as the phantasmagorical world of the *femme fatale*, since Zenia's power over male and female is mesmerising and destructive. In respect of the characteristics of strong (but in this case malevolent) woman, Warner finds this novel close to the work of Angela Carter. Zenia, the robber bride, is a powerful, intrusive female, a villainess, the embodiment of female evil; Zenia is an 'apparently unstoppable force of nature that rampages its greedy way through marital and family ties, friendship and history', as Maureen Nicholson notes in 'Unpopular Gals' (1994). King highlights the victim position, which Atwood demonstrates with eerie skill, '[...] the way in which victims acquiesce in—and sometimes actually will—their own exploitation' (1993).

Zenia as a robber bride is variously compared to Eve, Lolita, Jezebel, Medusa, Circe and Medea, in terms of both Gothic romance and fin-de-siècle iconography. She is also each woman's alter ego, a bad twin. The impact she has on others is more serious than anything she does individually. Her insidious effect is to turn each into a vulnerable version of their own worst selves, so that their worst fears come true.

For Sherrill Grace (1994), the novel is a postmodern fairytale emphasising our need for stories, with parallels in the cruelties of the everyday world, and Shannon Hengen relates the Gothic, fairytale and the learning curve women go through in the novel, as we do through reading fairytales in particular:

> 'we learn to sympathise for the downtrodden through fairytales and that we also learn to find solutions to our own problems.' Women who 'still remain caught between the traditional and pivotal woman's role of nurturer, and the new roles demanded of them in life in a difficult, complex world.' (Hengen 1994)

She argues that everyone needs some of Zenia's hardness or they get boiled (like the pigs in 'the three little pigs'). The novel is both realistic in setting and detail, and also Gothic and feminist because the women are toughened up, learn to live without their deceiving men, and Zenia herself is a tough, wilful character. Yet *The Robber Bride* also undercuts some of the myths of sisterhood, as does *Cat's Eye*, because Zenia is only a positive influence once the women have learned to construct more positive versions of their lives beyond her undermining.

At the end, multiple versions of Zenia's apparently final death and dismemberment offer some sort of closure (although a recent Atwood short story, 'I Dream of Zenia with the Bright Red Teeth' in *Stone Mattress* (2014), has her returning, 'a secret alter ego' (p. 159) to each woman, warning them about their lost or returned men). Each woman then begins to construct tales about Zenia in order to manage her.

There is just the one evil woman in this novel, while in *Cat's Eye* female solidarity comes under total threat, led by Cordelia, who has her own family crisis. Elaine Risley, the protagonist, is lured down and left in a ravine, presumably to die, and female spite dominates the tale, alienating Risley until she returns to see how part of her own history was self-constructed. In this latter insight, the novel resembles *The Robber Bride*. Reversing the Otherising, becoming aware of and refusing the control of damaging narratives, run throughout these two novels, as they also run throughout most of Atwood's work.

Conclusion

Atwood's interest in the Gothic and with rewriting fairytales and myths intersects with her engagement with politics and feminism. She has been described as giving:

> The impression of a quiet Mata Hari ... who pits herself against the ordered, too clean world like an arsonist. (Ondaatje 1972)

The Robber Bride is a Gothic, Canadian, postfeminist and occasionally comic, parodic exploration of the damage people do to themselves and each other, while *Lady Oracle* is a parodic Gothic romance. *Lady Oracle* is described as a comic novel colliding with Gothic conventions (Howells 2005, p. 65). Comparing *The Robber Bride* with Atwood's earlier novels, Howells notes the changes in her use of the traditional Gothic motifs, seeing this as a 'mutant form of female gothic' (Howells 2005, p. 65):

The Gothic takes many routes in Atwood's fictions, from Joan Foster, Gothic writer suffocating and trapped in her own labyrinths of Gothic romance plots, through to the Gothic vampire Zenia in *The Robber Bride*, and the consistent forms of duplicity offered by Atwood's lying or storytelling narrators, such as Iris Chase in *The Blind Assassin* and Grace Marks in *Alias Grace*. (Howells 2005, p. 65)

Such subterranean threats and horrors belong to the literary Gothic. Atwood's work uses the Gothic, myth, popular fictions, history and realistic details around her, people she knows and her own life, transformed into a whole which is always concerned with commenting on life and values, challenges and opportunities.

While the Handmaids are confined by regime, dress, rules, language, hierarchies and castes of imposed behaviour for women, internalising the limitations punished by death if they question or rebel, the Rapunzel figure is a key in Atwood's Canadian Gothic exploration, because she constructs her own tower, entraps herself in contemporary constructions of her opportunities, the way she should dream and be, the things she must not do. Canadian female Rapunzels construct their own towers and invent their own princes and witches. Margaret Atwood is a Gothic writer who combines the feminist, the Canadian and the postcolonial in her approach and perspective: the potential of the intrusive wilderness, the trajectory of quest set against the Arctic wastes, and the commodification of invasive American culture. Her treatment of the ways in which the Gothic challenges and problematises the narratives by which we live our lives, the social, cultural, gendered and personal stories we construct to understand ourselves and others, is central to her work. She explodes myths and engages us in undercutting security of any narrative.

This book focuses on issues prominent in late twentieth- and early twenty-first-century texts that are engaged with and vehicled by the Gothic. And with the work of Atwood, it looks at the construction of self and the world, influenced and affected by Gothic versions, by both constraining fairytale and contemporary cultural myth, and how haunted pasts affect versions of potential. In much of her work, Atwood unpicks the lies of Romantic fictions, turning the Gothic romance on its head, while elsewhere the Gothic lurks in her work focused on the ecological, sustainability, the dying planet and our insidious, often ignorant, role in this demise. Atwood is political, ironic. She is a writer of Canadian Gothic, a feminist, and a writer who uses all the strategies of the literary Gothic, as it causes us to see through narratives of disempowerment, offering insights which refuse to make us into victims and instead lead to opportunities for agency.

Bibliography

Brooks Bouson, J. (1993) *Brutal Choreographies: Oppositional Strategies and Narrative Design in the Novels of Margaret Atwood* (Amherst, MA: University of Massachusetts Press).
Grace, S. (1994) 'Atwood's Postmodern Fairytale', *Canadian Forum*, March, pp. 44–45.
Hammill, F. (2013) 'Canadian Gothic', in *The Encyclopedia of the Gothic*, W. Hughes, D. Punter and A. Smith (eds.) (Oxford: Blackwell).
Hengen, S. (1994) 'Atwood's Novel May be a Potboiler of a Modern Tale', Review, *Sudbury Star*, 6 February.
Hill Rigney, B. (1987) *Margaret Atwood* (Basingstoke: Palgrave Macmillan).
Howells, C. A. (2003) 'The Robber Bride or, Who is a True Canadian', in *Margaret Atwood Textual Assassinations*, S. R. Wilson (ed.) (Columbus, OH: State University Press).
Howells, C. A. (2005) *Margaret Atwood* (Hampshire and New York: Palgrave Macmillan).
McCombs, J. (ed.) (1988) *Critical Essays on Margaret Atwood* (Boston: G. K. Hall).
Ondaatje, M. (1972) *Canadian Forum*.
Palumbo, A. (1994) Review, *Paragraph*, Vol. 15, No. 3–4, pp. 40–41.
Ritchie, H. (1993) Quoting Atwood in 'Come into the Garden', *Sunday Times Review*, 10 October, p. 69.
Varma, D. (1986) 'Gothic Shadows in the Early Novels of Margaret Atwood', *Anglo-American Studies*, Vol. 6, No. 1, pp.31–43.
Warner, M. (1994) 'Atwood Dips into Plath Depths', *The Globe and Mail*, Saturday, 2 October, p. 39.
Wisker, G. (2004) 'Viciousness in the Kitchen: Sylvia Plath's Gothic', *Gothic Studies*,Vol. 6, No. 1.

CHAPTER 4

Cultural Haunting: Toni Morrison and Tananarive Due

This chapter explores cultural haunting in African American women's Gothic, looking closely at Toni Morrison's *Beloved* (1987), her later *Home* (2012) and at Tananarive Due's *Joplin's Ghost* (2006). It deals with the ways in which the Gothic exposes hidden painful histories of endemic racism, treatment of people as less than human because of their ethnicity and colour, and ways of breaking the silence, exposing the horrors, and rescripting life in order to move on. The three novels *Beloved*, *Home* and *Joplin's Ghost* revive moments in over a century of marginalised history, focusing on the legacy of the slave crossing, the horrors of slavery and its aftermath, and the continued silencing and marginalisation, even after the unsegregated practices of the Korean War (when African American soldiers were treated equally with other Americans), desegregation and the civil rights movement of the 1960s (which led to civil equality). It considers Gothic critique and the revelation of alternative ways of seeing, the exploration of self-worth through recognising, living with, then exorcising destructive elements of the ghosting of the past. In Morrison's *Beloved* the succubus of the dead baby's ghost is a lived presence of the harmful, corrosive internalisation of response to the experience of slavery. Her exorcism opens up the opportunity for recovering of both community and selfhood. *Home* as a title signals a contradiction for a homeless, moneyless, shoeless war veteran trying to make his way back to the South to find his sister. Frank Money's journeying reverses and retraces the historical underground railroad, and reveals the damage of repressed memories and racist abuse in the name of science. In Tananarive Due's *Joplin's Ghost*, Scott Joplin's music and the creative expression he represented is literally revitalised in the playing of lost, unheard, as well as more familiar music through a talented young woman aptly named Phoenix.

Haunting and trauma surround us:

> The process of mutual postcolonial abjection is, I suppose, one that confronts us every day in the ambiguous form of a series of uncanny returns. (Punter 2000b, p. vi)

As David Punter notes, there is a distinct similarity and conjunction between the postcolonial and the Gothic, each focusing on the return of the repressed, on alternative hidden histories and versions of the present.

Trauma theory (Madsen 2008) and Derrida's *Spectres of Marx* (1993) are useful theoretical lenses to combine with the strategies of the literary Gothic in order to clarify the ways in which these three texts express the past, alive in the present, in people, and in place. In *Spectres of Marx* Derrida considers the parallelism of different versions of time, 'this instant that is not docile to time', as the spectral appears in the daily routine, and time past, present and future elide, thus producing a different layered reading of 'now'. Spectres become a controlling metaphor for Derrida (1993), who locates in the postcolonial present a sense of layered, interlocking past moments, so that although we are in one 'post' of many 'posts' (moments after a movement, such as postcolonial, after and also in this case against colonialism), the lives of historical people and periods are always ever present in our lives. In the postcolonial we live in spectral moments, haunted by spirits and ways of the past, 'giving them the status of spirits haunting the apparently purged landscapes of the contemporary' (Punter 2000b, p. 62). All three texts suggest layers of the past ghosting the present. Each also makes politicised statements about values and community, using haunting histories to do so. Gothic stories play an important role in recuperating hidden histories, empowering those who have been marginalised and silenced.

In *Beloved*, when Sethe's mother in law, the herbalist and community preacher Grandma Baby Suggs, advises her against the futility of running away from their own house, haunted with the ghost of a dead baby, she indicates the extent of cultural haunting. There is nowhere to run; silenced histories and ghosts are all around them and in every home:

'what'd be the point?' said Baby Suggs 'not a house in the country ain't packed to its rafters with some dead Negro's grief.' (p. 5)

Morrison's concern is to reveal African American history, telling the stories she wanted to read herself, which were either not written, not published, or not available. Her work is political, engaged: 'I refuse to let them off the hook about whether I'm a Black woman writer or not, I'm under a lot of pressure to become something else. That is why there is so much discussion of how my work is influenced by other "real" writers for example white Southern writers whom I'm constantly compared to' (Morrison, interview with Stuart, 1988, p. 15).

Cultural hauntings permeate landscape, buildings, airwaves and the mind in the three novels considered in this chapter, reminding of a silenced and destructive past and present, through haunted houses, spaces, people and haunted music. But these ghosts will not lie down, and must be heard and lived with in a way which moves beyond the self-devouring and re-victimisation of continued resentment, and beyond mere retribution. In this trajectory of revival and reclaiming a positive narrative, the ghost, the revenant, the returned, is a catalytic figure. These stories insist on engagement with values. Their mix of history and the supernatural dramatises culturally sensitive material. They are essentially political in the broad sense of the word and remind us of the power of storytellers to speak out and offer alternate versions and ways forward. *Beloved*, *Home* and *Joplin's Ghost* use the literary Gothic for such disinterring of the past, decomposing the purely negative versions of history, and composing new scripts and versions.

The power of narrative to provide comment is emphasised by Chinua Achebe:

storytellers are a threat. They threaten all champions of control, they frighten the usurpers of the right-to-freedom of the human spirit—in state, in church or mosque, in party congress, in the university or wherever. (Achebe 1987, p. 153)

The novel is 'the stage upon which the great debates of society can be conducted' (Rushdie 1990, p. 7); '…it is the only [form] that takes the "privileged arena" of conflicting discourse right inside our heads. The interior space of our imagination is a theatre that can never be closed down; the images created there make up a movie that can never be destroyed' (Rushdie 1990, p. 13). Sandel also comments on the importance of narrative to identity and community:

> Political community depends on the narratives by which people make sense of their condition, and interpret the common life they share. (Sandel 1996, p. 350)

and:

> There is a growing danger that, individually and collectively, we will find ourselves slipping into a fragmented, storyless condition. The loss of the capacity for narrative would amount to the ultimate disempowering of the human subject. (Sandel, p. 351)

Morrison's engaged aim is a full record which recreates and revitalises history through factual testimony and a recreation of the imaginative world:

> What I wanted to do in my writing is to create an intimacy, share something with the reader. But I also wanted to write a book where your literary history wouldn't help you. So there are other voices in my work, like the folkloric, rather than the literary voices we are used to ... (Morrison, interview with Stuart 1988, p. 15)

Morrison, Achebe, Sandel and Rushdie know how radical, how transformative, storytellers can be. The right to recuperate, re-vision, re-tell and construct new stories in order to voice discontent and alternative versions combines with the opportunity to suggest that life might be otherwise. Through recovering and rewriting hidden histories and stories, re-evaluating, dramatically revitalising then taking them into a new place, the imagination frees us to see the world otherwise, so that a new view, a new version and change can follow. African American Gothic by contemporary women writers recovers a doubly hidden set of histories and stories through the Gothic, embodying the hidden and imagining the alternatives, or at least suggesting that there might be some. In this it recovers history as does traditional Gothic, but it also frees readers and any of us who are having our stories constructed and represented to move on into those we might construct differently, for ourselves. As David Punter has pointed out, there is a distinct similarity and conjunction between the postcolonial and the Gothic, each focusing on the return of the repressed, on alternative hidden histories and versions of the present. Contemporary African American and postcolonial Gothic can work to re-empower and revitalise—not just put back the coffin lid. Perhaps in some instances it is its slippage into combinations with speculative fiction that enables such developments.

Haunted and Haunting

Toni Morrison's *Beloved* does what every good Gothic contemporary tale should, it makes palpably real the everyday lives of people, the shocking, hidden histories which we have all repressed and which must be faced in order to be able to cope, return to wholeness and move on. In traditional historical Gothic, such histories were likely to be of illegitimacy, madness and murder and more likely to take place in a grand family, a castle ruins, the context constructing and embodying forth the disease of the hidden past. Morrison's contemporary Gothic tale here is based on a local example of the fate of Margaret Garner, an escaped slave, and the terrible history of a single family which is also that of a community and a nation, and more broadly of the history of the international transatlantic slave trade. The latter was a subject which took Morrison a long time to find a rich and sensitive enough way to express, and this she does without polemic, guilt or disgust.

Morrison's engaged aim is a full record which revitalises history through factual testimony and a recreation of an imaginative world. The year 1855 is a significant time, when the Northern States gave homes to freed slaves, but provided escapees with no protection from slave-catchers crossing to recapture their property. Cincinnati was the first state in the free North to which slaves escaped and Harriet Tubman and the underground railway supported them on their journey, using community, song and the individual and group bravery of those who would shelter escaped slaves. The slaves themselves made perilous journeys across swamps and open plains to safety. But they were still someone's property. In *Beloved*, although they escape to Cincinnati, Sethe and her family could be recaptured, re-enslaved and returned to the brutality of the plantation Sweet Home. Morrison's Gothic tale is triggered by history, the tale of Margaret Garner, 1854, who killed her own baby and attempted to kill her other children in order to prevent their re-enslavement. Morrison chose a moment of liminality, when some slaves were freed in the North and those in the South still remained enslaved, so that both ideas and geographical spaces indicated alternative ways of defining people and enabling them to live and develop self-worth or not. Into this liminal time and space, she gives us the ghost, the haunting figure of Beloved. The novel reminds us of the everyday horror of slavery, its geography and cultural imprinting: the brutality affecting whole towns and schools.

> Whole towns wiped clean of Negroes; eighty-seven lynchings in one year alone in Kentucky; four colored schools burned to the ground; grown men whipped like children; children whipped like adults; black women raped by the crew; property taken, necks broken. (p. 180)

The poignant, Gothic, Billie Holiday song 'Strange Fruit' (1939, written by Abel Meeropol) forces us to reimagine the landscapes in which lynchings and lynched figures represent a devastatingly gruesome, natural intrusion. Strange fruit is hanging; the trees could be seen to sprout lynched, burned bodies, which imprint upon this landscape the horrors of slavery and its aftermath. The Ku Klux Klan adopting ghostly white hoods was a recognition of the superstitious nature of the African Americans they preyed upon, since they believed that a ghostly figure would terrify, disempower and so render the slaves, and then free citizens, vulnerable and unable to escape or fight. Some of that vulnerability was seen as childlike, infantalising those whose superstitious and religious nature could be preyed on. Writing the Gothic also carries its own second-class citizenship, since for African American (and Black British) women, the forms of writing most accepted in the early 1980s, when their work started to gain a wider audience, was that of realism and testimony. This suggests that readers could only hear what they were saying if writers actually testified, as did the slaves whose stories we read in nineteenth-century slave narratives, such as Harriet Jacobs' *Incidents in the Life of a Slave Girl. Written by Herself* (1861). But testimony does not necessarily involve the imaginatively lived, the emotionally lived experience, as well as the factual. In her use of the Gothic, constructing a haunted house and developing the figure of a ghost returned into a Black household, Morrison knew she was taking a risk, because her use of the supernatural and of the strategies of the literary Gothic could themselves be seen as a simplistic mode. As Dale Townsend has also noted, much of the Gothic was seen as something immature and unserious because it came from and represented the powers of the imagination (Dale Townshend, Facebook post, September 2014). Beloved, the returned full grown ghost baby, functions ultimately to enable the family to free themselves from the mind-forged manacles of their past. The violence was real. Morrison uses modes of feminist Gothic writing; the body and the home are the sites which carry the pain and also the recuperation.

Incidences of rather patronising critical reception of Black women's writing, common in the 1980s, indicated the legitimising and recognition of only one form of Black women's writing —'a little Black pain undressed' (Burford 1987): life writing, testimony and social realism. Morrison herself was criticised for moving away from this stereotype. Sara Blackburn, for example, suggested that recording Black experience would be something she would grow out of, and the *Guardian* response to Morrison receiving the Nobel Prize for *Beloved* criticised her for constructing blatantly non-realistic characters: Pilate, the aunt with no navel in *Song of Solomon* (1977), and of course Beloved, the returned ghost baby and succubus. Speculative, fantastic and the literary Gothic were considered as lesser forms than the socially realistic, it seems, and also, Black women writers were only expected to write certain forms of fiction and tell certain kinds of story. However, against such repression, Morrison and others seek to express the imaginative life as well as the factually historical:

> The tone in which I could blend acceptance of the supernatural and a profound rootedness in the real time at the same time with neither taking precedence over the other. It is indicative of the cosmology, the way in which Black people looked at the world, we are a very practical people, very down to earth, even shrewd people. But within that practicality we also accepted what I suppose could be called superstition and magic, which is another way of knowing things. But to blend these two works together at the same time was enhancing not limiting. And some of those things were 'discredited' only because Black people were 'discredited' therefore what they knew was 'discredited'. And also because the press upward towards social mobility would mean to get as far away from that kind of knowledge as possible. That kind of knowledge has a very strong place in my world. (Morrison in Evans 1985, p. 342)

A vital way out of the prison house of the weight of silenced history is that of the imagination, and, in this instance, the alignment with the Black folk aesthetic, the supernatural world felt as real. This turns the tables on the Ku Klux Klan who wear/wore white costumes with white pointed hats, based on the belief that superstitious African Americans would believe them to be ghosts and be terrified. In *Beloved*, ghosting is seized as a way through and forwards, rather than a scare tactic leading to destruction.

'124 was spiteful.' The novel opens in a way which immediately defamiliarises us as readers, labelling a number, a house, as spiteful. The next phrase, 'full of baby's venom', is also confusing, as we normally associate babies with nurturing and not with poison. Signs of an angry, rebuked poltergeist follow. This baby has taken an active dislike to the family in the house, its own family, and every one of its actions serves to disorient, distress and endanger them. Food is spilled, dirty handprints appear on mirrors, mirrors are shattered. It wants to rid the house of their presence, it wants to harm them, at a liminal moment in a transitional space, the first location to which escaped slaves from the slave-owning South moved to be (ostensibly) safe in the free North: Cincinnati, Ohio, in a moment before emancipation, and in a road without name or number, a historical moment. The 'lively spite' in the house, which turns out to be a ghost of a dead baby, reminds them constantly and intrusively of their haunted past. The house with the 'pulsating red light' is passed in a hurry by everyone in the neighbourhood, none of whom will come inside. While it carries its own palpable haunted history because of the infanticide, the house is not alone. Morrison makes it plain that in many ways it is typical, touched by, imprinted on, still harbouring the ghost of dead slaves. Moving is pointless, you cannot escape this constant, insistent presence. 124 (the house number) is a microcosm of the society haunted by the all-pervading presence of the dehumanisation of slavery.

For Sethe the memories intrude on a daily basis, going about her business, or just as she's rushing across a field to wash the camomile from her legs, where we see her mid-step, suddenly flooded with the memories of the plantation, Sweet Home, and the interleaving of trees in leaf with lynchings. Sethe remembers the beauty of sycamores, but also the betrayal of that simple beauty, with an image of 'Boys hanging from the most beautiful sycamores in the world' (p. 6). It is only latterly we realise they are hanging because they were lynched by the brutal plantation owner, Schoolteacher and his workers. Even the lovely memories have death and pain in them—Sethe's own body brutalised by Schoolteacher's boys on the plantation, and this landscape filled with death. So Morrison establishes a haunted place, house, mind and body, inescapable and present. Sethe bears a tree of scar tissue from beatings on her back, a choke cherry tree, but it is also a tree of life, and her memories of pain and loss are also interlaced with the betrayal of the trees and a delight at being alive. In this ever present, lively haunting, we see both the permeating of the horrors of the past, and ways of moving on while never denying them, ways of acknowledging and incorporating, but not letting them swamp you; the major message of the novel.

The slaves at Sweet Home suffered from the legitimation of their degradation through language and education. Schoolteacher, an intellectual whose dehumanising cruelty to his slaves dresses up the denial of human rights in the cloak of academic authority, teaches the boys to put Sethe's human characteristics on one side of the page and her animal characteristics (a longer list), on the other. His misplaced use of the power of education, like much warped history, enforces a view of African Americans as not merely less than human but as deserving cruelty which is excessive and inappropriate for even a feared and abjected creature such as a snake (with which he compares them, when coming to reclaim his 'property', Sethe and her family).

We as readers dig back behind *Beloved* to find out about the experiences of women under slavery. bell hooks (1981) talks of and records details of slavery, lynchings, transatlantic slave crossing and brutalisation, all of which play out through the story of Sethe and her family. After Garner's relatively liberal behaviour, Schoolteacher's brutality is paradoxical in that his role is one of educating others. The male slaves of Sweet Home are burned, flogged, murdered and lynched; the women are raped, brutalised, treated and represented as animals (in Schoolteacher's teachings). In his hands, education, language and history all reframed slaves as non-people, which permits their lives and histories to then be subject to erasure. *Beloved* brings back to life and presence the ghost of the baby sacrificed when Schoolteacher returned to claim the objects of his possession, the slave family. Beloved herself returns as a full grown, insistent, confused, intrusive refugee from the swamp of that past. She does so through the help of supportive 'poor white trash', Amy Denver, and comes into the home which once could not protect her as a child, and back into the lives of her family. The novel brings her, her history and the palpable lived experience of that history into the lives of those who read the book. It builds on that shock, so that you have to find out the hidden history and stories of the slaves and ex-slaves, facing the horror which lies at the heart of the industrialised West: transatlantic slavery.

One of the Sweet Home plantation men, Paul D, returns suddenly. A stranger from the past, battered but resilient (at least externally), he walks invited into Sethe's life and into her home, and is able to cause some silencing of the ghost baby, at least temporarily. While the ghost might be seen as not evil, rather 'rebuked. Lonely and rebuked' (p. 11), it nonetheless causes emotional and physical disruption for the family. Initially it seems that this male presence from the past calms and removes the angry ghost when 'a kind of weeping clung to the air where it had been' (p. 10). However, they are all wrong to relax into the gap between its angry presence and the next event, the arrival of Beloved, the ghost in mature human female form, who enacts a realised presence in their relationship as well as their home space. The events suggest that trauma is not straightforwardly dealt with (see Madsen 2008). If people try and lock up memories and pain, try and exclude such ghosts rather than working through what they represent, they return stronger and more harmful. The novel's journey is a digging up, a revitalising, of the horrors which had lain dormant in memory, staved off by washing, sewing, cooking and working, but in fact constantly seeping in and infiltrating thoughts, as the battered domestic interior of the home attests. Every home in the whole country is affected by, haunted by the hidden and the everyday histories of the damage done by slavery, a damage of dehumanisation, considering people as objects, brutalisation upheld and reinforced by the powers of violence, of language and education.

The shocking dark centre of the novel is the moment of recapture by Schoolteacher and the slave-catcher. The moment is deliberately revealed, remembered, once Paul D and Sethe have settled into the beginning of a new life together, each revealing only small items of their past, in order to avoid re-entering the trauma of re-telling. Sethe escaped the brutality of the plantation with her children but her owner, Schoolteacher, has an economic and legal right to reclaim them all. Like the four horsemen of the Apocalypse, Schoolteacher, a slave-catcher and two henchmen come to recapture what is owned. The section begins 'when the four horsemen came ...', then goes on to detail, in an advisory tone, teaching us how to recapture an escaped slave, one depicted as childish, silly, in his futile attempts to escape:

> Caught red-handed, so to speak, they would seem to recognise the futility of outsmarting a whiteman and the hopelessness of outrunning a rifle. Smile, even, like a child caught dead with his hand in the jelly jar, and when you reached for the rope to tie him, well, even then you couldn't tell. The very nigger with his head hanging and a little jelly-jar smile on his face could all of a sudden roar, like a bull or some such, and commence to do disbelievable things ... (p. 148)

The intention is entirely economic: language dehumanises and in so doing removes the need to recognise human rights. He continues: 'unlike a snake or a bear, a dead nigger could not be skinned for profit and was not worth his own dead weight in coin' (p. 148).

The use of first-person language, of those recapturing the slave family, gives us insight into the mind-set of dehumanisation, and helps us understand why Sethe tries to kill her children in order to rescue them from the worse horror of slavery. We too accept the unacceptable (infanticide) as the lesser of two evils and the result of that worse evil: slavery. Strategies of the literary Gothic enable the immediacy, the language and the worldviews of the slave-catcher and slave owner, Schoolteacher, to be brought into our heads with all the darkness of their thoughts, and through the use of their thought processes and language, undercuts their paradoxical views of right and wrong, good and bad, black and white. It brings together into a drama and a space the horror of the interactions between those who believed themselves superior and acted only with inhuman brutality and negation of the rights of others, and those who were literally silenced (by the bit, the lack of history, the lack of education), brutalised, dehumanised.

History is portrayed as all around us, a tangible, visible existence that a community can experience and bump into. In this novel, the insanity and absurdity upon which an early capitalist society dependent on slavery is founded translates itself into the lived madness, the haunting of the past within the house where first Baby Suggs, the grandmother, then Sethe, the mother, and Denver, her daughter, live. Tangible history mixes with supernatural events.

Beloved is not a regular ghost, with a regular grudge to bear (such as murder, disinheritance, etc.), she is the ghosting of the past of America, the legacy of slavery lived within the times in which Morrison wrote the novel and in which we read the novel. The traumatic moment, one of many, which produces the return, this specific return to haunt the mother, is extremely localised and personal, confined to the family, to the body, to the house in the community. It goes beyond the personal, it is political, and it is both conceptualised in time and place and beyond both of these as a traumatic memory dealt with through the political, socially engaged imaginary that the Gothic enables. Eventually the realisation of the role of Beloved as returned ghost causes the community to recognise its complicity in the tragedy, and to step up and help exorcise its everyday destructiveness. It causes the reader to go through a whole host of responses: denial, refusal, followed by scepticism, i.e. did slavery really happen? Followed by some research, rejections (people can't possibly do this to each other, ghost stories, the format can't be true), then some more complex thoughts related to historical complicity (who gained what from slavery?). The complicity is much removed from the event. The event acts as a trigger for guilt, silence, denial and refusal, or awareness and confusion. The whole issue of slavery and racism is so big we can only manage to approach it in individual cases with which we get subjectively involved. We empathise with Sethe. The disgust of the community at the murder of her child resembles our disgust at communities and individuals who behave with violence, racism, sexism and genocide. Perhaps like Paul D and the community, we reject the victim as well as the victimiser; it is too difficult to unscramble. But this book forces us to recognise the standpoint and the confusion, the ways in which the community behaves, and the murder Sethe performs, which in her own eyes renders her guilty, damaged and soulless, but which was caused by the desire to rescue her children from a fate worse than death—slavery. We might identify with none of these characters directly but also might do so with the complexities of the damage done through internalising racist, sexist and genocidal arguments through education and language (the terrible objectifying, dehumanising language employed by Schoolteacher and the slave-catcher). It makes us aware of the reciprocal self-violence and internalised worthlessness, results of a reaction to this base behaviour (recognisable as elements of being human with which we need to deal, to overcome), and the collusion of the community, the larger collusion of wider communities, wherever we might engage or not.

We can see these complex behaviours playing out before us through the agency of the returned ghost baby. This is a full-grown adult problem, it insists its way into everything, refusing to see that there is no way forward. *Beloved* forces us to move through the stages of trauma and rejection, loss, guilt and silence, and then to engage with the debates, move beyond our own silenced, confused, lingering sense of third- or fourth-hand guilt, in order to make decisions to understand, internalise and to act in positive, community-orientated or individually orientated, values-led, positive human ways. It causes us to get inside the debates, and to understand the lived and imaginary.

Memory is alive. Morrison talks of a palpable memory which you can bump into. In *Beloved* she develops feminist forms of writing the body in a Gothic manner, to write the newly realised, adult body for the dead baby and that of the mother on whose body she latches and which she drains. The body of Beloved carries the interred pain. Her return offers no simple reunion of loved ones because the guilt of her mother is a microcosm of a national and international guilt, a family, individually located, feeling guilt, still alive on a daily basis. Sethe's story is retold in the bars, it keeps away the community who ostracised her, and it circles the little family in its own home. The boys ran away from both the poltergeist and the magic used against it, such as leaving soda crackers by the door, which actually fails to ward off the ghost, only sometimes temporarily allaying the attacks. Plates are broken, handprints appear on mirrors. Beloved as the ghost of slavery is a palpable presence summoned up by the beginning of a new life for Sethe with Paul D, and her educationally limited daughter Denver. The house shakes; it attacks. Beloved's own entrance as an adult is a raw, immediate reminder of the past in the lived present. Her return is a mixed blessing. Intruding on the relationship between Paul D and Sethe, she acts as a siren, upsetting trust and security. Her friendship with Denver is manipulative, and her relationship with her mother draining, like a succubus. Beloved steals Paul D from Sethe, and as Beloved grows with a phantom pregnancy, Sethe shrinks and shrivels. The guilty memory, the presence of this, eats her up. Like resentment, the tangible immanence of this presence rends the family and intrudes on its hard-won securities, fostering self-consuming worms of doubt. Paul can't stand it, and Sethe continues to shrivel. The family are trapped inside the haunted house. Denver's white employer, and Amy Denver, who helped Sethe on the crossing, are each reminders that Morrison is not constructing a simple indictment of white against Black, but in refusing to simplify she opens the haunting to everyone, from the immediately to the seemingly marginally concerned.

The women of the community who failed to warn Sethe of the slave-catcher's arrival finally return to exorcise Beloved from no. 124, utilising a pre-linguistic community humming sound, denying the dehumanising language of the white man. This enables them to cope with, recognise and place the ghost of slavery, thus ridding Sethe's house of the draining succubus of lived guilt and pain:

> They stopped praying and took a step back to the beginning. In the beginning there were no words. In the beginning was the sound, and they all knew what that sounded like. (p. 259)

Beloved is essentially a novel about the vitality and intrusiveness of memory, the memory of racial oppression under slavery. Memory or 're-memory' is acknowledged as present, solid, vital:

If a house burns down, it's gone, but the place—the picture of it—stays; and just in my re-memory, but out there in the world ... it's when you bump into the re-memory of someone else. (p. 36)

The novel uses figures and tropes familiar in the literary Gothic: the return of the repressed, revelations of hidden stories and secrets, silencing and voicing, language such as that of Schoolteacher, which deceives and hides. There are also liminal spaces, such as the swamp from which Beloved arises, and 124, the house which lies on the border between a free state and one relying on slavery, and the space in the clearing where the community reunites. Morrison recovers the past through haunting, suggesting that the legacy of a damaged past continues into every present until it is possible to live with, imagine and construct beyond the elements of such a damaged past, not ignoring but not letting them dominate either. As Deborah Madsen (2008) suggests, these are the processes employed in trauma narrative, at first a return, a repetition, and eventually an acknowledgement, then a management without full denial.

This book made me feel so guilty and silenced that I couldn't talk about it initially. The final words 'this was not a story to pass on' (p. 260) are tricky. We have to pass it on; we have to engage with it, we should not 'pass' on it.

What *Beloved* also does is exemplary of the best Gothic, it engages the reader directly with the issues which have been hidden, and it does so through its language, as well as the involvement with the family and with the returned ghost baby. While some elements of the Gothic can be trappings, stagy layouts and creaking artifices, cardboard villains and cardboard castles, bats on strings and equally creaking performances of Hammer Horror films, the home in which Sethe and her family live is a haunted house, one with its own destructive energies, and it is also the haunted house of the American South and its past.

Other examples of Morrison's work explore the haunted houses of relived, reimagined memory, including *Home*, *Love* (2003) and *Paradise* (1997), which each use locations which entrap or replay versions of the past, stories of marginalisation, silencing, disempowerment and the lack of human rights.

Home *(2012)*

In *Home* Toni Morrison uses strategies of the literary Gothic to explore cultural hauntings of racism and false science, deceit, power enabled by money, and entrenched inequalities, using the twinned motifs of journeying and returning to a new home. Morrison focuses on another key moment in American history, just after the Korean War, but before the Civil Rights movement. A homeless Army veteran ironically named Frank Money, journeys back to the South to try and help his sister, Cee. This, and the tale of his sister, uses Gothic strategies of parallels, silence, deceits, entrapping stories and spaces to question and trouble the notion of homeland and home, then restore it in a new form.

The novel opens with a terrible memory which is repressed, hidden throughout their adolescent and adult lives. Frank and his sister are in Lotus, Georgia, watching horses and men. 'They rose up like men. We saw them. Like men they stood' (p. 3). As they hide in the long grass, they marvel at the horses, which behave with more humanity than the men in front of them, since these men bury another alive, a body heaped on a wheelbarrow, shoeless, quivering, black with a creamy pink sole 'whacked into the grave' (p. 4). Frank's sister shakes. He believes he can handle it, but he suppresses this terrible memory for so long that recounting it to an interviewer who manages the story for the reader opens up the post-traumatic stress disorder brought on by the horrors of war, and the full story follows.

Although Frank is a veteran of war, his social position in his homeland is one of worthlessness. Much of his life post-war takes place in and out of jail. Damaged, he finds it difficult to hold his temper, maintain regular habits even when he is with a partner, and to hold down any job. He is dispossessed and demotivated, he has lost direction and there is no space for him to call home. His journey, often in broken shoes, is hampered by poverty and an ingrained, everyday racism. Even with Lily, with whom he lives for a while, he can find no peace. His dreams of the war intersperse with his perceptions of what is around him, including Lily, altering his perception, so 'a tired cruelty laced her voice and the buzz of her disappointment defined the silence'. Lily's face seemed to resemble 'the front of a jeep, relentless headlight eyes, a bright scouring above a grill-like smile' (p. 20).

Frank behaves in ways that are antisocial. He is bemused and disorientated, and is seen as guilty (of something, anything) just because he is poor and Black. These are negative responses to his journeying and his somewhat troubled sense of identity. However, he also gets help from an ordinary African American with his own home and child, but little money, and also from a religious man, and as he gets further south, from a white preacher who offers support but wants to keep him out of the house, at arm's length, despite the preacher's Christian generosity. It is a dark and hellish journey for Frank, a form of pilgrim's progress. The weather is inhospitable, he is frequently off course, but he eventually finds his old home. He also finds the house where his sister, seeking a real home, became imprisoned, in a death trap. Gothic tropes of journeying through dangerous places, misunderstanding, undermining of identity, misreading, disempowerment, unsafe spaces of danger, are accompanied by those of incarcerated spaces.

Frank's sister, Cee, made a poor choice in a flamboyant partner who ran off with her car, his real love. Penniless, she sought a job in a white Southern doctor's establishment. Secure for the first time, she is told by the housekeeper, Sarah, that the doctor, Beauregard Scott, is 'No Dr Frankenstein' (p. 60), an allusion which alerts the reader to Gothic possibilities, particularly of misdirected experimentation on humans. This ostensible haven is a kind of white, Southern, gingerbread house, ostensibly nurturing and full of sustenance, but actually deadly. In this 'babes in the wood' tale, Cee, one of the two lost children, is trapped and deceived. The place, and especially the cellar of the treatment room, resembles a modern-day torture chamber, a Dr Frankenstein's surgery and operating table. Scott's work on poor Black girls is carried out in secret, though sometimes shared with another doctor, and Sarah's interpretation of the growing illness and demise of these girls is naïve, but as alert readers, we grow suspicious. The wife, medicated on laudanum, watches 1950s sitcoms while in his office the doctor keeps texts on race and eugenics such as *Heredity, Race and Society*, and *The Plans of the Great Race*, a collection that aligns his interest with those of Hitler and the experimental eugenics of the Nazis. But Cee is too comfortable to notice either this or the problems of practices upon her, since at last 'this was a good, safe place, and Sarah had become her family' (p. 65).

When Sarah takes a knife and cuts up a melon described as 'female', this presages the violence done to Cee and other African American women in the name of science. One reviewer picks this up as a metaphor for the richness of the text:

> slice it anywhere and you will find striking moments, dialogue that sings with life, and the mythic American landscape and its people surviving within it. (Akbar 2012)

Cee loses her rights to her own body, which becomes a site of experimentation. The unethical practices resemble those of the Tuskegee syphilis case, a disgraceful piece of racist research in the 1920s and beyond, in which African American men with syphilis were given placebos but thought they were being treated, in the name of medical science. Beauregard Scott's gynaecological experiments are a culpable, insane way of dealing with humans as subordinate, useless forms of life. The treatment of Cee and the girls on whom Beauregard Scott experiments, whom he imprisons and objectifies, represents an indictment of science without ethics, the dehumanisation of others. It is a Gothic horror scenario in the name of unethical racist science, involving issues of power, identity, gender, culture and exploitation, all acted out in the doctor's experiments.

Frank and Cee are twin halves, one static, the other journeying. Frank is out on the road, buffeted by everything and denied rights, money and self-worth, but dedicated in his travelling back to what was once an abusive home, while Cee is trapped inside, imprisoned, static and experimented on. Neither care about maintaining their own bodily safety, but both survive. Once reunited, they find redemption. Frank rescues Cee. Their being together, brother and sister, rescues both of them. They return to their old home, once no home at all, haunted by the history of an abusive childhood, and they reclaim their sense of self-worth. Home, where abuse and violence were allowed, unnoticed, covered up, is finally restored to a place of calm and growth. Cee begins to heal, cared for by Miss Ethel and a community of women who make and sell quilts. The men fix things and there is at last some harmony.

Miss Ethel relates Cee's dehumanising treatment to that of slavery, advising: 'don't let Lenore or some trifling boyfriend, certainly no devil doctor decide who you are. That's slavery, somewhere inside you is that free person I'm talking about, locate her and let her do some good in the world' (p. 126). As one reviewer, Ron Charles, notes, in *The Washington Post*:

> Despite all the old horrors that Morrison faces in these pages with weary recognition, 'Home' is a daringly hopeful story about the possibility of healing—or at least surviving in a shadow of peace. (Charles 2012)

Another reviewer comments on the significance of the motif of *Home*, a land shared by everyone who lives there whatever their skin colour and history:

> Part of Morrison's longstanding greatness resides in her ability to animate specific stories about the black experience and simultaneously speak to all experience. It's precisely by committing unreservedly to the first that she's able to transcend the circumscribed audience it might imply. This work's accomplishment lies in its considerable capacity to make us feel that we are each not only resident but co-owner of, and collectively accountable for, this land we call home. (Hager Cohen 2012)

Postcolonial and postmodernist writing is a form of ghosting, the repressed hidden histories of the past lingering alongside those of the present. Gothic strategies can enact that ghosting, those haunted histories. However, both Toni Morrison and Tananarive Due recognise that the Gothic is not for everyone, and might be seen as mere entertainment, shrieks, spooks, not a serious way of challenging marginalisation, racism and sexism. Morrison talks of African American insight as a 'discredited' view (1985, p. 65). Here she argues for the importance of the supernatural, superstition and the spectral, alongside palpable, felt reality, vehicled by a mixture of historical realistic detail and the Gothic, to explore and express how temporal, physical and metaphysical layers of life are experienced. Tananarive Due also felt that she might not be taken seriously if she used Gothic literary strategies. However, they have the Gothic critics on their side. Jeffrey Weinstock's *Spectral America* (2005) reinstates the value of the imaginative and the supernatural. Weinstock identifies the contemporary, revived fascination with ghost stories as having affinities with poststructuralist thought insofar as they disrupt the complacency of a single received version of reality and history, and instead, offering alternatives:

> The ghost is that which interrupts the presentness of the present and its haunting indicates that, beneath the surface of received history, there lurks another narrative, another story that calls into question the veracity of the authorized version of events. As such, the contemporary fascination with ghosts is reflective of the awareness of the narratives of history. (Weinstock 2004, p. 5)

Contemporary Native American, African American, postcolonial and other ghost stories revision history from alternative perspectives, filling in the gaps: 'To write stories concerning exclusions and invisibilities' is, as Avery Gordon notes, 'to write ghost stories' (Gordon 1997, p. 17). These haunted tales remind us of parallel, often hidden, as Morrison calls them 'discredited' lives, histories and interpretations. They return, and replace what has been silenced or denied.

Tananarive Due, *Joplin's Ghost* (2006)

> Your music can help free our people from their binds, so no one can make slaves of us again. (Freddie Joplin to Scott Joplin, Due 2006, p. 212)

Miami journalist and daughter of Civil Rights activists, Tananarive Due, constructs African American located Gothic in *The Between* (1995), in which a middle-class man is haunted by the sense he should have died, feeling his time stolen. She also writes the African Immortals series of four novels. This is a mixture of thriller and vampire tale focused on an alternative, religious community of immortal Life Brothers living underground in Africa, one of whom, Dawit, married a mortal woman, Jessica, and has a child, Fana, through whom these different beings can be reconciled. Among the vampire-like Life Brothers there is a reverse racism, in which humans and women are seen as lesser beings. Separatism and predatory arrogance over the ownership of life-preserving miracle blood resembles racist and sexist behaviours.

In *Joplin's Ghost*, Due, like Toni Morrison, uses the infiltration of a ghost, and in this case also his music, into and through a contemporary, female musician, to revitalise and replace the silenced stories and sounds of African American history. Due relates Gothic horror to a duty to retell the full variety of histories:

> I like to scare people ... In terms of folklore, I'm trying to mine stories from our own traditions and history, since so much of that has been overlooked in literature thus far. (Due 2005, p. 160)

Tananarive Due writes action-packed adventure horror which troubles racial and gendered otherising. Due's *African Immortals* is an engaged saga which challenges racially inflected hierarchies and gendered distinctions. *Joplin's Ghost* turns to contemporary America. Both Morrison and Due reimagine, re-infuse, recreate and express anew themes, and in the case of Due's *Joplin's Ghost*, the very sounds which have been ignored and silenced. Living history is re-visualised, updated and gendered in folk tale and other forms of cultural expression, rewritten from a female point of view and infused with the ideological influence of their historical and contemporary cultural context.

Joplin's Ghost continues a postcolonial and African and American trend in rediscovering the power of music as a living history of people who were often dispossessed in history, their languages stolen. So Sri Lankan Canadian Michael Ondaatje recuperates the history of Buddy Bolden, the acclaimed but totally unrecorded father of jazz in his novel *Coming Through Slaughter* (1976). Toni Morrison injects this idea of rediscovery and re-recording into two of her novels, *Jazz* (1992) and *Love* (2003), the first of which is postmodern in form, as is Ondaatje's. These novels use storytelling and interwoven tales to explore a powerful moment in Black history, the Jazz age, the Harlem Renaissance, while Morrison replays the literary Gothic in *Love*. Coming closer in form to Due, in *Love*, Morrison operates by reinvigorating the memories of the dead in the lives and music of the living, settling old debts, admitting old guilt and celebrating life.

Morrison's concern is with the past as a way to understand the present, recovering African American history from the Second World War to the 1990s, unblocking her material and setting free the sounds of the relative freedom of some examples of Black life, here in Cosey's bar and restaurant, with its lingering music. This can reinvent and reinvigorate a ghosted setting of versions of this past which are accessible, as are the sounds and characters of the musicians.

In making use of the ghosting trope, both writers take a very American tradition into African American and Canadian/Caribbean contexts and interests.

Tananarive Due's *Joplin's Ghost* explicitly focuses on the motif of creativity and the past as influence and transfer down the years, as the spirit of Scott Joplin, troubled and physically debilitated musical genius, enters the life and piano playing of a contemporary African American singer and composer, Phoenix, changing her directions and behaviour without draining her individuality. Joplin's music represents the hidden sounds of a hidden history recuperated though the playing of Phoenix, who by channelling and reproducing his music celebrates its influence and referencing in the work of contemporaries and musicians of the twentieth century, establishing a continuity of African American history hitherto literally unmentioned. Joplin and his music are guests in the body of Phoenix, her music, and her lover Carlos.

Colonisers have the authenticated histories on their side. The tales of the dispossessed were not written down. Due's Scott Joplin was not so much a victim, but his economic position was unstable and his access to the opportunities for recording were, like Ondaatje's Buddy Bolden's, rare and mostly ungraspable. As with the music of the 1940s and 1950s in segregated America, from Cosey's resort in *Love*, there are few traces and only the major popular works remain.

Due acknowledges that her mission is empowerment:

> I want to create stories that are so outside of the realm of our everyday human struggles that they give me greater insight into how to manage the everyday battles we all face in life. I think empowerment is a good word for what I'm seeking as a writer writing for myself. (Due 2005, p. 161)

Her tale parallels the life history of Scott Joplin, author of 'The Maple Leaf Rag' and 'The Entertainer', among others, with that of hip hop singer Phoenix, who expresses her own creativity in her attempt at fame, urged on by her manager father aptly nicknamed 'Sarge', for his controlling behaviour. Phoenix's relationship with the gangster and music producer G. Ronn almost gets her killed, while her nightly haunting by the ghost of Scott Joplin gives her a new infusion of reasons to live. But the first sign of the ghostly presence is dangerous. As a teenager, Phoenix is run down by Joplin's ghostly piano, a gift from Freddie, the wife who supported Joplin and his work and who Phoenix grows to resemble when, late in the story, she slips back and forth in time from his period to hers and their lives and music intersect. Joplin's ghost needs her voice and her abilities through which to play his last pieces, including the lost opera 'Treemonisha', which initially met with discomfort and silence and latterly with acclaim. Phoenix, as if in a trance, finds herself playing Joplin's music on prime time TV. But she does not merely channel Joplin's lost work. With this music increasingly comes a political message about equality.

Occasionally the ghost of Scott Joplin is frightening and intrusive, more often latterly it is seen as inspiring and hopeful. Phoenix, in her aim for instant success in the music business, has sold out on her talent, and her sell-out reflects the betrayals of a history which somehow managed to exclude Scott Joplin, denying his talent, and that of friend Louis Cochrin, who was never recorded. Joplin's desire for immediate appreciation among his fans and his refusal to work for permanent recognition through recordings, politics and the political life all contrived to hide his work and his talent. Because Joplin's contribution was kept from public view, it is important that his ghost returns it to its rightful place and somehow revivifies it through the playing of Phoenix. Her channelling of Joplin's work is first recognised by Milton, his museum keeper, then it suddenly breaks out into the playing of unrecorded compositions, on prime time TV. Joplin's ghost's designs upon her, however, almost take over her everyday life. This is enriching, necessary, erotically represented, and ultimately dangerous. Phoenix almost remains in the past with Joplin as a new version of his wife Freddie, and he almost remains in the present with her, inhabiting the body of her lover, Carlos. As with Morrison's *Beloved*, it is important, the text suggests, that the ghost is heard and acknowledged but that the ghostly presence in the body is but a stage of development, a coming to terms with a newly heard past, a prelude to moving on. In this case, Joplin gets the airing both of his views on equality and his work. However, as with Morrison's Sethe, Phoenix and through her the readership must be freed from a debilitating guilt. It is important that Phoenix rise above being only the vehicle for Joplin's reignited talent, the channel for his music.

One gift she gives him is a sense of his own legacy in contemporary music. Phoenix plays Scott his legacy in chosen extracts from modern music, a living history of great works influenced by him:

> She didn't use Scott's ears because his ears were failing him. She gave Scott her ears, her future memories, searching in lightning speed. The soul could hear so much better anyway, especially music. The soul heard music best. She gave him Miles Davis and Duke Ellington, she gave him BB King, Otis Redding and Marvin Gaye. She gave him Mahalia Jackson and Shirley Caesar, Miriam Makeba and Jelly Roll Morton, Sly and the Family Stone, Gil Scott-Heron and Louis Armstrong. She gave him Dizzy Gillespie and James Brown. She let him hear Paul Robeson singing 'Olman river', and Billie Holliday singing 'Strange Fruit'. She let him hear 'Respect' sung the way only Aretha could. She gave him Earth Wind and Fire and Arturo Sandoval, Al Green and Eric Clapton … last she let him hear Phoenix. That music came from a different place in her memory, because most of it had yet to be written. But she heard it and so did he. Scott Joplin's face didn't change but she felt his soul's glow. 'You matter, Scott,' she said in a whisper. (Due 2005, pp. 445–446)

Joplin's ghost inhabits the body of Phoenix's lover Carlos, her mind and her everyday actions as well as her music. This is overwhelming, and she is torn between being a conveyor of his music, and wanting her own life back. The ghosts of the past, the book suggests, must be heard but not overwhelm and drain the living. While it is important that Joplin gets the airing his work needs, latterly it is important that Phoenix rise above the reignited talent which he embodied and produce her own composition. Scott Joplin's ghost inhabiting Phoenix and her work has enabled his own legacy to come to life, and also her own talents and identity to shine through.

In focusing on the musician and composer Scott Joplin, who died of syphilis, a turn of the century artist who was genuinely largely unrecognised in an era of intense racism, and on Phoenix, rising star, suppressing her creative voice for fear of failure and selling out for success in the hip hop generation, Due utilises a liminal space for music as interpretation of the past, of hidden history and of a cultural legacy. Through Phoenix's channelling, Joplin's music and views get a real audience. Once Phoenix has learned to work with it, the channelling enhances her own work and enables her to be true to her own interpretations.

Scott Joplin's wife, Freddie, points out:

your real gift is for making negroes feel proud. (p. 212)
   you can help us all get better seats on the trains, and equal treatment everywhere. Your music gives you a platform Scott, you'll be heard. (p. 213)

The historical effacement of Scott Joplin is set to rights. With the ghostly inhabiting and channelling through Phoenix, his work literally rises from the ashes of history and is not only played and recorded, but seen to be that of an ongoing African American historical legacy, embedded in the great performers and writers who followed him; history inscribed, revitalised.

CONCLUSIONS

African American women's Gothic fictions engage with and dramatise issues of oppression, silencing and empowerment in relation to gender identity, history and ethnicity.

Toni Morrison led the way with the ghost narrative *Beloved*, using Gothic strategies to indicate ways in which the legacy of slavery and its effects are still tangible and palpable as a pall—in this case in the form of a returned ghost baby acting as succubus on her mother, Sethe, and who must be exorcised to allow people to move on. Creating a readership *ensures* it will be passed on. *Beloved* directly confronts racism in a novel which combines lyrical beauty with an assault on the reader's emotions and conscience. It traces, embodies and focuses on the legacy of slavery, using forms derived from a traditional Black folk aesthetic.

Tananarive Due's channelling and reviving the more historically ignored music of Scott Joplin in *Joplin's Ghost* revives and replays what has been silenced, without overwhelming the variety, originality and talent of the new and living, in this case of Phoenix, the contemporary musician. We need our ghosts but they must not only remind and hold us back, instead they must feed the present and the future.

In these contemporary African American women's Gothic fictions, as we shall see in Chap. 6 in the work of Nalo Hopkinson, ghosts are revived, hidden histories are replayed, and the past is re-read.

Both Morrison and Due use the conceit of guests in the body, a spirit or ghostly possession of women and nested genre structures in the body of the text, to engage with and dramatise issues of oppression and empowerment in relation to history, gender and ethnicity. Postcolonial and postmodernist writing is a form of ghosting or haunting, where the repressed hidden histories of the past linger alongside those of the present. Gothic and speculative fictions can re-read the past and the present through their projections into a future or alternative reality. And they have designs upon us to consider values, specifically in relation to the texts discussed here, to engage with and dramatise issues of oppression, silencing and then empowerment in relation to gender identity, history and ethnicity. As Salman Rushdie comments on the role of the writer:

> A poet's work is to name the un-nameable, to point at frauds, to take sides, start arguments, shape the world and stop it from going to sleep … and if rivers of blood flow from the cuts his verses inflict, then they will nourish him. (Rushdie 1988, p. 97)

Morrison, Due, Hopkinson and others write the histories of African Americans in periods in which they seemed silenced—hidden from history—and they write the books not written, which is an act of empowerment in itself. This creative act shows that through using the imagination, where values operate as well as horrors, the worst can be recognised and faced, and ways forward constructed. Their work uses the strategies of the Gothic to engage us, and enables us to imagine a better future.

Bibliography

Achebe, C. (1987) *Anthills of the Savannah* (London: Heinemann).

Akbar, A. (2012) '*Home* by Toni Morrison', 20 April, http://www.independent.co.uk/arts-entertainment/books/reviews/home-by-toni-morrison-7660995.html

Burford, B. (1987) 'The Landscapes Painted on the Inside of My Skin', *Spare Rib*, June, p. 37.

Charles, R. (2012) 'Book Review: Toni Morrison's "Home," A Restrained but Powerful Novel', 30 April, http://www.washingtonpost.com/entertainment/books/book-review-toni-morrisons-home-a-restrained-but-powerful-novel/2012/04/30/gIQAKiWSsT_story.html

Derrida, J. (1993) *Spectres of Marx: The State of the Debt, the Work of Mourning & the New International* (Paris: Editions Galilee).

Due, T. (2005) Interview, *Femspec* 6, Issue 1, p. 160.

Due, T. (2006) *Joplin's Ghost* (New York: Washington Square Press).

Gordon, A. (1997) *Ghostly Matters: Haunting and the Sociological Imagination* (Minneapolis, MN: University of Minnesota Press).

Hager Cohen, L. (2012) 'Point of Return "Home", a Novel by Toni Morrison', 17 May, http://www.nytimes.com/2012/05/20/books/review/home-a-novel-by-toni-morrison.html?pagewanted=all&_r=0

Madsen, D. L. (2008) 'On Subjectivity and Survivance: Rereading Trauma through *The Heirs of Columbus* and *The Crown of Columbus*', in *Survivance: Narratives of Native Presence*, G. Vizenor (ed.) (Lincoln: University of Nebraska Press).

Morrison, T. (1985) in M. Evans, *Black Women Writers: Arguments and Interviews* (London: Pluto Press).

Punter, D. (2000b) *Postcolonial Imaginings: Fictions of a New World Order* (Edinburgh: Edinburgh University Press).

Rushdie, S. (1988) *The Satanic Verses* (New York: Viking Books).

Rushdie, S. (1990) *Is Nothing Sacred?* (New York: Granta Books).

Sandel, M. J. (1996) *Democracy's Discontent: America in Search of a Public Philosophy* (Cambridge, MA: Harvard University Press).

Weinstock, J. (ed.) (2004) *Spectral America: Phantoms and the National Imagination* (Madison, WI: Popular Press).

CHAPTER 5

Postcolonial and Cultural Haunting Revenants—Letting the 'Right' Ones in

Postcolonial Gothic women writers expose the double oppression of gender and race, and in so doing they use figures of the ghost, vampire and zombie, revenants reminding us of hidden histories, a silenced past. Jean Rhys' *Wide Sargasso Sea* (1966) begins this process for me. Through rewriting Charlotte Brontë's nineteenth-century Gothic classic, *Jane Eyre* (1847), Rhys uses characteristics of the literary Gothic to expose colonialism, racism and sexism and to rewrite perspectives on history through focusing on the demonising and abjection of the foreign female Other, a mad woman kidnapped and incarcerated. This figure represents all that the dominant culture insists must be hidden away and denied, including any traces of the theft of the wealth of other nations, and the potentially disruptive power of female identity and sexuality.

Rhys started to rewrite how imperial and colonial history was represented. They have been developed more recently with Malaysian Beth Yahp's cultural hauntings, Singaporean Sandi Tan's exposure of the imperial deceits and ghostings of the fall of Singapore to the Japanese in the Second World War, and Singaporean Catherine Lim's Gothic social critiques in her ghost stories, and her exposure of conspicuous consumption and worship of success at the expense of humane behaviours. Contemporary women's postcolonial Gothic offers both revisitings and revitalisations, frequently though exposing haunted spaces laced with the misrepresentation, mislabelling and disenfranchisement of a colonial past, and through the figures of revenants, ghosts, duppies, zombies, vampires and soucouyants. The revisitations and the new stories recover marginalised lives, replaying and recuperating hidden histories and suggesting different perspectives and revaluations, and the importance of awareness and agency.

As David Punter and Alison Rudd comment, the colonial past is always with us:

> The process of mutual postcolonial abjection is, I suppose, one that confronts us every day in the ambiguous form of a series of uncanny returns. (Punter 2000b, p. vi)
>
> The presence of the Gothic allows a space for the unspeakable and haunted past to force its way to the surface, particularly in a culture characterised by loss and transgression. (Rudd 2010, p. 10)

Postcolonial places are haunted places where historical silencing and erasure leak back into the everyday. Against this effacement and silence, the postcolonial Gothic offers counter-narratives to rationalism, romanticism and modernism, as it does to legitimated official histories. Who are the 'right' ones to let in to writing and reading experiences? Historically, many voices have been silenced and 'discredited': women's voices, the voices of colonised and displaced or 'resettled' people. For many whose stories remain unheard, there is also a triple marginalisation, that of form and voice. Those who use culturally contextualised and originated forms of writing and expression of lived experience through oral form-based myth and folk tale which influenced ways of telling and seeing often remain unheard outside their immediate context. This is also a fate suffered by storytellers who express their views through the strategies of the literary Gothic, acknowledged by African American writers Toni Morrison and Tananarive Due (Chap. 4). Postcolonial women's Gothic often requires readers to read differently, more aware of context and history, including *imaginative* history and the way people interpret their experiences, moving beyond the bald dates and facts. It enables silenced voices to speak against established interpretations, and encourages us to read in ways which acknowledge and 'let in' different, haunted, metamorphosed experiences and forms of expression inflected by culture and gender. It offers new ways to hear the subaltern voice. The culturally inflected postcolonial Gothic with its wealth of folklore, oral forms, versions of histories and ways of looking at the world might present particular reading issues for readers from cultures less familiar with such views and forms, so ways of reading might need adjustment to see what is being revealed, or suggested.

The history of colonialism and imperialism was in many ways one of displacement, brutality, renaming, disenfranchisement and deliberate reconfiguration and reimagining of places, spaces and lives, which preceded its violent rupture, whether that involved settlement, imperial, colonial rule or obliteration. A problem for those whose forefathers spread colonialism and imperialism across swathes of 'terra nullius' could well be a limited means of appreciating the histories, contexts, civilisations and cultures which were overrun, misrepresented or destroyed. Every location has a history which can be reimagined, read back through presences which have been curated, are still alive, or through the traces of presences that thought has erased. The postcolonial Gothic has this rereading and revitalisation as a core purpose.

Considering context, loci of enunciation and reception Cora Kaplan points out that some cultural, historical background could be necessary in which to locate texts from origins other than our own:

> Unless we are actually specialists in the area from which these foreign anglophone literatures come, and teaching them in that context, our more than usually fragmented and partial knowledge of the history, politics and culture in which they were produced and originally read frequently leads us into teaching and thinking about these texts through an unintentionally imperialist lens, conflating their progressive politics with our own agendas, interpreting their versions of humanism through the historical evolution of our own. (Kaplan 1986, p. 177)

Absence and silence are brought straight into England with Rhys' *Wide Sargasso Sea*, and the haunted places are all around us if our histories have been affected at all by colonial and imperial power. Elsewhere (Wisker 2007, pp. 401–425), I commented that in the UK, many people have and many have not had first-hand experience of marginalisation based on racial difference. Many have not been refugees or asylum seekers, have not directly suffered the kind of physical and psychological abuse as those who have suffered under the harsh denials and silencing of colonial or imperial rule, from white settlers, slave-owners or colonial and imperial masters. However, the obliteration and silencing of the work of others made such work, such voices, an absence for everyone. Betty Govinden, a South African critic, argues in such circumstances, in the context of

South Africa, in her own case, that with such deprivation and silences, with those protected absences, we have all have been 'subjected to colonial discourse and simultaneously prevented from criticising empire "textuality"' (Govinden 1995, p. 175). We might well have been starved of the reading, the insights, the cultural awareness, of experience and articulation of their experience by colonial and postcolonial writers. This is not the polite inquisitiveness of the complacent: we need to know, we need to share, but not to appropriate.

In focusing on the lioness's tale rather than that of the hunter, on the female 'hisstorian' of female, colonial experience, Grenadian, Black British writer Merle Collins' poem 'Crick Crack Monkey' (1984) presents a series of reinterpretations of events, places, beliefs and people in history. While culturally powerful views present one prioritised interpretation, from another perspective event, their underpinning values and interpretations can be seen quite differently. Her poem begins with a premise which offers new insights by mentioning the work of William Wilberforce. Wilberforce played a vital part in curtailing transatlantic slavery, and was active in the liberation of slaves. However, his efforts would not have been necessary, Collins argues, if the impetus for historical events had started from a different set of beliefs and behaviours. The poem questions various premises upon which heroic histories are built and suggests that ending slavery would have been unnecessary had there been no slavery. What is depicted as enlightened in colonial history is re-depicted as a response to the brutal excesses of the Enlightenment, the forces of reason which denigrated others as subhuman. Merle Collins' poem has a memorable last few lines suggesting that the (female) subaltern has much to say. The lioness (no longer the hunted) will eventually tell a different tale when she is her own historian ('hisstorian' in this poem). Collins and other postcolonial women writers are 'writing back' to the established readings of history which present such negative views of their lives and their values. In the context of Aboriginal women's writing, for example in *Talking Up to the White Woman* (Moreton-Robinson 2000), this has been expressed as a deliberate refusal of the interpretative power of the white woman. When using the strategies of the Gothic, such challenges to established, compliant readings are infused with the powers of the imagination, of metaphor, to undermine the seemingly fixed, and offer a range of alternative perspectives, leaving interpretation in a constant state of creative flux. But the Gothic and its origins and strategies, along with the supernatural, metaphor, symbol, and representation rather than asserted fixed facts and reality are often misunderstood, seen as suspect, discredited versions and interpretations.

Toni Morrison talks of knowledge of the supernatural and the spiritual, as 'discredited' (1988). She and Tananarive Due each note that not everyone can interpret the revelations, the different ways of seeing which this discredited knowledge enables. However, for many of us it is another valid way of knowing and expressing our understanding of being in the world, interpreting the vibrant living remains of history and its celebrated or silenced narratives. Steering a course through reading which ignores any Gothic overtones or Gothic texts is like walking around with blinkers on, blindly selective. We miss too much, dismissing as nonsense, secondary, undecipherable and irrelevant the voices of other ways of seeing, of arguments which might not be mainstream. We could falter short-sightedly in a manner resembling that of blundering over the lands, lives and beliefs, stories and ways of interpreting existence in the way that colonial and imperial past-masters cleared the bush and filled the empty spaces. Language is a weapon in this misrepresentation and concealment.

In *It's Raining in Mango* (1987), a text with Gothic undertones, Australian, Thea Astley exposes deliberate misrepresentation in the defamiliarised context of the Aboriginal lands being cleared for European settlement. The protagonist stumbles across a casual genocide of Aboriginal people, and is told by the men clearing the land that 'they're not human'. Such labels excuse scientific experimentation on animals (the 'dog model', the 'rat model') and here the destruction of a people. '"They looked human", she persisted. "They had all your features"' (Astley 1987, p. 27). The protagonist responds, shocked and horrified, refusing to be part of the cover-up, but not powerful enough to act directly, or to reverse the damage.

When considering postcolonial women's Gothic writing there are a number of difficulties in deciding what work to select and why, and the selection has been fuelled by sensitivity concerning labelling and simplifying. Postcolonial spaces and places are found in the imperial lands as well as the lands and peoples invaded, colonised, displaced and 'settled' (a peaceful sounding term for genocide in Australia and elsewhere). Gothic, in some contexts, emerges from the alternative worldviews of indigenous or colonised peoples, from those displaced from Africa and Asia (for example) and settled as indentured labourers, or from those whose lives existed alongside such colonised, displaced and invaded people. The perspectives will be different, the sense of displacement and haunting different, and no doubt many blithely feel no sense of history and haunting. It is ever the role of the Gothic to jolt that kind of complacency. Who knows what histories are hidden beneath our feet and the floors of our comfortable buildings? Or just out of shot in our photographs?

Homi Bhabha (1994) considers the postcolonial as a condition of silencing, and for the colonisers and colonised alike, often a condition of self-silencing, springing from a sense of the abject self. The uncanny and the abject are key concepts of the postcolonial Gothic, and women writers of postcolonial Gothic offer an awareness of a double displacement and defamiliarisation, the unease at that which should be or seems to be familiar but which is now strange. The Gothic slips into a rejection of that strange, that Other, as Gothic and horror (which tends to be more violent) are aligned in the notion of abjection. This is explained by French feminist psychoanalytic critic Julia Kristeva in *The Powers of Horror* (1982) and in *Strangers to Ourselves* (1988). In the first, Kristeva reveals the basis of abjection, Otherness. In the second she clarifies ways in which those in power, most commonly from the North and the West, construct those who are not themselves, as Other, to be rejected with disgust in order to reveal a certain sense of self; a psychoanalytic turn most commonly seen as an identity development stage in the development of a child (assumed a male). Her basis for relating this argument to Otherising those different (from whoever 'us' is) in terms of ethnicity has its roots in observing racism in France. Exposing Western patriarchally based horror, its boundaries, repressions and rejections, Kristeva emphasises the importance of equality in terms of gender, race, religion and politics. However, *we* construct the Other and offload onto it whatever disturbs us and often what attracts and frightens us also: desire and disgust.

> Our disturbing otherness is what bursts in to confront the 'demons', or the threat that apprehension generated by the protective apparition of the other at the heart of what we persist in maintaining as a proper, solid 'us'. By recognising *our* uncanny strangeness we shall neither suffer from it nor enjoy it from the outside. The foreigner is within me, hence we are all foreigners. If I am a foreigner, then there are no foreigners. (Kristeva 1988, p. 192)

This resembles David Punter's (2000b) comments about ways in which postcolonial Gothic exposes how imperial and colonial texts characterised, and erased, colonised foreign subjects as objects, the Other. Women and foreigners are each constructed as Other, abject, victims or monsters. In this context:

> as the great globalising project of modernity, which has its own controlling relationship to the postcolonial, rolls on, one of its more curious current effects is that, perhaps against expectations we live increasingly in a world of ghosts, spirits, phantoms. (Punter 2000b, p. 61)

Punter also indicates the constant presence, the reminders, the ghosting and haunting of those silenced Others (who are often also women). I argue that their voices become the channels for contemporary postcolonial women writers of the Gothic to reimagine and rewrite. From a position of ostensible double disempowerment and silencing, women postcolonial Gothic writers have a privileged position of insider—alive to (some of) those histories and their constant presence in the everyday lived experience. Salman Rushdie characterises immigrated peoples (to the UK) as 'outsiders with beady eyes and without Anglo Saxon attitudes' (1990, p. 7). These insider outsiders in an economy privileging white middle-class male power can take a piercingly perceptive view of the narratives that leave out the experience of the colonised/invaded, enslaved, obliterated from memory and existence. Instead of such narratives, these insider outsiders offer an askance view on the smug certainties of master narratives and worldviews which engineered both the silencing and obliteration, the devaluing of the voices of those considered Other to the imposed cultural mainstream. They find voice and forms to revive the silenced other voices, their voices. In this respect, the narrative strategies of postcolonial women Gothic writers very often include those Gothic tropes of ghosting and haunting, shape-shifting figures and reminders, revivals, and rewritten hidden histories. They offer alternative views and often also alternative expression, opening up familiar forms to reveal the potential for Others, referring out and back to oral storytelling, circular forms, to the everyday normality of the supernatural, bringing metaphor in as possessing equal weight to fact, cutting through external pretence, neat categories and neat interpretations and valuations. Theirs are essential, radical, different versions springing from radically different views, demystifying elements of the taken for granted world and its power-infused tales, rules and histories, and placing the alternatives as real and of equal value. An example of this is Nalo Hopkinson's *The New Moon's Arms* (2007), in which slaves leap from a slave ship and find their freedom as mer-people, an embodiment of the need for alternative ways of being. Hopkinson splices the Gothic with the speculative to add energy to the suggestion and embodiment of alternatives, and so other postcolonial Gothic women writers similarly trouble and develop the genre into hybrid forms, splicing it with fantasy, sci-fi, crime and romance, imagining ways forward from the contradictions and silences they have exposed.

Alison Rudd (2010) emphasises the widespread nature of postcolonial hauntings and ghostly traces and uses Ken Gelder and Andrew Hock Soon Ng's arguments about the Gothic's ability to open up new crucial insights into imperialist texts, and those which appear to have only Gothic trappings, revealing the supernatural, ghosts, duppies, zombies, soucouyants and local mythical beings, including the Lagahoo and Anansi. Descriptions of landscapes and buildings also emphasise the strange, Other and the untamed, the places and people who refuse to be defined and described in ways infused with imperial and colonial values and interpretative modes. If the Gothic is ignored, if somehow we can't read it in texts we might expect to be realistic records or sometimes straightforward tales of everyday life, then the texts are read as if depoliticised. They remain culturally silenced; we overlook and cannot hear what spaces, places, constrictions, people and events are telling us about the traumas and legacy of the colonial and imperial past. Recognising the Gothic features of contemporary women's writing from postcolonial contexts introduces a radical and revelatory critical insight exposing the inequalities of the legacy of slavery, the horrors of the transatlantic crossing, of indentured labouring, physical abuse and silencing. This re-reading exposes subtexts and shadow texts, or turns textual confusions into clarities. *Myal* (Erna Brodber 1988) is a good example of this (Chap. 6). Recovery of memory and the inevitable return of the spectres of the repressed past into the locations of the present are all features of postcolonial Gothic disabling historical interpretations; sets of behaviours and readings can be questioned or undermined, and histories rewritten, which can lead to a new sense of self-worth, history and location.

A key text which used the Gothic to open readers' eyes to a very different perspective on the interpretation of colonial experience, and issues of gender power, occluded, offstage in the great nineteenth-century novels, is Jean Rhys' *Wide Sargasso Sea* (1966).

MAD WOMEN: *WIDE SARGASSO SEA*, JEAN RHYS (1966)

'Qui est la?' cries the burning parrot at the end of Rhys' *Wide Sargasso Sea*, reminding us of loss, confusion, lack of certainty and of the power of the voice of authority, how gendered and culturally inflected it is. Anyone not fitting the version of the master's view and the master's voice is silenced and removed. The burning bird (a parrot who mimics the speech of the owner) tries to decipher the voice and presence even at the end, even as it goes up in flames, taking with it the house of empire and wealth, its lies, incarcerations, mistranslations, and enforced renaming of values, place, colonised others and in particular of women.

Through rewriting that culturally embedded women's Gothic novel, *Jane Eyre* (1847), Jean Rhys, colonial Other, Dominican-born, displaced colonial traveller, offers a startling challenge to entrenched versions of narratives about empire, the colonies and racial hierarchies, and to interpretations of history from the perspectives of the wealthy white male. She offers another view, another perspective, that of women, and of colonised peoples doubly disenfranchised and silenced. Rhys also reopens a classic novel which itself set off much of our critical thinking about the strategies of women's Gothic to undercut established narratives of values, power and hierarchy. This is achieved through the novel's dual action of undercutting the promises of romance, wealth, the big house, happily ever after, and lies concerning empire. It exposes the constantly leaking history of a previous first wife, mad, locked in the third floor (not exactly the) attic, the poisoned past of male–female relationships, and the silenced but shrieking woman. Jane marries her hero Edward Rochester, but not until she has moved beyond the fairytale romance of winning the Lord of the Manor, discovering his hidden secret, the hidden secret of England, the construction of the Other as foreign female, mad and to be denied, on which the success of patriarchal, imperial England was based. Rochester, as the second son, has connections with the colonies so could well have been sent there to bring back a wealthy wife. The mad first wife, Bertha, haunts Jane in reality, screaming in the upper rooms, escaping from restraints, appearing in Jane's room, trying to set her on fire and ending up burning herself to death, as she brings the house of empire and power down. As readers we saw the disturbed narrative and celebrated Jane's insistence on freedom, self-worth, her own inheritance and her agency, as well as 'winning her man'. But perhaps we cannot rest now with the relatively straightforward reading of nineteenth-century women's Gothic fiction, because we have to see that other parallel version, the one influenced by Jean Rhys' rewriting of the novel. We are also now more able to interpret the tale using the strategies of postcolonial feminist Gothic because of our enhanced reading abilities influenced by Gilbert and Gubar's *The Madwoman in the Attic* (1979) (see Chap. 1, and for comments on Neo-Victorian Gothic, see Chap. 10). Novels do not remain stable; we return to them and find them changed, as we are changed, and perspectives and interpretations hide or reveal themselves. In Rhys' narrative, Antoinette loses her name, and her inheritance is taken by Rochester, the second son, one of those usually sent abroad to make their fortunes. In the Caribbean, where these two are brought together, the landscape, lush and foreign, defamiliarises him and Antoinette's erotic power over him is described as maintained by obeah. The foreign Other, Antoinette/Bertha, must be renamed, and incarcerated as punishment for these strange ways. Dealing with a fictional figure, Antoinette/Bertha, Jean Rhys takes over *Jane Eyre* (1847) and not only rewrites it from a different perspective but invites reader awareness of the importance of perspective, silencing, power, economics, control over history and the right to speak about different versions of history; an awareness essential in the appreciation of postcolonial writing.

CROCODILES AND SHAPE-SHIFTERS: BETH YAHP, *THE CROCODILE FURY* (1992)

The wise grandmother in Malaysian Beth Yahp's *The Crocodile Fury* warns of the power of ghosts and spirits who represent alternative versions of events. Ghosts are real, and only strong women are a cunning match for them.

> Grandmother says: People who strike bargains with ghosts or demons sometimes lose out in the end. People who give their promises recklessly have been known to regret it. Ghosts know things that people don't. The favour a ghost grants always has strings attached and often turns out to be a nightmare benefit for the one favoured. Never think you can outsmart or outbargain a ghost, unless you happen to be a powerful wisewoman, well-versed in the arts of magic. Unless your hair is firm at the roots and your eyesight as sharp as a piercing. Sometimes even powerful wisewomen get caught out. (Yahp 1992, p. 313)

Hidden histories are found wherever colonialism and imperialism tracked across the lands and lives of people, and often emerge in the form of hauntings. Singaporean Catherine Lim's hauntings remind of domestic violence and the brutality of a rush into a world of commodification and consumer capitalism in Singapore, ex-British colony and trade centre of the world. Beth Yahp's Malaysian Gothic, like that of Tash Aw in *The Harmony Silk Factory* (2005), rewrites and revalues space and stories, landscapes, lives and houses. She exposes the appropriation of wealth and resources and the disempowerment of women, each seen as objects of ownership. Yahp's *The Crocodile Fury* parallels and interrelates the mythic figure of a jungle bandit in crocodile form, one who invades property and upsets enforced imported rules, with that of a shape-shifting sea creature, a crocodile figure of the lover of the great imperialist landowner who built on Malaysian land and imported and stole precious artefacts with which to fill his imposing house. The crocodile bandit and the now long dead lover are figures of otherness representing refusal of the oppression of colonial rule, and their spirit enters the child whose story we follow, granddaughter of a bondmaid who suffered at the hands of the great imperialist landowner, who owned her labour, and her body.

The novel is set in a convent school which was once a rich house built on colonial wealth, filled with imported and exotic things, set on the edge of jungle and rubber plantations in Malaya. The colonial is seen as an imported strangeness, the jungle as a wild, alternative, encroaching presence. The granddaughter, a young girl student in the convent, encounters the lizard boy and the bully, each wayward alternative versions of behaviour and of perspective, and finds herself affected by, aligned with, shifting into the strangeness and wildness they represent and which is also represented by the bandits, the crocodile fury, the shape-shifting lover stolen from the sea by the rich man.

Set on Mat Salleh (mad sailor) Hill, the grand house (convent, also called the ghosthouse) is a relic of colonial days when the land was taken and developed. Historical research also reveals that Mat Salleh was a nineteenth-century rebel who led other rebels against British imperialism, and that hill forts and locations such as the place where the great house/convent stand, exist as record and memory of the alternative energies he and his followers represent. The grand landowner who owned the great house stole goods and objects from the region and the world and he stole a woman, his beloved. She appears from the sea as if herself a sea creature, wild and difficult to adapt, suggesting the energies of rebellion and Otherness. These energies are figured in the crocodile fury, the pirates, the wildness of the young girl student who is the bondmaid's grandmother's granddaughter. As a building the great house embodies colonial theft, violence and usurpation. Native sweat and blood went into its building, stolen exotic artefacts into its rooms:

> when he lived there it was filled with exotic treasures. The gardens were filled with exotic plants and trees brought back from the rich man's travels: the Rose of India, the juniper, the raintree, the great hog plum. The rich man was a collector of the exotic ...
>
> The rich man cut back the jungle and built the mansion from stones carved from a foreign country ... Only the natives who built it left traces of a local presence in the rich man's mansion: their drops of sweat mixed in with the foundations, their blood and crushed limbs marking the beams that held the ceilings up. (Yahp 1992, pp. 4–5)

The place has layers of history, which seeps through its cracks. Its spatial fabric and ideological wholeness are each undermined by the power of the jungle, seen as female energy. It is:

> A mansion abandoned for years by everyone except the jungle. The mansion had been ransacked long ago. It was filled with rubbish and decaying furniture, its fine marble floors were heaved and prised apart by jungle roots as thick as a young girl's thigh. Its windows were hung with jungle creepers allowing only a feeble light. (Yahp 1992, pp. 4–5)

Magic and superstition are tangible presences in the house, part of everyone's everyday lives. People wish for cures, and for evil to be cast on their enemies and they pay for these supernatural services as easily as buying food in the market. The girl, her mother and grandmother made different choices about coping with the constraints of their position. The grandmother, fierce and spell-wielding, offers an alternative energy. The mother colluded; the girl inherits the radical views of the grandmother.

Tales of the crocodile, the bandit, the stealing of the lover from the sea and her burning up and disappearance are repeated, elaborated, as the girl uncovers and reconstructs the histories, exposing fissures in authorised versions of historical events. The story of the imperialist landowner's catching the shape-shifting mermaid lover elides the identity and bodies of the bondmaid forced into bed with the woman from the sea. Historically, the landowner forced this natural female energy, this mermaid, into a shape he could manage and own:

> The sharp glint of a knife. The rich man gripped. He pulled. The catch of breath in his throat scraped at my throat. The suck of the sea on his mermaid shape almost pulled my arms from their sockets. My feet thrashed wildly in bed ... His fingers on the dragon shape, the reptile-shape, the fish-shape eased themselves around a single scale. (Yahp 1992, pp. 135–136)

But as the story proceeds, the historical, mythical tale is understood differently.

> The rich man could not hold her. The dragon-shape twisted to savage him, the reptile-shape slashed its tail, the fish-shape pressed serrated teeth to his flesh. ... I reached to tear the lover's gown from my neck. My face was wet with tears. (Yahp 1992, pp. 281–282)

The historical body of the shape-shifting lover returns through the girl student, whose life we follow through adolescence until she inherits then reconfigures the love, violence, magic and myth of the crocodile in the wild mountain forest and escapes colonial and convent rule, hand in hand with the legendary lover.

> The lover clings to my hand like a promise, her hand fits the palm of my hand. Her joy is something I can touch. Our laughter shakes the birds and small animals from their perches, the jungle leaves from their trees. Our thirst is a scraping that makes us run and run. East, towards the sea. (Yahp 1992, p. 329)

Against the theft, possession and imposition of the colonial is the wildness arising from the jungle, from the sea, refusing the disempowering versions of history. *The Crocodile Fury* is a novel about rewriting history, using myth and oral storytelling forms, and it is also a novel about shape-shifting as a mode of rebellion and refusal, since those who refuse to be disempowered shift into crocodiles, sea-beasts, bandits and the Other. It interweaves *bildungsroman* and oral storytelling formats, setting different readings of events in history against each other through versions of the stories and through the girl's consciousness, so conformity and silence, superstition, magical powers, mythic and supernatural occurrences and readings jostle together. As readers, we are finally aware that the jungle must be allowed back and allowed in. Its energies and wildness are versions of self; what is damaging is the restructured history of imposition and theft which accompany repressive colonial rule. Both the imported, dangerous strangeness imposed on the jungle by colonial wealth and the tendencies of each culture to ostracise and 'Otherise' anyone who is different are exorcised and indicted through Gothic strategies. Layers of stories are uncovered through reimagining versions of people, the ghostly lover, the bandit, the grandmother, mixing and reconfiguring, version upon version a kind of palimpsest being peeled away so that the reader starts to piece a more coherent reading together from what is unsaid and hinted at.

In *The Crocodile Fury*, Beth Yahp uses postcolonial Gothic to explore hidden colonial histories of theft, repression and abuse, romantic lies and hidden passions. She reminds the reader of both the wildness of the jungle and the creative wildness of the Other, which lies both within and outside the self. A feminist critique of the oppressions of gender, power and a postcolonial awareness of their interlacing with colonialism, imperialism and patriarchy run throughout this novel as they do Singaporean Catherine Lim's *The Bondmaid* (1997). Enslaved or indentured women of history, whether the possessions of colonialists or of wealthy local people, are portrayed as revenants, returning with intent either as ghostly presences or through the bodies and spirits of others. This they do in Yahp's work, where the land and house are imbricated with colonial violence, and the granddaughter infused with the crocodile fury, the renegade rebellious spirit of revolt and agency.

Conclusion

Ghost stories grown from a gendered inflection to colonial and imperial history expose lies, bad memories, pretences, deceits, murders and displacements. Postcolonial ghosts haunt the spaces and places of the abused, misread and silenced past of imperial and colonial history, revealing as violent crimes acts to legitimate power based on gender, ethnicity, and wealth. In Julia Briggs' (2012) terms, ghost stories give us supernatural explanations and solutions to crimes committed while for Jeffrey Weinstock (2004), they also trouble received versions of history. In the case of the texts discussed here, these received versions have been handed on and maintained by the continued control of (most often Western, Northern) imperialist and patriarchal voices, who sanction selected narratives and histories. Weinstock's *Spectral America* (2004) identifies the contemporary, revived fascination with ghost stories as having affinities with poststructuralist thought, insofar as they disrupt the complacency of a single received version of reality and history, instead offering alternatives.

> The ghost is that which interrupts the presentness of the present and its haunting indicates that, beneath the surface of received history, there lurks another narrative, another story that calls into question the veracity of the authorized version of events. As such, the contemporary fascination with ghosts is reflective of the awareness of the narratives of history. (Weinstock 2004, p. 5)

Postcolonial spaces, people's lives and histories are haunted by the buried, silenced troubles of destructive acts in the past. Women's lives in particular have suffered the 'triple burden' of gender, race and economics: poverty with the accompaniment of powerlessness. In contemporary women's postcolonial Gothic these hauntings are often of domestic spaces, families and the woman's body, and they expose the triple dispossession and subordination of race, economics and gender. Part of the achievement of the postcolonial Gothic by women writers is to embody, write through, articulate and express such haunted presences, speaking out from silence, refusing what Gayatri Chakravorty Spivak (1998, p. 252) famously described as the 'subaltern' position. Expurgation is an aim, coming to terms with damaged histories, revealing lies and grand deceits, and preventing any more damage being done, sometimes offering a settling of memories, however temporary, some resolutions and some potential movements forward.

BIBLIOGRAPHY

Astley, T. (1987) *It's Raining in Mango: Pictures from the Family Album* (New York: Putnam).
Bhabha, H. (1994) *The Location of Culture* (London: Routledge).
Brodber, E. (1988) *Myal* (London: New Beacon Books).
Govinden, B. (1995) 'Learning Myself Anew', *Alternation*, Vol. 2, No. 2, pp. 170–183.
Kaplan, C. (1986) 'Keeping the Colour in *The Color Purple*', in *Sea Changes* (London: Verso).
Kristeva, J. (1988) *Strangers to Ourselves* (New York: Columbia University Press).
Moreton-Robinson, A. (2000) *Talking Up to the White Woman* (Brisbane: University of Queensland Press).

Punter, D. (2000b) *Postcolonial Imaginings: Fictions of a New World Order* (Edinburgh: Edinburgh University Press).
Rhys, J. (1966) *Wide Sargasso Sea* (London: Andre Deutsche).
Rudd, A. (2010) *Postcolonial Gothic Fictions from the Caribbean, Canada, Australia and New Zealand* (Cardiff: University of Wales Press).
Weinstock, J. (ed.) (2004) *Spectral America: Phantoms and the National Imagination* (Madison, WI: Popular Press).
Wisker, G. (2007) 'Crossing Liminal Spaces: Teaching the Postcolonial Gothic', *Pedagogy*, Vol. 7, No. 3.
Yahp, B. (1992) *Crocodile Fury* (Sydney: Angus & Robertson).

CHAPTER 6

Testing the Fabric of Bluebeard's Castle: Postcolonial Reconfigurations, Demythologising, Re-Mythologising and Shape-Shifting

Postcolonial, feminist Gothic is a powerful combination. It deconstructs oppressive narratives based on colonial and imperial, patriarchal worldviews, rewriting, reconfiguring and reconstructing versions and voices of the Other.

In uncovering unheard and unseen versions of lives and worldviews and histories, and in finding a hybrid form with which to express discredited perspectives, postcolonial Gothic is powerful and political. But Jean Franco warns against literary touristic delight in the foreign otherness, the frissons of difference born of reliance on certain valorised ways of speaking, seeing and remembering:

> the discourse of recognition becomes possible when heterogeneity is valorised by the increasingly routinised metropolis. At this moment, the Third World becomes the place of the unconscious, the rich source of fantasy and legend recycled by the intelligentsia, for which heterogeneity is no longer a ghostly, dragging chain but material that can be loosened from any territorial context and juxtaposed in ways that provide a constant frisson of pleasure. (Franco 1988, p. 95)

Ghosting and haunting were themes of Chap. 5, the return of the repressed, the silenced histories, the lands and places and readings laced with misinterpretations and silences evoked and expressed anew, returned, to be accounted for. This chapter considers in the main the challenge to oppressive narratives and constructions figured here as 'Bluebeard and his castle' to suggest both the mind-set and the fabric of repressive patriarchal and colonial narratives and constructions which control women's lives, and which the postcolonial Gothic helps to dismantle.

Canadian/Trinidadian writer Nalo Hopkinson works with the metaphor of the house of patriarchy and imperialism and her role as a woman writer, from a postcolonial context, when she directly links power, patriarchy, the image of the house, and her right to write:

> What do you think of Audre Lorde's comment that massa's tools will never dismantle massa's house?
> in my hands massa's tools don't dismantle massa's house—and in fact I don't want to destroy it so much as I want to undertake massive renovations—then build me a house of my own. (Hopkinson and Mehan 2004, p. 7)

This reminds me of Bluebeard's castle and the several extant versions of his story, originally an oral tale passed down by women, then developed into 'Fitcher's bird' in which a sorcerer entices and murders two of three sisters, their body parts found by the third. She is wily, preserves an egg, and on her wedding day disguises herself in feathers, as a bird, to escape his plot. In both 'Fitcher's bird' then later, by way of the collector of folk and fairytale, Charles Perrault, as the tale of Bluebeard, women are vulnerable, and either rescued by men, often by their brothers, or wily enough to contribute to their own escape. The variations on the Bluebeard tale are favourites for women writing the Gothic, whatever their origins, and particularly so for those from postcolonial contexts, since Bluebeard's story is, I argue, one of imperialism and colonialism played out through gender and power. There are fascinating parallels between the bases and the trajectory of the tale and the liberating work of postcolonial Gothic women's writing.

Patriarchal Bluebeard is an imperialist whose castle or grand house and whose narrative of care and ownership seduces and forces compliance, offers and restricts knowledge, disempowering and destroying both those who do and those who don't collude, the more wily women, such as in Nalo Hopkinson's 'The Glass Bottle Trick' (2000), where elements of 'Fitcher's bird' appear in references to preserving eggs (see below). Collusion is silencing and marginalisation; non-collusion is most often death for any woman who even slightly questions, pries, queries or offers alternative ways of behaving, driven by a little individualism, a little agency. Denying the right to questioning and the quest for knowledge, Bluebeard drives his many wives to explore his locked rooms with a key from which the blood will never be removed. Like colonised, nameless, powerless peoples, particularly subaltern women (Spivak 1988), these wives inevitably challenge his power and his version of life, and most die as a result. This tale has a strong message. It seems to say, question, challenge and you will end up with nothing: dead. This is a warning to women, and particularly those whose economic situation and status as colonial Others positions them as relatively powerless.

In this chapter, we look at the unravelling and rewriting of oppressive versions of the narratives of disempowerment, the prison-house of knowledge and power in which we can be locked, including that of education, in *Myal* (1988), and several versions of the more domestic prison-house, as represented in the Bluebeard story, in Nalo Hopkinson's 'The Glass Bottle Trick', Helen Oyeyemi's *Mr Fox* (2011), and Shani Mootoo's *Cereus Blooms at Night* (1996). Refusal of constraining constructions and tales lead to rewriting, reconfiguring something different, creating a new self and agency. Reimagining, retelling, reconstructing, changing shape or shape-shifting are different, empowering modes of response. As Nalo Hopkinson expresses it, it is not a matter of reconstructing Massa's house, the house of the oppressor and silencer, but of producing something completely different, in exposing the oppressions and silencing and reclaiming the language and spaces for new expression, revaluing the devalued and taking agency through shape-shifting and speculative fiction. Shape-shifting is a way of reconfiguring the self, split selves, metamorphoses, sometimes adopted as a mode of escapism, of hiding the self, sometimes of protection under duress, enslavement or marginalisation. Often it is an active response of subversion. When in a different shape it is possible to speak out, act out, behave differently, and change more than one's shape, rewriting familiar myths and casting them in a different light. Many of Hopkinson's tales in *Skin Folk* (2001) use shape-shifting, as do Helen Oyeyemi's *Mr Fox*, and Shani Mootoo's *Cereus Blooms at Night*.

BLUEBEARD AND HIS HOUSE RESHAPED

The original Gothic tale of Bluebeard highlights the dangerous contradictions of promises of stability, love and wealth, grandeur and domestic comfort in home and marriage, which entail obedience and denial of free will. Those who seek knowledge or question control suffer entrapment, oppression and destruction. It is a Gothic warning which, nevertheless, most frequently relies on male rescuers. Angela Carter's 'The Bloody Chamber' (1979) rewrites the tale, initially emphasising women's naïve collusion born of poverty, and a desire for sexual awakening. Carter enables the vulnerable young woman to use her wits, her warrior mother to use her strength and the monstrous male who owns the power and money to be dispatched, while the young woman loses neither love nor agency. Rewriting narratives dominated by oppressive male power, often the power of imperial, colonial or economic wealth, is a favourite choice of contemporary women writers of the Gothic, particularly those of postcolonial descent. Bluebeard's castle is a form of incarcerating domestic space, a mind-trapping worldview, a postcolonial haunted house. The castle/house of the dominant, attractive male/society and Bluebeard's own patriarchal and colonial power depend for their success on women's internalised versions of dependency. Carter's 'The Bloody Chamber' reveals the grander collusion of women in this destructive tale in the context of social constraints which grow from financial dependence, age, value, lack of power and lack of self-worth. Women exchange self and body for a myth of protection and cherishing.

In postcolonial Bluebeard tales, Bluebeard's house and the haunted house of the colonial past each are seen as constructed from patriarchy and imperial male power, effective where once colonised peoples and disempowered women internalise their own victim position in an economy in which they are always only a commodity. In postcolonial re-readings and rewriting of the Bluebeard tale by Hopkinson, Brodber, Mootoo and Oyeyemi, what we find instead is the dismemberment of Bluebeard, his house and his power. Colonial haunted houses are seen as constructed upon the prison-houses of history, gender and power. Self-recognition can lead to challenge, escape from the prison-house of Bluebeard and gendered, racialised history, and a regaining of power, self-worth and agency. With Nalo Hopkinson's work and that of Erna Brodber, Shani Mootoo and Helen Oyeyemi, what emerges is neither silencing nor mimicry of the dominant voice. Instead, their postcolonial Gothic derives from local folk cultures and women's experiences, reimagining previously disempowering texts or those from which they were entirely absent. It re-educates, reimagines and re-voices.

Talking of African American women writers, but relevant to postcolonial women writers more generally, some of whom are writing in the diaspora, Lorraine Bethel argues that:

> Women in this country have defied the dominant sexist society by developing a type of folk culture and oral literature based on the use of gender solidarity and female bonding as self-affirming rituals ... a distinct Black woman-identified folk culture based on our experiences in this society: symbols, language and modes of expression that specifically reflect the realities of our lives as Black females in a dominant white/male culture. (Bethel 1982, p. 179)

Gothic writing by postcolonial women writers moves beyond the tropes of incarceration and silence into something positive and new. A model for this trajectory considered here is Mootoo's *Cereus Blooms at Night*, where a silenced older woman manages to survive in, and then leave the house dominated by her abusive father, who she killed in self-defence, overcoming the abusive and hidden history and regaining her powers. Mootoo's story is one of revitalisation. Similarly challenging and newly affirming are Nalo Hopkinson's celebration of middle age, *The New Moon's Arms* (2007) her tale 'Precious' (2001), a rewrite of the King Midas story and 'The Glass Bottle Trick'.

Zombies and *Myal*, Erna Brodber (1988)

Myal, by Erna Brodber, deploys zombies and spirit theft to indict oppressive narratives embedded in religious teaching, popular culture and an education system established by imperial powers. In *Myal*, zombification results from a dominant, historical, racialised worldview peddled in popular culture and history and through warped education. When a young girl, Ella, disputes this worldview, these narratives, she frees herself and helps develop an alternative history of the island. The zombie and duppy (a Jamaican originated, usually malevolent spirit or ghost often entrapped in a bottle or jar) are popular expressions of abjection and cultural anxieties, duplicity and self-alienation, relations between innocence and guilt, but as Marina Warner argues, imperial control produced a loss of soul as a condition of slavery which has informed a complex use of both figures in Caribbean literature. Warner references Paravisini-Gebert, noting that:

the figures of the duppy, the soucouyant and the zombie have been disseminated through Caribbean centric tales since the 19th and early 20th centuries. For Paravisini Gebert the representations of the Caribbean in Gothic literature were a means of addressing the violence of colonialism but drew on the region's African-derived belief-systems of Haitian Voodoo, Jamaican Obeah and Cuban Santeria. (Warner, in Rudd 2010, p. 32)

These figures were traditionally used to depict Caribbean people as backward and savage, another form of silencing and denigration. In a response using the Gothic figures of zombie and duppy, undermining this, the destructive, dominant narrative is deconstructed and hollowed out, exposing the collapse of the ruling elite.

Myal is a powerful novel set in the first 20 years of the twentieth century in St Thomas parish in a fictionalised Caribbean location, both specific and representative in the ways in which its people have been silenced and misrepresented, in effect, zombified. Brodber explores the widespread traumatic experiences of migration, imperial and colonial disempowerment and disenfranchisement and does so by focusing on the lives of people in Grove Town, principally two young women: mixed-race Ella, whose culture is stolen in performance, and Anita, who suffers spirit theft (by male power), each an example of patriarchal control. We can never be complacent about our reading of *Myal*. It is a writerly text (Barthes 1973), and its use of the postcolonial Gothic is a major contributing factor to its destabilising of oppressive, collusive or simplistic readings. Denial of the values of others, marginalisation, undermining Black women's identities and body image lie at its heart, as does an indictment of the prison-house of oppressive versions of history and education. One of the novel's initial surprises is its use of an oral storytelling format, circular, returning to elements of the tale to more fully explicate or offer another reading. It uses both spirit theft and zombies to suggest the oppressive mind-sets which would keep a people spellbound, disempowered, zombified from the effects and forces of imperialism and colonialism. As such, then, it directly identifies colonialism with spirit theft and zombification—uniting the postcolonial with the Gothic. It is also postfeminist, moving beyond divisions between Black and white women to celebrate boundary crossers such as Maydene Brassingham, the reverend's wife, a positive character in a text which locates oppression in male power as much as in colonial lies.

Myal immerses readers in the complexities of realistic and spirit worlds to explore the historically constructed spiritual and real identities of the young women Anita and Ella, who are both victims of patriarchal and imperial power. Anita's spirit theft is initiated by landowner, Baptist and obeah man, Mass Levy, to cure his sexual impotence. Education is seen as used for good or evil, both as a challenge to colonial oppressions operating through education and as a way of enforcing imperialist versions and views. Ella O'Grady, with her absent Irish white father and her Jamaican mother, recites the imperialist representation of colonised people, Kipling's 'The White Man's Burden' (1899), at public shows, and has her identity shaped by English education through *Peter Pan* and 'The Dairy Maid'. Ella's sense of self is next influenced by her American capitalist husband Selwyn Langley (who will not have a child with her for fear of miscegenation), through theft of her history and re-representation of it in a 'coon' show, 'Caribbean Days and Nights'.

Gayatri Chakravorty Spivak's theory (1988) concerning the subaltern's inability to speak because of the necessity and inevitability of mouthing the language of the oppressors is enacted through Ella, whose identity, history and culture are misrepresented on stage. Sold on cosmeticised versions of the ideal white, blonde haired, blue-eyed woman, Selwyn Langley portrays a version of Ella, which she cannot recognise. Her hybrid identity is her own, it has both enabled her to pass for white and so gain an education and place in poetry recitals, as well as marriage to a white husband, yet it has also somewhat separated her from those of her own ethnicity. Seeing the white, blue-eyed blonde version of her on stage, Ella grasps the full meaning of her acceptance into white society as both a curiosity and a unique doll-like entity. Langley refuses to have children with her because of his fears of mixed-race births, the colour returning somewhere in the children, the bad blood. Ella was unaware that she had colluded with the version of herself which singled her out as truly unique because she would never be allowed to bear children who might look or be like her. Langley's staged 'Coon Show' forces her awareness of all this and for a while she suffers what Frantz Fanon (1952) has identified as psychological and physical psychosis.

Ella suffers from exoticism and cultural fetishism, while more generally on the island, the people are taught lies to keep them silenced, obedient and subaltern, little more than zombies, their spirits removed. Education is a powerful force for good or evil, and in her new job as a teacher, Ella recognises the powerful control of language and minds, worldviews and identities in the teachings of the imperialists and colonialists. The accepted reading of *Mr Joe's Farm*, a controlling children's book, enforces notions that without white paternalistic management, local people would be entirely directionless, powerless. Like George Orwell's *Animal Farm* (1945), *Mr Joe's Farm* resembles Stalinist rather than nurturing authority or democracy.

A colonial education system negates and denies representation of varied cultures, an erasure translating into low self-image, a kind of invisibility, acknowledged by postcolonial critic David Dabydeen when talking more generally of education under colonialism:

> We never saw ourselves in a book, so we didn't exist in a kind of way in our culture and environment, our climate, the plants around us did not seem real, did not seem to be of any importance—we overlooked them entirely. The real world was what was in books. (Dabydeen 1988, p. 78)

There are other voices than those of the oppressive set books, and other versions of space, time and power. Ella is able to engage with these too. Dialogues between Willie (Ole African), Perce (Mass Cyrus) and Simpson, who are both 600 years old *and* contemporary, testify to a vital race memory, and to African and Afro-Caribbean modes of worship. With such dislocation of the narrative through various voices and the circling forms of oral storytelling, we must trust the voices. Simpson/Dan identifies everyone whose worldview is curtailed as duppies, zombies, obeying orders and lacking vitality and independence. The disempowerment and disenfranchisement exposed in the text are played out at a realist level—education, books, performances—and a spiritual level through the discussions of Willie, Perce and Simpson. Radical political history is referenced through Simpson, based on Baptist preacher Paul Bogle, who led the Morant Bay rebellion and was subsequently hung. Simpson speaks of a 'fellow in St Ann', Marcus Garvey, who campaigned for the return of ex-slaves to Africa. Garvey had a literal escape, Simpson a more local and spiritual escape. However, Garveyism (which underpins Rastafarianism) cannot solve Anita and Ella's problems and the local African-derived religion of possession in St Thomas depends on Miss Gatha and Kumina (a local African-originated, Jamaican religion) as followers.

Ella's story is interleaved with Anita's, and the choral testifying of Simpson/Dan, Willie and Perce, who provide a comment on silencing, zombification and through their expression, a subtext, a Gothic but everyday critique.

> We said folk should keep their ...
> – Power.
> – They split man from his self. A working Zombie.
> – Split them from us. Made us a joke. Made us a blot.
> – And 'those tacky old ships'. Remember that Dan? Six hundred years ago, five hundred years ago, four hundred years ago and here in those 1760s: 'we'll quiet them and send them back to their tacky old ships'. Remember?
> – Can I forget?
> – They sold out our sound. (pp. 66–67)

In her teaching, Ella challenges the zombification of the children through their work on set texts which reference the meaning of subordination. 'The children are invited into complicity—she continued' (p. 97). Willie, Perce and Dan recognise her insights and discuss them, exploring silencing leading to zombification, and ways of overcoming it. Ella explains to Rev Simpson that the dominant narratives and education have undermined the children and the local people. They have:

> Zombified them. That's the word you need. –
> Meaning –
> Taken their knowledge of their original and natural world away from them and left them empty shells – duppies, zombies, living deads capable only of receiving orders from someone else and carrying them out. –
> Is that what I am to teach these children, Reverend Simpson? That most of the world is made up of zombies who cannot think for themselves or take care of themselves but must be taken care of by Mr Joe, and Benjie? Must my voice tell that to children who trust me? (pp. 106–107)

The spirits of Grove Town take on global capitalism in league with the female go-between, liminal space crossing Maydene Brassingham, Simpson's white wife, a postcolonial and Gothic figure herself and someone who works for unity and helps reunite the community alongside Miss Gatha's spiritual unity. Maydene emphasises the misrepresentations of history, asking:

> How much did Napoleon take? How much did Drake and Hawkins take? How do you measure men? In litres, pounds, in quarts? How much to sweeten how much tea? How much to make a garland for my lady's neck? Napoleon said to George: 'You see the stones in this necklace?' and George

said to him, 'you see the jewels in my crown? People strung together in a chain.' And the Reverend shook his head. 'Separating people from themselves, separating man from his labour. Should be preparing to meet their God stead of stringing chains for aging queens. Spirit thieves!' (p. 37)

A significant influence on Ella and others in Grove Town is Myalism, after which the novel is named. Several dictionaries and encyclopaedias define Myalism as black magic, obeah; however, it was the first Pan African religious movement of Jamaica in the 1760s, and challenged tribal divisions of slavery, in dialogue with an African past. Myalism has the interesting characteristic of refusing gender differences in the spiritual realm, so male and female spirits converse, and in the novel, Miss Gatha takes on the dangerous task of cure. Miss Gatha's magic is in opposition to a destructive obeah magic as she and the community join to help Anita against the control of Mass Levy.

Through her rereading and reconstruction of *Mr Joe's Farm* and the inspirational religion of Myalism, Ella reinterprets and so enables others to see they do not need to remain secondary and controlled, effectively zombies. Settling back into her own body and its differences, her own words and power as a teacher literally revitalise her in a novel whose dominating image is that of zombification. Ella reclaims a new voice in her challenge to the propagandist allegorical schoolroom text, *Mr Joe's Farm*, which would disempower generations of Black Caribbean children.

As Ella's spirit theft dissolves, so too does that of her parallel, Anita, who has literally had her spirit stolen by Mass Levy, a powerful man who achieves sexual control over a series of women. The community bonds together to call him out and cast him out. He is overcome by Miss Gatha, the local obeah woman, and a neighbourhood exorcism, which returns power and identity to Anita.

Myal is a complex novel which politicises the figure of the zombie as bonded sufferer of imperialist and colonial spirit theft, which embodies a form of mind slavery to a Bluebeard of historical imperial and colonial power, whose control of the secret room of knowledge is covered in the historical blood of the colonised and enslaved peoples. This control, this misreading is to be thrown off, leaving the ex-sufferer re-empowered. Brodber uses narrative experimentation—storytelling, oral/shifting, narrative voice and a mythical, spiritual world of equal reality to any historically 'realistic' world. She does so to develop debates about religion, education, culture, history and politics, and to challenge the imperialist and colonialist theft and translation of African/Afro-Caribbean/African American lives, particularly those of women, into controllable forms through education and entertainment. In so doing it reasserts Myal's healing community power, African roots and history, the power of magic and spirituality, the strength of local culture and of women. *Myal* makes demands on the postfeminist, postcolonial Gothic reader to weave their way through spirituality/reality/women's lives/colonial powers/ideological hierarchies of race, culture and gender—which test our tendencies to translate the spiritual into the real. The novel deals with history, identity, sexuality, the spiritual and historical, colonial legacy, silencing, women's identities, and rights.

Creative Gothic fantasy and horror enables a breaking down of boundaries of the imagination, opening up new perspectives, historical and culturally engaged fiction. For postcolonial women writers more generally, the expectation that they will focus on realistic writing, 'a little black pain undressed' (Burford 1987), initially limited postcolonial Gothic creativity. As David Punter notes, the literary can make connections between lived experience and imaginative alternatives, as absences and possibilities:

> the peculiar condition of the literary will always be to effect a link between the actuality, the presence of such conditions, however powerful and terrifying, and the imaginary, universality ... in its proper position, in absence. (Punter 2000b, p. 189)

'Massa's house' of oppressive beliefs and education can be reimagined and reconstructed, in a different shape, for different ends.

NALO HOPKINSON: DISMANTLING 'MASSA'S HOUSE'

Some contemporary African American and Caribbean women writers (Tananarive Due, Nina Kiriki Hoffman, Toni Morrison, Toni Brown, Erna Brodber, Jamaica Kinkaid and Olive Senior) use elements of the literary Gothic, myth, the supernatural and the fantastic to critique the legacy of slavery and racism, and deal with current issues such as power and identity inflected by gender, race and history. Their work is a radical challenge to gendered and racialised constructions of the abject. Ghosts, vampires, werewolves, voodoo, mer-creatures, various Gothic horror figures and formulae both entertain and act as vehicles through which to review and revise.

Postcolonial, feminist Gothic texts problematise and reconceptualise. Liberating powers of the imagination record different histories and present and envision alternative futures. Wilson Harris sees the power of such disruptive and newly creative energies as:

> the imagination of the folk involved in a crucial inner re-creative response to the violations of slavery ... the possibility exists for us to become involved in perspectives which can bring into play a figurative meaning beyond an apparently real world or prison of history. (Harris 1981, p. 27)

From her early short stories *Skin Folk* (2001) onwards, Caribbean/Canadian Nalo Hopkinson uses metamorphoses, shape-shifting ghosts in the body, body swaps, Caribbean soucouyants, vampire-like figures and duppies, zombies, witchcraft and mer-people to explore issues of gender, ethnicity and power. She often rewrites European folk and fairytales, spliced with Caribbean and African figures such as the Lagahoo and Anansi, to engage with and dramatise issues of gendered and culture-based oppression, and to move forwards to awareness and empowerment. Hopkinson uses strategies of the postcolonial/African diasporan literary Gothic and speculative fiction to rewrite fairytale and myth and undercut constraining personal, gendered and racialised narratives. This rewriting creatively enacts the re-visioning impetus behind postcolonial criticism, as suggested in the work of Tiffin and Lawson, who argue that theory and critical analysis expose ways in which alternative forms of knowledge and expression can be constructed and expressed:

> Colonial discourse analysis and postcolonial theory are thus critiques of the process of production of knowledge about the Other. As such they produce forms of knowledge themselves, but other knowledge, better knowledge it is hoped. (Tiffin and Lawson 1994, p. 8)

Hopkinson's collection *Skin Folk* (2001) uses shape-shifting and metamorphosis, and she rewrites a number of similar tales in a Caribbean/Toronto context emphasising speaking and acting out against male, colonial and historical narrative controls. Gendered silencing is an issue in her short story 'Precious', in which Hopkinson considers use of a gift in the body and develops an up-to-date female version of the tale of King Midas. Here, the protagonist, Isobel, blessed by an old woman for offering kind words, now spits precious stones and gold nuggets when she speaks, cutting her mouth, and so is effectively silenced. Her worth is represented in the precious gems and gold, but the trajectory of her relationship with her husband Jude turns from love to manipulation and abuse. Abusive and greedy, he first tickles, then starts to scare her, this unusual access to wealth turning him into a greedy, debt-ridden bully. Her only way out is to reclaim her gift for herself, through speech. She talks faster, telling him how much she wants him back and appreciates him, resulting in heaps of precious stones and a final huge ruby that knocks him out. He only wanted her for her money and gems. Released from this version of self, Isobel finds her speech is now her own; words, not gems now pour from her mouth. This act of rebellion is a catalyst for positive change and recognition of self-worth, at which point the precious curse ceases. The tale ends in her reclaiming her own sense of self-worth and value, being precious in herself, without the economic wealth which was a curse rather than a gift.

'The Glass Bottle Trick' is Hopkinson's Caribbean, Canadian rewrite of the Bluebeard tale, and another folk tale, 'Fitcher's bird', involves women, an incarcerating prison-house of conformity and silencing, murders and, here, Caribbean folklore. Through her tale, she addresses the destructive racial and gendered teachings which have been internalised by the rather safe, stuffy Samuel who courts Beatrice, who has been considered a little too liberal with her ways and needs to settle down. Beatrice is taunted by her ex-friends as 'Leggo beast ... Loose woman' (p. 90), so marriage is a version of woman's escape in this instance not just into relative wealth (as normally is the case in a Bluebeard story) but also respectability. Beatrice decides to settle for serious, 'stocious' (p. 87), 'cultured', 'punctual', 'courteous', 'self deprecating' (p. 91), darker skinned, bookseller Samuel, with his respectability and lovely house. However, gradually she realises that his negative comments about skin colour spring from having internalised a racialised self-loathing of his own black skin, which turns him into a controlling husband, terrified of producing dark children and willing to kill off a series of wives who often unwittingly challenge this.

Hopkinson mixes Caribbean with European folklore in a Gothic kaleidoscope, a bricolage, making something new which can present a version of Bluebeard and link it with more than gendered power, also with internalised disgust of the signs of race, which have been adopted by Samuel, who is locked in his own personal, racial, torture chamber. Commenting on the possibilities of Caribbean folklore, Hill also uses kaleidoscope and glass images to indicate a new construction:

> Caribbean folklore is fresh and lacks an ancient history, it is wider than indigenous cultures of the continents from where it came. It holds pieces from all those areas, like a kaleidoscope with bits of glass (but not the entire glass), in ever shifting patterns. It is combinations of ancestral lore, remembered in fragments, and fit and refit to new ... For this reason, it seems to reflect the contemporary world very well, more so than grand old traditions. (Hill, D.R., 2007, p. 6)

Samuel keeps duppies of his late wives in glass bottles in his tree. This is a Caribbean folkloric custom, but also a form of control. 'Is just my superstitiousness, darling,' he'd told her. 'You never heard the old people say that if someone dies, you must put a bottle in a tree to hide their spirit, otherwise it will come back as a duppy and haunt you? A blue bottle. To keep the duppy cool, so it won't come at you in hot anger for being dead' (p. 86). Beatrice is no expert in folklore, since separating duppies from the body is unusual, and indicates that Samuel fears their wrath. Containment of this intensity is only to control dangerous, angry spirits likely to wreak revenge. He argues that 'no woman should have to give birth to his ugly black babies' (p. 97). Beatrice begins to understand his reason to keep her out of the sun as she darkens up, no longer 'Beauty. Pale Beauty to my Beast' (p. 94).

Samuel hides the bodies of his two murdered previous wives in an air-conditioned room, separated from their duppy spirits. Glass bottles, hidden rooms and secrets represent his control and internalised self-loathing. Another feature in the story is the Trinidadian myth of the egg-swallowing snake, significant when relating to the punishment wreaked on wives who would bear children. Beatrice's father had always empowered her with the childish rhyme 'eggy law' (which also references the preserved egg in 'Fitcher's bird'), and she empowers herself when, discovering the bloody wives in a form of suspended animation inside the locked room, she goes outside to the tree and breaks the duppy bottles, releasing their spirits. Nobody knows if the duppy wives will embrace her as saviour and a once potential victim like themselves, or take some awful non-sisterly revenge on her: 'The duppy wives held their bellies and glared at her, anger flaring hot behind their eyes. Beatrice backed away from the beds. "I didn't know" she said to the wives, "don't vex with me. I didn't know what it is Samuel do to you"' (p. 100).

Hopkinson uses Gothic and Caribbean images and narratives, challenging both the damage done by internalising racialised self-loathing, and the traditional tale's conventional underlying warning to women which reinforces vulnerability, innocence and lack of agency. Writing postcolonial Gothic fusions of culture, myth, folk tale and speculative fictions enables a wide readership, and also the kind of positive forward energy of speculative fiction, which moves beyond the limiting constraints of gendered and racialised narratives. She comments on this powerful creative opportunity of adding the speculative to critique:

> Mosley says that sf makes it possible to create visions which will 'shout down the realism imprisoning us behind a wall of alienating culture.' I don't want to write mimetic fiction. I like the way that fantastical fiction allows me to use myth, archetype, speculation, and storytelling. I like the way it allows me to imagine the impossible. Mosley also said something to the effect that human beings first imagine a reality, then figure out a way to make it manifest. When women sf writers first began imagining women in positions of authority, the idea seemed risible to many. (Hopkinson, http://nalohopkinson.com/blog/nalohop)

Hopkinson's work aims to free thought so that readers can speculate about alternative ways of seeing and being. As Gothic, it rewrites folk tales, using duppies, zombies, mer-creatures, shape-shifting and recuperation from (often) self-constructions of abjection. She locates tales in enclosed spaces, the domestic hothouse, closed rooms, encircled, entrapped cities (*Brown Girl in the Ring*, 1998), small islands (*The New Moon's Arms*, 2007), but also opens up new vistas and reclaims a different version of a victimised past. In *The New Moon's Arms*, slaves transported by boat prefer to jump overboard and become liberated mer-creatures, while for the protagonist the return of her magic reignites her will to live, re-fruits her father's dead orchard and brings a mer-child temporarily into her care. For Hopkinson, Bluebeard is a colonial, imperial patriarch or a man whose mind has been enslaved and would enslave and deny others. She does not just dismantle 'Massa's house' in her work, she builds something totally new. Nalo Hopkinson's contemporary women's Gothic uses Gothic locations and entrapped spaces, female bonding, community, family, a critique of predatory romantic relationships ('Precious'; 'The Glass Bottle Trick') and in 'Greedy Choke Puppy' (2001) the role of the grandmother in managing selfish waywardness. Her fusion of the Gothic and the speculative offers new ways forward.

Shani Mootoo: Hothouse Flowers and Shapeshifting—*Cereus Blooms at Night* (1996)

A postcolonial and patriarchal haunted house lies at the centre of Shani Mootoo's *Cereus Blooms at Night*, where the Bluebeard figure is the protagonist, Mata/Poh poh's own father, Chandin. Acknowledging her own experience of abuse prompted Mootoo to write short stories, *Out on Main Street* (1993), followed by *Cereus Blooms at Night*, her first novel, set in the town of Paradise on a fictional fantastical Caribbean island, Lantanacamara, colonised by the 'Shivering Northern Wetlands', in a space indicating colonial fable—El Dorado park, Paradise town. The entrapping house is both physical and a product of sexual abuse. Mootoo's young woman is no willing victim, but suffers at her father's hands once her mother has died, and her sister has escaped. Mootoo also looks at the demonising of older women, since at the novel's opening Mata/Poh poh is seen as an aged witch-like crone, an ancient Sleeping Beauty in a walled overgrown house and garden, her only companions bugs and moths and the pungent cereus, which attracts insects (and casts an erotic stupefying power over people through its scent) when it blooms.

At the start of the novel, Mata/Poh poh is abused by local children who taunt her because she is strange, different, a recluse, inside her walled garden and boarded-up house. She is a woman silenced by the brutality of her father, and the insularity of her world, on an island which, moving from imperialist rule, slavery and indentured labouring, has left her in a static, vegetative stage. She is hemmed in, keeping the secret of her father's death, the death of colonial reign, her own subordinate status, walled up inside her as his body is walled up behind furniture. Mata/Poh poh is released from this spell when the son of her former lover discovers her and her historical crime of self-defence. Instead of merely falling into disgraced old age, Mata/Poh poh finds a new identity and relationships in the care home to which she is consigned, dancing, courted, telling her tale. She can move on.

Her home is shuttered up, but the garden filled with moths and the remains of small creatures is somehow magical, overpowering, dominated by the power of the cereus, which flowers on a particular magical night of the year, drawing creatures to its overwhelmingly attractive scent. The cereus' heady flowering scent releases passion and danger:

> It was one of the brightest moonlit nights ... she witnessed the slow dance of huge, white cereus buds ... the moonlight reflected off the blossoms' pure whiteness and cast a glow over the yard. (p. 144)

Close to midnight the buds had opened fully. The smell in Mata's yard drenched the air and flowed across town. Neighbours in deep sleep stirred, suddenly restless. Some were pried awake but were soon pleasantly besotted by the perfume and swept back into deep sleep. (p. 149)

Oral storytelling forms circle round, revealing Mata/Poh poh's tale by digging back from her current isolation in the care home. Historically, Mata is an enslaved female, subject to the ceaseless control of her abusive father, Chandin, himself a colonised subject. She supports her sister Asha, and at night, like a soucouyant (a vampiric creature, who sheds her skin at night, flies like a ball of fire, and usually preys on the young), slips into the fairytale houses of other sleeping families, touching, never harming, freed to roam, feeling herself a protector of children.

Ambrose E. Mohanty wooed her, bringing dancing and music via a portable gramophone, his visits giving her the strength to endure her father's night-time attacks. Mata has a Sleeping Beauty version of her own life: 'She thought privately of him … and of herself as the lady who would one day be rescued by him and revealed to all the world as a princess stolen by the commoners at birth' (p. 226). However, in fact, she is more than a Sleeping Beauty, instead she is entrapped in Bluebeard's house, Chandin's house, and the position of dutiful daughter in a constrained society, abused regularly by her father, her hopes of being rescued cut short by his jealous violence. Chandin refuses her nascent relationship with Ambrose, claiming ownership 'I ent go let nobody tief my woman. No man, no woman, no damn body go tief my property again. I go kill he, I go kill she, too, if it comes to that, I go kill meself, too' (p. 238). Confronting the lovers, the father erupts into unstoppable violence and is accidentally killed by Mata/Poh poh (her split self seen in her double name). She walls him up behind the heavy furniture and once he is walled up, she walls herself up in her house, her garden of moths and snails, her encroaching madness.

When Ambrose's son rediscovers Mata/Poh poh, he also finds the father's body, breaking through the wall of furniture. The police visit and Mata is taken to the care home, under arrest. This is not a negative ending, however. She has been rescued from more than the walled-up Bluebeard's castle. Beyond that incarcerated existence, of the Sleeping Beauty in the Bluebeard house and the heady scents of the night blooming cereus/frangipani, Mata herself blossoms gradually into a new life. She shape-shifts in human form through friendship with the gay male nurse Tylor, in which dancing and the loosening of memory heals both of them emotionally. Tylor is also active in linking Mata to more positive elements of her past and she is reunited with Ambrose through his son. Tylor comments 'Before our visitors arrive I wash her, mildly rubbing her skin with frangipani petals from Mr. Hector's hedge and pay special attention in dressing her' (p. 267).

> On visiting days she wears a garland of snail shells about her neck or a crown of wreaths that we wove with feathers and the wings of expired insects. (p. 267)

Beauty is made from the deaths she protected herself with earlier, in the house, which held such secrets. The love shown to Mata helps to heal her, while the dancing, music and frangipani odours indicate a new wholeness and recovery.

The novel dramatises the abuse, silencing and entrapment of a subaltern subject, a woman held captive by her father, by her own guilty secret and silence, and by the Otherising of the local children. Ostracised but walled in, she represents a traumatic response to a destructive, disempowering past exacerbated by age, but her freedom to tell her story and have it told, to dance and find again a version of herself is a positive, enabling ending, offering a sense of creative resilience. She finally escapes the Bluebeard-dominated haunted house, her role as Sleeping Beauty and her label as murderess. Mootoo crafts an imaginary space in which to play out hidden histories and redressing of wrongs, both colonial and personal, and in so doing reconceptualises the construction of the ageing woman. When Mata's stories are revealed and the ghosts laid to rest, this seemingly aged crone can return to music and dancing, blossoming to herself and others. Freed and freeing herself, she frees others into celebration, dance and performance of their sexuality.

HELEN OYEYEMI, *MR FOX* (2011)

Oyeyemi's first novel, *The Icarus Girl* (2005), was published when she was nineteen and waiting to go to Cambridge University, and since then there have been four more, *The Opposite House* (2007), *White is for Witching* (2009), *Mr Fox* and most recently *Boy Snow Bird* (2014). She splices Yoruba mythology and folk tales with British and European, and two of the novels also include Cuban folk tales. Her Gothic is enriched by all of these cultural infusions. In *White is for Witching* the girls are both entrapped in a witch tale which they produce and continue. The postcolonial condition of immigrating into another country's ways and the liminal spaces of a house in Dover, an immigration space, matched by the opposite house and the dual names, suggest split colonial subjects.

Some of Oyeyemi's work deals with the complexities of hybridity, using images of opposites and twins—so *The Icarus Girl* has two sets of twins, each with a living and a dead twin: Jessica who discovers she has lost a twin, Fern, and is given both an English and a Nigerian name (further twinning) but feels at home with neither, and Tilly Tilly, whose name is already doubled, a Nigerian friend who reappears in England and lives locally. The issue of hybridity is represented as abject by relating the dead twin to the live, since in tradition, if the live twin cannot replace the dead with a traditional Yoruba icon (the Ibeji), they cannot form a sense of self, their sense as apart from the dead twin leading to an abject hybridity. Julia Kristeva's notions of abjection are useful when considering the difficulties of hybridity, where one half of the self can seem abject. Stouck (2010, p. 104) suggests that Yoruba's understanding of twins recalls the dynamics of abjection: 'Not only are the shifting reactions to twins of joy and horror typical of the abject dynamic as depicted by Kristeva, but the concept of a twin, an other self from which one does not part, can be interpreted as a form of abjection which dramatically destabilises the boundaries of self.'

Twins are seen as a problem in West African society, as explained by Fernand Leroy, Taiwo Olaleye-Oruene, Gesina Keoppen-Schomerus and Elizabeth Bryan who clarify both the traditional problems with twins and more recent responses. They note that, historically, given high infant mortality in West African society, one twin was likely to die at birth; however, more recently twins have been seen less as a supernatural occurrence, less problematic. They comment that, 'In traditional African societies, twins were considered of preternatural origin and raised emotional reactions oscillating from fear and repugnance to hope and joy' (2002, p. 134). Now more accepted, twins are still seen as different, as sharing one soul and able to cross boundaries between the three worlds of spirit, real life and the 'bush'. Oyeyemi frequently uses twinning, which is also a motif in *The Opposite House* (2007). In *Mr Fox* there are twinning, opposites, spirit travel, ghostings, and a rewrite of the Bluebeard tale centred on a writer, his muse and his long-suffering wife.

Oyeyemi's *Mr Fox* is a mixture of a rewritten fairytale, 'Reynardine', a version of the Bluebeard tale, speculative fiction, and a university campus novel. Ralph Fox, an author, reproduces manipulative versions of women in his novels, and is brought up short somewhat when he is suddenly visited by his muse, Mary Foxe. Mary Foxe is no pushover, but instead as wily as her name suggests. Transferring the Reynardine/Bluebeard name to the woman immediately suggests that the Bluebeard academic male will have less control than he hopes and imagines over the women he thinks he creates as a muse. Mary Foxe plays the dual role of siren and muse, and critic of his sexist behaviour. The other woman in the novel is the wife, Daphne (another name from myth, this time from Greek myth), long-suffering and manipulated. Oyeyemi replays the complexity of collusion in power and sexual promise at the heart of much of the Bluebeard myth, in the context of intellectual as well as economic male power, through the character of Ralph Fox. In doing so she writes from and beyond Carter's exploration of sexual awakening in the earlier rewrite of Bluebeard, 'The Bloody Chamber'. In *Mr Fox*, Oyeyemi introduces the abuse, manipulation and sexual hierarchies in terms of power between Black and white, male and female. Mary Foxe as a character in Fox's fictional works might be a sexual fantasy and willing victim, but when she actually appears, she points this out, offering other perspectives and seizing her own power. She reverses the power roles, able to appear and disappear at will.

Critics appreciated the play on the Bluebeard Reynardian tales. Anita Sethi (2012) sees both the English fairytale and that of 'the robber bridegroom' (rewritten in Atwood's *The Robber Bride*, 1996). Fox, like so many other male authors, needs to construct objects of desire, then kill them off. (Thomas Hardy's Tess in *Tess of the D'Urbervilles* (1891) is an example of this.) As Fox attempts to write, in comes Mary, whom the fairytale warns to be 'bold but not too bold'. Mary points out that Fox is stuck in a misogynistic rut. He must reject his sexist focus on women as victims and change the endings of his novels accordingly. Sethi (2012) notes that 'Within the feisty framework of this engrossing main narrative are stories-within-stories, unfolding like Russian dolls.' She identifies Oyeyemi's work as magic realism, but actually it is more than that, as is so much of Angela Carter's work. Its darkness, its rewriting of established constraining fairy tale and popular cultural expressions (women as muses, victims, objects of novelists' desire and the need to control and destroy), its defamiliarisation of the campus novel and the novel concerning writers writing, place it as a Gothic tale.

While St John Fox controls his wife Daphne, and makes up female characters only to kill them off, he mistakenly believes that he also controls his fictional character, Mary. 'She's not real, honey,' he reassures Daphne. 'She's only an idea. I made her up.' Mary, however, challenges him for control of the fiction and the pen, and they then vie with each other over the power of fiction, and together write the nine tales of seduction and death which form this novel. In the stories they co-write, Reynardine appears as a murderer from the fairy story and a medium for Yoruba ancestors. A Yoruba girl dances with her dead husband; Mary Foxe rolls in a bed filled with words; and a fox tears the word 'fox' from a dictionary, hoping through owning words and names to become human. As Sethi (2012) notes, 'Oyeyemi peoples her text with ghosts, dreams and talking animals, burrowing through the surface of the everyday to reveal the bizarreness beneath.'

Oyeyemi's *Mr Fox* rewrites Bluebeard and 'Fitcher's bird' as well as the folk tales about Reynardine and its plucky potential victims turned heroes/heroines. This aligns her postcolonial Gothic challenge to constraining myths and representations of women with those of Hopkinson, Brodber and Mootoo.

Postcolonial Feminism Revisited

Talking more broadly of women's writing and the historical debate about feminism being a white (American initially—this was a 1980s initiated debate which continued) women's activity, excluding the voices of women from a fuller variety of cultural contexts, Vaid et al. (1993) suggest:

> In terms of women of colour undermining feminism, 'minority women feel their needs and values have been largely ignored by the organized women's movement, which grew out of white, middle-class women's discontent' (Wallis 1989, p. 82), and racial-minority women feel they cannot participate in the feminist movement because of white women's racism. (Vaid et al. 1993)

Hall and Rodriguez historicise this position as a process during second-wave feminism, while avoiding falling into the trap of presuming contemporary versions of feminism are able to encompass the wide diversity of women's lives and needs (Hall and Rodriguez 2003). The postcolonial, postfeminist Gothic of Hopkinson and Brodber moves beyond the historically powerful assertion that feminism is a white Western construct which marginalises Black women. Each text uses doubles, spirit theft, the supernatural, fantasy, futures, zombies and transformation to express postcolonial and feminist reclamation of identity, history, voice and the body.

Each develops a postfeminist focus on performativity and moving beyond artifice and simulacra (see Baudrillard 1983; Butler 1990) to conscious, gendered sexuality and a culturally aware self.

Through their use of Gothic fantasy and horror, postcolonial feminist writers engage imaginatively, directly and critically with issues such as material, gendered and culturally inflected experience. The texts considered here engage with internalised self-damage, negative self-image, a direct result of racist, sexist denial, destruction and demoralisation, which paralyse action. The cultural contexts in which racial and gendered hierarchies and norms have historically operated are based on a post-Enlightenment binarism which casts as secondary anyone who is not white, and not male. These tales use the strategies of the postcolonial, postfeminist Gothic—images of fantasy and horror, a reversal of postcolonial abjection—and enable re-reading, a reclamation of history and of versions of self and identity. Hopkinson's, Mootoo's, Oyeyemi's and Brodber's female protagonists regain and re-establish self-worth in the face of that which would deny them. In this sense, each tale enacts a transformation and offers a radical challenge to gendered and racialised constructions of the abject, using aspects of the literary Gothic in postcolonial contexts to postcolonial ends. Ghosts, vampires, zombies, werewolves, voodoo horror figures and formulae are vehicles to review, indict and re-vision versions of what it is to be part of Black subculture, being both Black and a woman. Hopkinson revises and reinterprets Afro-Caribbean and international folk tales, placing them in contemporary Canada and the Caribbean. Brodber uses images of zombieism and spirit theft to criticise colonialism and patriarchy's effacement of self-worth and identity. Their critique leads to the reclamation of ontological security, and refuses undermining performance and educational propaganda.

For the women in Hopkinson's, Oyeyemi's, Mootoo's and Brodber's tales, this appears as a newly found comfortable oneness with their own history, rewriting and refusing internalised, alienated cultural denigration. In Ella's case, celebrating the inspirational religion of Myalism can be seen as re-empowering a reinterpretation of the disempowering story *Mr. Joe's Farm* told to schoolchildren. In this context, transformation lies at the heart, since zombieism results from inappropriate dramatisation for Ella and spirit theft for Anita.

Textual choices, forms and treatments are vehicles for shaping, guidance, control and limitation. As Elleke Boehmer has pointed out, colonisers use a variety of textual representations in order to render recognisable the unfamiliar and new. Treaties and declarations, records, logs and the couching of descriptions of the new and strange in familiar forms, myths, endowing them with familiar names, paralleling them with those from back home are all ways in which colonisers have sought to feel comfortable in new worlds, familiarised and then owned through redescription (Boehmer 1995, p. 14).

Conclusion

This chapter looks at recuperation and revaluing, using shape-shifting Gothic figures to reclaim gendered and racialised histories and identities and a sense of agency and worth. Gothic Bluebeard tales and haunted houses in the hands of Hopkinson, Brodber, Oyeyemi and Mootoo remind of the triple power games of gender, economics and the social and cultural power endemic within slavery and indentured labour, retelling this historically, and each turns the entrapping, devaluing, sexist world upside-down.

The Bluebeard myth which seeks to show women entrapped in the patriarchal colonial house is exposed and rewritten, the house totally re-owned and rebuilt. Reshaping and re-storying are important in the work of women writers of contemporary postcolonial Gothic. Postcolonial women writers of the Gothic write familiar narratives, shifting their shape and reshaping to their own. Nalo Hopkinson ('The Glass Bottle Trick'), Helen Oyeyemi (*Mr Fox*), Shani Mootoo (*Cereus Blooms at Night*) and Erna Brodber (*Myal*) undercut and rewrite Massa's/Bluebeard's deadly narrative of power and disempowerment, remaking, re-owning his house, his castle, or building a house of their own. Nalo Hopkinson, Erna Brodber, Helen Oyeyemi and Shani Mootoo dismantle Bluebeard's house and his repressive stories, shifting into new shapes in new contexts.

Rewriting the Bluebeard tale helps build a new house, not just one recognisable as a rebuild of Massa's in his shape, with his values. Recuperating and revaluing Gothic constructions of mer-people, vampires, soucouyants, zombies and various shape-shifters offer ways forward to new versions of history and life.

Bibliography

Barthes, R. (1973) *The Pleasure of the Text* (Paris: Editions du Seuil).
Baudrillard, J. (1983) *Simulations* (New York: Semiotext(e)).
Bethel, L. (1982) 'This Infinity of Conscious Pain: Zora Neale Hurston and the Black Female Literary Tradition', in *All the Women are White, All the Blacks are Men, but Some of Us are Brave: Black Women's Studies*, G. T. Hull, P. Bell Scott and B. Smith (eds.) (New York: The Feminist Press).

Boehmer, E. (1995) *Colonial and Postcolonial Literature: Migrant Metaphors* (Oxford: Oxford University Press).
Brodber, E. (1988) *Myal* (London: New Beacon Books).
Burford, B. (1987) 'The Landscapes Painted on the Inside of My Skin', *Spare Rib*, June, p. 37.
Butler, J. (1990) *Gender Trouble: Feminism and the Subversion of Identity* (New York: Routledge).
Carter, A. (1979) 'The Bloody Chamber', in *The Bloody Chamber and Other Stories* (London: Gollancz).
Dabydeen, D. (1988) *Handbook for Teaching Caribbean Literature* (London: Heinemann).
Fanon, F. (1952) *Black Skin, White Masks* (Paris: Editions du Seuil).
Franco, J. (1988) 'Beyond Ethnocentrism: Gender, Power and the Third-World Intelligentsia', in *Marxism and the Interpretation of Culture*, C. Nelson and L. Grossberg (eds.) (Basingstoke: Macmillan).
Hall, E. and Salupo Rodriguez, M. (2003) 'The Myth of Postfeminism', *Gender & Society*, Vol. 17, No. 6.
Harris, W. (1981) *History, Fable & Myth in the Caribbean and Guiana* (Georgetown: National History and Arts Council).
Hopkinson, N. (2001a) *Skin Folk* (New York: Aspect).
Hopkinson, N. (2001b) 'Precious', in *Skin Folk* (New York: Aspect).
Hopkinson, N. (2001c) *Skin Folk* (New York: Aspect).
Hopkinson, N. (2001d) 'Greedy Choke Puppy', in *Skin Folk* (New York: Aspect).
Hopkinson, N. and Mehan, U. (2004) *So Long Been Dreaming: Postcolonial Science Fiction & Fantasy* (Vancouver: Arsenal Pulp Press).
Punter, D. (2000b) *Postcolonial Imaginings: Fictions of a New World Order* (Edinburgh: Edinburgh University Press).
Rudd, A. (2010) *Postcolonial Gothic Fictions from the Caribbean, Canada, Australia and New Zealand* (Cardiff: University of Wales Press).
Sethi, A. (2012) 'Mr Fox by Helen Oyeyemi—Review', 13 May, http://www.theguardian.com/books/2012/may/13/mr-fox-helen-oyeyemi-review
Spivak, G. C. (1988) 'Can the Subaltern Speak?', in *Marxism and the Interpretation of Culture*, C. Nelson and L. Grossberg (eds.) (Basingstoke: Macmillan Education).
Stouck, J. (2010) 'Abjecting Hybridity in Helen Oyeyemi's *The Icarus Girl*', *Ariel: A Review of International English Literature*, Vol. 41, No. 2, April.
Tiffin, C. and Lawson, A. (eds.) (1994) *De-scribing Empire: Post-colonialism and Textuality* (London: Routledge).
Vaid, U., Wolf, N., Steinem, G. and hooks, b. (1993) 'Let's Get Real about Feminism: The Backlash, the Myths, the Movement', *Ms.*, Vol. 5, pp. 34–43.
Wallis, C. (1989) 'Onward, Women!', *Time*, 4 December.

CHAPTER 7

Vampire Bites

Vampires are the ultimate Gothic creatures, a living dead contradiction able to vehicle the angst, desires and fears of whatever time, place and cultural context produces them. Sexier, better dressed and more able to pass as romantic leads than zombies, their use as a measure of the gendered cultural concerns and contradictions of time and place is so varied as to enable a simultaneous fascination and repulsion. They project what we desire and what disgusts us. Their liminality is a cultural index of unease, dis-ease and apprehension. It is not surprising, then, that in the hands of contemporary women writers, vampires should be used as a metaphor, as vehicles for the contradictions of our gendered worlds and experiences. As Poppy Z. Brite and Nina Auerbach point out, vampires are embraced as cultural metaphors, as figures of radical, alternative energy:

> The vampire is the only supernatural creature who has become a role model. (Brite 1994, p. ix)
>
> Vampires were supposed to menace women, but to me at least, they promised protection against a destiny of girdles, spike heels and approval. (Auerbach 1995, p. 4)

Auerbach specifically identifies the vampire as metaphor and role model, offering herself and other women an alternative to restrained, dull conformity.

The figure of the vampire, archetypal male seducer, villain, a seductively voracious and devouring femivore (Schlobin 1989) has been reappropriated, reconfigured and rescripted by late twentieth-century women writers such as Poppy Z. Brite (who now identifies as male, as Billy Collins: I only look at her earlier vampire themed work), Anne Rice, Pat Califia, Jeanne Kalogridis, Jewelle Gomez, Sherry Gottlieb and a host of others. They challenge the conventions of horror, of female victims and sexually voracious monsters, and revive and reinterpret the vampire to their own radical ends. They critique and re-empower the figure of the Mother, and infuse their work with the disruptive powers of the erotic, centre-staging the vampire in a variety of forms: flâneur, rock star, gay/lesbian/queer. In this rescripting, they enable social critique, highlighting and questioning the constraining meta-narratives and the enforced fixity of gendered roles and behaviours.

Contemporary women writers of vampire fictions let their vampires enter numerous aspects of life to perform and enact perennial terrors and fantasies, and expose the entrapment of the mundane. The figure is alternately threatening, destructive, icily honest and dangerously, thrillingly, radically Other. In late twentieth-century women's vampire writing, liminality and new radical sexual energies are enacted and celebrated.

This chapter considers exciting, radical examples, and the ways in which feminist writers of the 1970s onwards have appropriated the traditionally male, sexually dominant, invasive vampire who represented fears about inheritance, heritage, purity of the blood, land ownership, and control over women's sexuality. A number of contemporary women writers turned this figure into one whose sexuality and sexual choices are less likely to be heteronormative, whose ability to be a cultural index both enacts the angst and terrors of the age: war, homelessness, lack of community, destruction as a response to outsider behaviour, the damage done through the traditional mothering role, and entrapment in domestic and romantic deceits. Their radical work offers alternative relationships, new energy and agency.

Male vampires in much women's fiction are often dapper, erotically charged potential partners, either offering to take the female protagonist away from all this (castle, status, ageing, death, for example in the First World War in Sarah Smith's 'When the Red Storm Comes', 1994), or, representing the flipside of romantic love, they betray deliberately or casually ('The Lady of the House of Love', Carter 1979c) and seek only invasions, devouring and desiccation, enthralment and servitude. Love bites, but the woman is left drained and in thrall, as in Poppy Z. Brite's 'The

Sixth Sentinel' (1994). The demon lover, the betrayer and enslaver are each seductive terrors from women's fantasies and fears. Vampire fictions also expose the false romantic dreams of eternal bliss and the protection of paternalism, revealing deceit, treatment of women as property, and a disempowerment produced by societally reinforced fantasies about women's vulnerability and need for rescue, entrapped by their own gullibility, and powerless before seductive allure.

Historically, women represented as vampires were seen as threats to order, whether of ownership, property and heredity, since the vampire invaded the home, the body of the beloved, and upset every comfortable complacency. Dracula's three voracious female vampires (Stoker 1897) are kept like dangerous pets, occasionally tossed a screaming child or an unwary traveller, while the British women whose bodies he invades—Mina only slightly, Lucy, fatally—fall unwitting prey to his physical night bites. Women, however, are depicted as both victims and the cause of the problem, scapegoats for a repressive society which needed to control women's sexual energies and heredity. But Lucy's attempts at challenging patriarchally validated control and reinforcement of laws governing women's sexuality and agency, leads to a second sexual invasion in the name of God and virtue. In order to punish her/rescue her from being turned into a vampire by Dracula, she is staked at the hands of men who loved her, her fiancé Arthur Holmwood, with the collusion of her ex-suitor Dr Seward, Quincey Morris the American, and Professor Van Helsing.

Historical and traditional vampire fictions (*Dracula*, 1897; 'Carmilla', 1872; *Blood of the Vampire*, 1897) emphasise, enact and then punish what is constructed as women's vulnerability, gullibility and latent sexual weakness. The female vampire of the fin de siècle resembles the many other female figures represented as alluring, deadly creatures, often pictured as spliced with animals. Bram Dijkstra's *Idols of Perversity* (1986) has a number of images of women as half snake, half mythical creature, each deadly, each an example of the terrifying fantasy of the vagina dentata, where women's sexuality and her sexual allure for men is directly linked to the perverse and murderous intent of castration. In *The Monstrous Feminine* (1993), the critic Barbara Creed explores this transfer of lust and loathing onto demonised versions of woman born of desire and disgust, terror and guilt at that desire. Radical women's vampire fictions of the 1980s onwards expose this construction and representation as born of male fear of women's sexuality, and its power over men, evoking fears of disempowerment and castration. This narrative can also be reproduced in some conventional women's vampire fictions. However, radical women's vampire fictions refuse it, undercut it, ignore it and offer instead critiques of the ideals which underpin such a dichotomy of desire and disgust. These include a questioning and denial of binary opposition between male and female in which the female is always weaker, and a challenge to the investment in heterosexuality and eternal romantic love ending in wedded bliss. Instead, romance is often exposed as a deadly trap, fear of women's sexuality seen as either pathological or irrelevant, and women's agency is celebrated.

Poppy Z. Brite's 'The Sixth Sentinel' (see Wisker 2014), exposes romantic love as deadly, an eternal bondage. Families and domestic bliss, the stuff of complacent, conventional life narratives for women, are turned on their heads. In Melanie and Steve Tem's 'Mama' (1995), the vampire mother eats flies in the kitchen and embarrasses then tyrannises her teenage daughter. Anne Rice challenges concentrations of women's power and powerlessness with the mythically, monstrously maternal and dominant Akasha in *Queen of the Damned* (1988). Many contemporary radical women vampire writers move on to offer alternative readings of women's sexuality and agency, celebrating the lesbian vampire and the S&M relationship alongside the re-reading of the vampire narrative as one which can empower women rather than destroy them. The norms of romantic narratives tend to be exposed in contemporary women's vampire fictions. As cultural indices, vampires expose lies and contradictions, and also offer new opportunities for agency.

HISTORY—VAMPIRE WOMEN

Many cultures have myths of vampires, and there is thought to be a factual history to the representation of women as vampires, the most famous European potential vampire being Elizabeth Baathory, the 'Sanguinary Countess' (as Angela Carter calls her in *Vampirella* (1976)). Elizabeth Baathory was a contemporary of Vlad the Impaler, the tyrannical ruler from the Carpathian mountains in Transylvania (now part of Romania), on whom *Dracula* is believed to have been based. There seems little actual evidence of her vampirism, although she was extremely violent. However, if we believe the version of the tale that sees her as a notable noble woman with vampiric habits, she apparently bathed in the blood of over 600 virgins to remain youthful, establishing a link between women's desire for beauty and eternal youth. Historically, there are also menopausal vampires, one of whom could well have been Elisabeth Baathory. Victorian writer Arabella Kenealy also wrote of such a figure in 'A Beautiful Vampire' (1896) (see Swenson 2003) although there seems to be less interest in the figure currently.

Either factual or mythical or a mixture of both, women vampires offer influential models. Their take up and development in fiction and film is a cultural index of desire and disgust, a thermometer of response to women's power and sexuality, either seen as demonic or liberating. For men who might be threatened or become the victims of female vampires, the vampire teeth remind one of the fin de siècle pictures of the monster half animal, half woman, the vagina dentata, siren above, castratrix below. These are versions of woman and women's sexual allure constructed by popular culture and the desire and disgust of Victorian men, who found thrills in a sexual challenge which was dark, denied and thus rendered dangerous and vile. Bram Dijkstra's *Idols of Perversity* (1986) offers many visual examples of this form of representation of woman, born of a refusal to recognise sexual impulses and relationships, and an offloading of self-disgust onto a construction of woman as seductive, devouring and destroying. As Barbara Creed comments, theorising the demonising and abjection of woman through the construction of the vampire figure, and building on Kristeva's notions of abjection (1982, 1988):

> The female Dracula or vampire figure is masculinized because she penetrates her victim. She becomes an active predatory seducer. (Creed 1993, p. 70)

One of the great fears here is a reversal of roles, a challenge to the constructed binary oppositions between male and female in which one, the male, is active, and penetrates, the other meant to be passive, and seen as terrifying if she refuses that role. The female vampire also represents potential dangers of sexual licence. Female vampires were terrifying constructions of heated brains, threats to masculinity and wholeness of self, as well as moral pretence. And they threaten normality:

> The female vampire is conventionally represented as abject because she disrupts identity and order. (Dyer 1988, p. 54)

[D]riven by her lust for blood, she does not respect the dictates of the laws which set down the rules of proper sexual conduct. Like the male, the female vampire also represents abjection because she crosses the boundary between the living and the dead, the human and the animal. (Creed 1993, p. 110)

The vampire's initial liberation of excess energies and disruption of normality is a very temporary affair. Social order is quickly restored, the cathartic experience nailed down again to the relief of the conformist audience/readership. This has, of course, always been the role of horror, and of much gothic. (See also Punter 1996)

Vampires are a product of their time and place, a half living, bleeding, metaphor for whatever we fear as uncomfortable, threatening and deviant. Ironically perhaps, they are also a celebration of those deviances in times when deviance is exposed as culturally constructed, and in times when we might question what those who are conservative and conventional consider to be deviant. Before the 1980s, brought up on *Dracula*, by way of Hammer Horror movies, we were most likely to expect vampires to be men in black frock-coats in gloomy foreign castles whose intent was invasion of property and heritage. Their main focus was luring in and then turning vulnerable women into vampires. The women were then punished for their vulnerability or their easy succumbing to the deadly vampire embrace. Their voracious vampire appetites were as much for sex as they were for blood, and their punishment, as vampires, was as much for their unnatural behaviour in terms of conventional gender norms, devouring children, seducing naïve young men (or women), as it was for their terrifying borderline state as creatures of the night. Staking such creatures punished them for social and sexual deviance, as well as rendering them no longer able to drink the blood of unsuspecting others.

The historical Elizabeth Baathory was finally found guilty and sentenced to immurement, walled up and left to die, because of her cruel deeds, but versions of her live on in the contemporary women's vampire fictions which replay such demonising, or which explode the myths which women themselves have internalised, making them collusive and vulnerable against their own best interests. In tales which derive from this first scenario, where behaviour is exposed as collusive, there are vampire women who are victimised because of their power and sexual energies, women who fall for the promise of eternal romantic love, women who prey on other women and women who foolishly seek eternal beauty (and/or eternal life), having bought into the beauty myth. Then, turning the tables, lesbian vampires appear as celebrated figures rather than demons to be punished and destroyed. Instead, they represent the celebrating of sexual energies, the challenging of conventional constraints, roles and agency.

Demon Lovers—Romantic Love, Vampires and Escape

The Gothic figure of the vampire both plays out and exposes the flaws in popular narratives of romance, sexual relationships and an eternity of love. Vampire lovers can offer seemingly unlimited romance and sexual gratification, of a kind, and much popular fiction reconstructs the only temporarily dangerous seducer of romantic fiction as a vampire, either ultimately as tameable such as the craggy, lantern-jawed, seductive renegades of Mills and Boon, Harlequin romances, and Barbara Cartland (Wisker 1998), or finally rejected en route to a more dependable and rewarding (and conventional) love of one's life. In much romantic vampire fiction, the potential disruptive seducer is unmasked and dispatched, or rewritten. Interestingly, in alignment with conventional popular romance, the vampire Edward Cullen in the *Twilight* series (2005–2008) is only a predator when he needs to be and is, in the main, a trustworthy, romantic companion: a vampire recuperated and re-energised to serve convention, an interesting about-face (Chap. 8), as I have explored elsewhere (Wisker 2014). There can be twists in the vampire romance which challenge romantic fiction's promise of an eternity of love.

Escaping time and place with the intrusive, socially destructive stranger/demon/vampire lover both replicates and disrupts conventional romantic fiction fantasies in Sarah Smith's 'When the Red Storm Comes'. This tale utilises romantic fiction tropes, rewarding the vampire hero's chosen partner with material and temporal transcendence, everlasting love, and escape from the tribulations and horrors of the lived history of the world. Like Angela Carter's 'The Lady of the House of Love', the tale is set at the advent of the First World War, working with familiar settings and scenarios of nineteenth-century romantic fiction: a lower-middle-class heroine, thwarted by her restricted life, condemned to a pointless dull existence whether married or unmarried, and the romantic offer of a dashing, good-looking stranger. In a conventional romance such as Jane Austen's *Pride and Prejudice* (1813), such a potential match (Wickham) would be rejected as dangerous, unstable, lacking land and money, and the hero, the good match (Darcy), would reinforce the values of property, economic security, inherited wealth, honesty and upper-class values alongside true romance. Austen also enables her lively heroine, Elizabeth Bennett, to be valued for her energy and individuality within marriage.

Sarah Smith's story 'When the Red Storm Comes' sides with the dangerous, good-looking, aristocratic and well-travelled hero and in so doing both challenges and rewards romantic fiction formulae. The young heroine seems condemned to a life of cutwork when in Portsmouth, USA, in 1905, she meets a dashing young foreigner, Count Ferenc Zohary, who, spotting her copy of *Dracula*, seduces her with both his love-making and his offer of eternal power, a power which will enable her to rise above the coming carnage of the First World War, born of patriarchal rigidity and imperialistic boundary disputes. Under the vampiric tutelage of the Count, she sees ahead in time to the war, through visions of destruction, and a sea heaving with bodies and blood. He offers to help her realise her own desires to escape and transgress, to cross boundaries between obedience and conformity into the marginalised but insightful vampire position. He also offers the erotic opportunity to actually achieve her own sexual desires through crossing the living/dead boundary. There is no contest:

> I could sit down beside them, drink tea, and listen to the orchestra for the rest of my life. For me there would be no vampires ... The blood, crusted at the base of his fingers, still welled from the slit he had made in his palm. It was bright. Bright red. I bent down and touched my tongue to the wound. The blood was salty, intimate, strong, the taste of my own desire. (Smith 1994, p. 159)

She can escape the carnage and the thrall of history, particularly the horrors of the First World War, and do so while also gaining eternal life and a version of romance. It is an irresistible offer. Becoming an abject creature is an irrelevance.

The dangerous sexual promise of vampire lovers is also replayed in Sherry Gottlieb's *Love Bite* (1994), a mixed-genre vampire/crime/romantic fiction playing with the formulae of all three. It also emphasises the erotic charge of the (venomed) vampire embrace, which effectively physically persuades the victim that this particular sexual encounter is worth dying for. Gottlieb splices crime fiction with romantic erotic thriller and vampire fiction, so crossing genre boundaries as her novel also offers the crossing of life and death boundaries. It begins as a police procedural narrative as Jace tracks down the photographer Rusty/Risha, with whom he then falls in love. Rusty, who lost her partner, Gregor Bathory (referencing Countess Elizabeth Baathory, and Gregor from Kafka's *The Metamorphosis* (1915), is a night-time photographer whose photographs of 'LA City of Angels' successfully expose the underside of the city. With such a job, she can be both anonymous and nocturnal, hunting with a knife that gashes her prey, her venom causing a sexual 'high' before a victim dies. She, too, seeks a mate with whom to spend more than a lifetime and Jace, who has Huntington's chorea, is a dying lover and candidate for vampiric transformation. Their love is unpunished, as are their vampiric crimes.

Both transgressive and celebratory, much contemporary women's vampire fiction rescripts popular romance narratives by rewarding the expectation of 'eternal love' beyond the grave. Not surprisingly then, rescuing friends and lovers from fatal diseases into vampiric being is a common humanitarian act.

Revamping the Vampire

For more radical contemporary women writers in particular, the late 1970s and 1980s onwards was a period of full-scale overhaul of the tired romantic lead of the male vampire and the demonising of women which resulted in their being turned into vampires, then punished. Instead, they created energetic, socially critical, often female or variably gendered vampires who successfully challenge behavioural gendered norms. Radical feminist energies found the figure of a vampire as a perfectly formed conduit for social cultural critique. They recuperate the vampire as metaphor for exposing a number of problems, fears and concerns of the contemporary world, whether they be a materialistic life drained of values which treats people as throwaways (Poppy Z. Brite, in *Lost Souls*, 1993), an exposure of the constraints and contradictions of the domestic condition (Melanie and Steve Tem, 'Mama', 1995) or the compulsion of heteronormativity (Anne Rice, *Interview With the Vampire*, 1976; Pam Keesey's *Dark Angels*, 1995, and *Daughters of Darkness* tales, 1993).

At what point did women vampire writers refuse to swoon at the frockcoated mythic figure? When did they reverse the romantic myth underlying sexual invasion and demonising of women's sexuality and energy?

When did they find vampiric women equally sexually attractive? When did they reconfigure the sexually voracious, socially unacceptable vampire as the next-door neighbour, the Other, as well as the draining and daring mother? In effect, when did they begin to both critique the conventional social mores which lay behind the literary vampire and replace these with something more exciting, deviant, energetic and which questioned conventions?

The revolution in taking the kind of approach that I have just done, recognising vampires as culturally constructed, exploring those gendered cultural and social conventions, recognising that the figure of the vampire was a product of their time, place and cultural mores, and which could be unpacked, re-scrutinised as a vehicle for cultural critique, could well have begun with second-wave feminist work, such as Angela Carter's 'The Lady of the House of Love'. From unpacking the instructions for good behaviour embedded in a range of myths and fairytales, including the dark tale in which we find the vampire and other metamorphosing creatures, and exposing the latent message of gender role conformity and punishment, Angela Carter and other feminist writers radically rewrote the female vampire figure. Carter's two early women vampire figures derive from male fears of femininity and female sexuality, which is to be controlled. The descendant of Dracula, in the castle ('The Lady of the House of Love') alone, is under a curse passed on by masculine constructions of the passive victimhood of women. The puppet who wreaks revenge ('The Loves of Lady Purple', 1986) is a whore constructed by male insecurities and that mix of desire and revulsion which Kristeva identifies as abjection. While the first Carter vampire descendant exposes the lies of romance but then dies, the second vampire-like puppet has more agency, walking off to wreak destruction on those who would objectify her.

It is with a critique of fears of women's sexuality that radical women vampire writers engage most fully. As a first step, the vampire with its penetrative teeth, bleeding and swooning, seen as a metaphor for sex, can be a figure critiquing sexual licence and desire, *or* one exposing the disgust and desire which fuels this transfer and deferral onto the vampire figure, *or* one who turns the tables and celebrates the characteristics of the vampire, teeth, penetration, non-normative sex.

> Vampirism itself—depicted as uncontrollable desire and as sensual swoon for both victim and vampire—stands as a euphemism for sex, forbidden by social mores. And the sex itself is not of a normative nature. (Brownworth 1996, p. xi)

The radical turn is built on Julia Kristeva's psychoanalytically inspired rejection of Lacan's gendered interpretation of identity development. In Lacan's version, which grew from his work on and from Freud, in the mirror phase of development, the establishment of identity involves rejection of others identified as not the self. In order to establish a firmer sense of self, it is necessary to reject with disgust anything which is not the self, including faeces, menstrual blood, vomit and other abject substances, and then that first Other, succouring not the infant self, the figure of the mother. I am not suggesting this is a conscious equation—mother = faeces—but a subconscious or unconscious need to reject the Other, to abject (reject with disgust) the mother in order to survive as separate. What can be developed in pathological variants of this (separation is normal, though disgust, rejection and demonising do not normally need to accompany it) is a terror, disgust and abjection of women. A warped next step leads to disgust at the sexuality women represent, and then women themselves who represent this sexuality. Woman's sexual power is seen as dangerous, to be denied, and following or giving in to sexual impulses is seen as potentially a weakness which could destroy the (male) self. Kristeva comments, 'Fear of the archaic mother proves essentially to be a fear of her generative power. It is this power, dreaded, that patrilineal filiation is charged with subduing' (Kristeva 1982, p. 102).

This is the stuff of numerous horror and slasher films, including *Psycho* (Hitchcock 1996), and a narrative behind popular literature and film representation of sexually charged serial killers. We can recognise terror and disgust at women and sexuality, which also produces traditional versions of women as vampires. However, theorists such as Kristeva, and critics such as Creed and Dyer, have exposed and explained this demonising trajectory. In the next creative step, radical women vampire writers expose and reject the psychoanalytical turn which demonises women's active sexuality. They refuse the demon vampire lover male lead, and instead revitalise the female vampire as a creature who revels in her alterity, is sexually liberated and energised. Many contemporary women's vampire fictions use the boundary-breaking liminality of the vampire to test a range of other boundaries, such as the constructed divisions between male and female, straight and gay, dead and alive and in so doing represent examples of Hélène Cixous' celebrating energies in *The Laugh of the Medusa* (1975), which refuses binaries as limiting constructions.

Whether heterosexual or lesbian, the woman vampire in more radical contemporary women's vampire fiction enjoys sex, thrills, and the dark side of the night. The energetic sexual vampire is no longer the vile unnatural condemned creature of man's heated fearful fantasies; she is the liberated radical feminist finding sexual pleasure and eternal love with whom she and her chosen companions please. Vampire figures in the hands of feminists are used to unpick and expose limiting, damaging conventions with which women were portrayed, constructed socially and culturally in texts. They are used to expose political, social and cultural lies and mistakes. One example is that of Poppy Z. Brite's transient, valueless castaway generation, products of the Vietnam War and capitalist values which construct so many people as unnecessary (*Lost Souls*, 1992). They are also used as ways of imagining alternative relationships—lesbian, gay, trans body, trans creature—the crossing of boundaries, the breaking of conventions and the playing in liminal spaces. All the delights and disturbances embodied in the vampire are a promise and a possibility for change rather than merely a threat to conventions which would bring forth some social, cultural or religious wrath. Radical feminist vampires are wild, dangerous, sexy—they delight in cruelty and they ridicule the conventional; they are exciting.

Much feminist vampire writing in the latter part of the twentieth and now twenty-first century recognises the thrill of the dark side of the night, of undermining conventions and intellectual, aesthetic and personal limitations. Latterly, however, the boundary traversing vampire is replaced by the vampire next door and by vampire family fortunes (Chap. 8).

Lisa Tuttle reminds us that:

> We all understand the language of fear, but men and women are raised speaking different dialects of that language. (Tuttle 1990, p. 5)

Fear is conditioned by gendered spaces, places, behaviours: all have different resonances for men and women and this varies in different cultures. Why is this interesting in terms of the Gothic? And the vampire?

Comments about gender differences and sources speak to the construction and representation of the vampire, since a woman writing the vampire figure might find other issues and behaviours to inspire terror, and regard some of those which disturb and terrify a male writer or reader perfectly acceptable. Lesbian vampires, romances turned sour, domestic threats, an eternity of love (seen as curse or promise) and vampire neighbours are all products of interests more broadly familiar in women's writing. Domesticating sits alongside questioning of what it is that is acceptable as a configuration of the outsider, of the other, and what can then be challenged.

The vampire is the Gothic's favourite boundary breaker. Challenging and crossing physical, psychological, and cultural boundaries of life/death, male/female, myth/real, self/Other, the vampire tests and questions the resilience of the human need for such boundaries. Vampire fictions show, in the light of the philosophical, psychoanalytical and critical work of, in particular, Julia Kristeva, that such boundaries are constructions born of our own fears and desires. An embodiment of the abject, a figure of desire and disgust, the literary and filmic vampire has been seized on to entertain, explore and express ways in which we celebrate or abject difference. Vampire fictions, in particular, trouble, break and cross boundaries between genres, enacting their radical, liberating transgression which takes place at the level of narrative and interpretation. A variety of fictional and filmic horror and vampire texts challenge and cross boundaries and vampire and horror fictions intersect with romantic fictions.

Contemporary women writers have found in the figure of the vampire marvellous potential for radical reappropriation and boundary-crossing gender writing. They splice their representation with crime (Laurell K. Hamilton's *Anita Blake, Vampire Hunter* series, 19 novels from 1993–2010), family sagas (Anne Rice's novels), time travel (Chelsea Quinn Yarbro's *Count Saint-Germain*, 19 novels from 1978–2010), lesbian Gothic (Pam Keesey's *Dark Angels*, 1995, and *Daughters of Darkness* tales, 1993), homoerotic and youth culture horror (Poppy Z. Brite), popular cultural teen slasher thrillers (*Buffy*, 1997), neighbourhood gothic (Charlaine Harris, *True Blood* series from 2008), and replays of the Dracula myth and tale in Kostova's *The Historian* (2005). Jeanne Kalogridis's (1995–1996) vampire tales continue the original Dracula story through first-person narratives and diaries of relatives, exploring the experiences of Zsuzsanna and Mary Windham Tsepesh (Vlad the Impaler = Vlad Tsepesh). The women, still often victims, take a more active role. The vampire tale is still spliced with romantic fictions which, with Stephanie Meyer's *Twilight* series (since 2005, Chap. 8), actually offer an opportunity to reinforce conventional romantic traditions of the tall, dark, handsome demon lover, rather than to trouble the romantic traditions (which they do in, for example, Sherry Gottlieb's *Love Bite*).

In Poppy Z. Brite's work and the more radical lesbian vampire fiction there is a self-aware element revelling in and simultaneously exposing performativity. Many contemporary women's vampire fiction writers align vampires themselves with a new feminist carnivalesque, infusing the age-old figure with new life and new potential to comment on what it means to be (at least somewhat) human.

Rock 'n' Roll Vampire Transients—Critical Comment

I once gave a paper entitled 'Vampires and Westerns' (at the International Conference on the Fantastic in the Arts, 2002), arguing that there are many similarities between the conventional outlaw, the swaggering villain, the light-and peace-bringing sheriff, and the polarised characters who inhabit conventional vampire tales. Radical vampire writing, however, disturbs both stereotypes.

Poppy Z. Brite's vampires are products of a period of disillusionment, representative of disaffected post-Vietnam war and transitory youth. Her early work is defined as 'postmodern southern gothic' by Jason K. Friedman (2007, p. 203), the dress and attitudes deriving from Goth subculture (Siegel 2005, p. 72). Vampires dressed as Goths and performers rely on image and the investment others make in their performance, which is presumed artifice but is actually real. Joshi (2004, p. 208) accuses Brite's work of an emphasis on superficiality, on style, but ironically this is also what she exposes in this novel and her short stories: a fatal investment in delusion and performance. Talking of her mix of Goth trappings and her position as an observer offering a moral comment, James Campbell (2013) notes: 'Like Goth performativity, this mode playfully parodies, while also participating in, the now ubiquitous Southern Gothic.' The travelling vampire youth *seem* to be what they are, vampires. *Lost Souls, Drawing Blood* (1993), and the short story collection *Swamp Foetus* (published in the United States as *Wormwood*, 1994) see vampires and other troubled youth as products of a society with a vacuum at its moral heart.

The ever-changing troupes of vampires prowling America's freeways and byways, feeding on despair and rejection, are products of their society, emptied out, focused on defining others as waste. Transient, homeless, violent, they pick up strays from families who throw them out, symbols of a context and period which promised a lot—ownership of goods, family values, stability, winning wars—but could not deliver. The contradictions of late twentieth-century America are enacted in Brite's teenage and twenty-something sexually various vampire travellers whose own lives and intrusions into the lives of others usually lead to sadness, violence, rending and death. Brite reclaims the vampire's engagement with and expression of contemporary issues, creating a place of lost hopes, emptied out values, a kind of liminal space in contemporary America. She says of her novel *Lost Souls*:

> *Lost Souls* is a homoerotic, Southern Gothic rock'n roll vampire tale set partly in New Orleans and partly in my fictitious town of Missing Mile, North Carolina. I had never been especially fascinated with vampires before this book, I chose to write about them now because it was 1987 and I was interested in and involved with the Gothic subculture—the beliefs distilled from dark music and darker emotion, the black lace and torn velvet, the affinity for graveyards, the bloodletting. That was what I wanted to write about and vampires are an essential icon of that culture. Those kids are beautiful, alienated, at once craving wild experience and romanticising death. Is it any wonder they identify with vampires? (Brite 1995, p. viii)

Vampires as cultural icons are at the heart of these fictions. Poppy Z. Brite's vampires are, like Anne Rice's, homosexual or bisexual performers. They are Southern Gothic rock 'n' roll youths daring the limits of life and death as youthful rebellion in a post-Vietnam age of complacency and hypocrisy. Brite's imagery resembles that of Jacobean revenge tragedies: tactile, brittle, brilliant and visceral. Sex and death combine in tantalising unity. They are also often not merely decadent and violent, but eroticised. She has produced two collections of vampire erotic tales, *Love in Vein* (1994) and *Twice Bitten (Love in Vein 2)* (1996), and for the novel *Lost Souls* won a prize for the best new writer of the homoerotic. Brite has always said she identifies more as a gay male (something Anne Rice has also said—when looking at the perspective taken in her novels), and following her writing about restaurants and cooking as locations for challenging events, she now writes a column as Billy Martin, a gay male author. Brite has been a part of the rock 'n' roll lifestyle, the transgendered challenging of restrictive simplistic delineation, the kind of challenges offered by the figure of the vampire. These young, decadent, destructive, performative vampires court drugs, liquor, sex and death:

> The vampires got into town sometime before midnight. They parked their black van in an illegal space, then got hold of a bottle of Chartreuse and reeled down Bourbon Street swigging it by turns, their arms round one another's shoulders, their hair in one another's faces. All three had outlined their features in dark blots of makeup, ... they wished they had fangs but had to make do with teeth filed sharp, and they could walk in sunlight as their great grandfathers could not ... (Brite, *Lost Souls*, 1993, p.59)

Fascination with the vampire is frequently more radical than this seeming escapism, however. Molochi, Zillah and Twig, Poppy Z. Brite's androgynous vampire trio, swagger into town like a bunch of outlaws, boozing, celebrating their status as marginal, but ultimately powerful, Others. Outlaws crossed the widescreens of cinemas and then our TVs, replayed in black and white or colour endlessly on wet winter Sundays, where John Wayne was always able to restore order against their leering, skulking, bad behaviour. In the traditional western, another dark figure, the gunslinger, is added to their number, dressed in black, something of a dandy, like a Victorian flâneur; he roams the high plains and dusty valleys, heading into the border towns with the deadly protection of his art. This figure resonates with that of the dark caped Victorian outlaw, Count Dracula. These contempoary vampires now occupy the same spaces that have been vacated by the westerns. Poppy Z. Brite's Gothic youth also own the streets. Their relationship with those who attend their concerts, and want to be a part of their cult, is predatory. These vampires are beautiful, amoral, their success a characteristic of a society whose moral values are questioned, emptied out. Brite's fascination with their energies, both celebratory and critical, enacts the desire and disgust provoked by more conventional vampire figures. They are a construction of and an indictment of a particular period and culture. The vampires in *Lost Souls* adopt the rejected child Nothing, who is a representative of the waste of a culture more focused on conquering Vietnam and on sidelining its veterans than on moving towards positive change, or social care. Nothing turns out to be related to them, but there is no parenting or care offered. The values of the vampires in post-Vietnam America are emptied out, along the freeways and the outskirts of towns where they prey on rejects, the destitute and the wayward. They also enact their own rituals including a kind of devotional cannibalism.

For vampires, the celebration involves the carnal (literally the *carnelevare* of the word 'carnival's' source—the taking away of meat from a saturnalia or Twelfth Night riotous holiday—see Stallybrass and White 1986), the devouring of the victim/lover's blood. It violates the ultimate taboo against cannibalism while offering eternal life for the chosen ones, a promise which is also a central feature of various religions, including Christianity. Lovingly, Poppy Z. Brite's Southern Gothic rock 'n' roll vampires lay out and drain their dead companion vampire:

> Tenderly they laid Zillah out on the bed and used his pearl-handled razor to slit him open from sternum to pubic bone. Nothing saw strangely

shaped organs glistening in the pale aperture. They lifted the organs out and arranged them carefully, lovingly, on the bed around him. Then, one by one, they thrust their heads into the long wound and licked the husk of Zillah clean. (Brite 1993b, p. 348)

Campbell (2013) comments that 'Brite's association with the "splatterpunk" movement is a reminder that each grisly spectacle is also a product for consumption. These texts may repel the squeamish, but they also fascinate those interested in the aestheticization of violence.'

Brite's fascination with liminality, the transitory pain and beauty, in a Goth subcultural context, peaks with the construction of a young Vietnamese American transsexual, Tran-Tran Vinh and 'Vincent Tran' in *Exquisite Corpse* (1996). He is in a liminal space between genders, identities, cultures and places; he loses himself in the graveyards and underworlds of New Orleans, and is caught up in the decadence and destruction of a Gothic vampire existence followed by death. This novel is a tour de force of glittering, decaying excess and death, a nihilistic vampire overload. Following *Exquisite Corpse*, *The Lazarus Heart* (1999) brings dead lovers together again. Brite's gender and name change accompanied the writing about cooking and the dark side of New Orleans. In the more recent works, there are no vampires.

INTERVIEWING VAMPIRES—ANNE RICE

Anne Rice was pioneering in her revitalisation of the figure of the vampire, coinciding with Angela Carter's 'The Lady of the House of Love' and the 'The Loves of Lady Purple'.

In *Interview with the Vampire* (1976) Daniel, a young interviewer, interviews a vampire as one would a novelist, or a celebrity. His transcript is credible because it is the product of a (relatively) conventional interview. What is recorded, however, contributes significantly to vampire lore. Rice sets her vampire history initially in New Orleans, a favourite of Poppy Z. Brite's, and focuses on families, history and inheritance, then questions both sexuality and power. The first novel of the *Vampire Chronicles* series, *Interview with the Vampire*, takes the reader through time and space from historical New Orleans, plantations, slavery and land ownership, to the present day, while *The Vampire Lestat* (1985) concentrates on the decadent era exemplified by the Rolling Stones' 'Sympathy for the Devil', where the updated rock 'n' roll vampire Lestat, newly returned from his recovery after being burned alive and notionally killed, lives the life of a rock star. Rice's trajectory in these two novels offers a parallel with the decadence of the twentieth century in New Orleans and that of 1960s and 1970s Britain and America, where dandyism and excess are so normal that vampires can walk among us unnoticed. Lestat, the age-old vampire, turns Louis, a plantation owner, in order to enable him to have eternal life. Instead, however, the great house is burned and they have a transitory, predatory existence with Louis reluctantly surviving for the most part on small animals rather than humans.

Rice's initial entrance into writing vampire narratives stemmed from the loss of her own daughter, Michelle, aged six, from a blood disease. In an interview she revealed the connection between loss and the channelling into something constructive, the fictional vampire:

> They are dealing with death at a symbolic and metaphorical remove ... My theory is that you don't have to run away from what you are suffering when you read these books. You can experience your thoughts and feelings about it, one step removed. (Rice 1996, p. 26)

The tragedy challenged her thoughts about life after death, and blood. She produced a fully-fledged revival of vampire mythology long before other writers (except Angela Carter) became interested again in the vampire as a figure, since at that time the Gothic was not the popular mode of choice. Anne Rice's work on the mythology of vampire history, law and relationships over time and place includes fin de siècle France, antebellum slave plantations in the Deep South and New Orleans, and ancient Egypt. Based in ancient lore, the Egyptian-set narratives centre on 'Those Who Must Be Kept', Akasha, the Queen in *The Vampire Lestat*, with her unmoving husband Enkil. Akasha appears more extensively in *Queen of the Damned*, in which Rice considers issues of female power, the archaic mother, mothering and the loathing this can produce (Kristeva 1982, p. 102).

Queen of the Damned interrelates the spiritual and the material, making political comments about gender, history, culture and power. Onto the figure of the female vampire is loaded all the fear and loathing of libidinous enactment. Seen as potential castratrix, she appears as dangerously powerful, sexually voracious and engulfing, equated with the powerful, fecund Mother who has the power to procreate but cannot let the child be itself; she cannot let go. Akasha has legendary sexual powers and is a mythic, terrifying force, the life-giving and devouring first mother of all. Her simplistic response to the evils of patriarchy is to kill all men.

Rice's postfeminism inspires a highly ritualistic moment when Akasha is destroyed, and her heart and liver ingested by her descendants, red-haired twins Mekare and Maharet. Her power, now cleansed, lives on in one iconic, female twin, Akasha's replacement.

Rice's vampires are transgressive, crossing boundaries of time, place and space with ease. Probably basing his suggestion on the traversing of gender binaries in Rice's work, Gelder argues that Rice's treatment of the vampire actually contradicts arguments about gender difference, which I believe is an ideal, but not one Rice actually realises:

> Ironically, the return to the mother is what allows Rice to kill off and transcend feminist politics ... sexual difference is a dead issue. (Gelder 1994, p. 117)

In the conventional vampire exchange, birth is a sexualised, potentially fatal experience in which gender roles are confused. The vampire (male or female) acts as mother, birthing a (usually) adult child, either victim or new vampire lover. The vampire mother is life-giving, seductive, and terrifying. Suckling is displaced from the breast to the neck, and milk replaced with blood. Disgust and horror at the Mother/vampire's generative, engulfing and destructive powers are mingled with the erotic. Conventionally:

> Vampirism combines a number of abject activities: the mixing of blood and milk; the threat of castration; the feminization of the male victim. (Creed 1993, p. 70)

Rice unites international vampire lore and myth, focusing on identity, inheritance, relationships, gender, hybridity, power and the duplicity of offers of eternal love. She also problematises normative sexual encounters and engages with issues of performativity in the contemporary world. Her vampire flâneurs walk among ordinary people and see only waste, artifice, and a pursuit of ephemeral human pleasures.

Rice's vampire narratives are motivated by questions of life and death, patriarchal and matriarchal power, the ethics of giving and taking life, performativity, identity and freedom. Rice comments on the imaginative, liberating potential of the vampire, identifying how fantasy can enable release, exorcising and speculation:

> the fantasy frame allows me to get to my reality. I'm telling all I know about everybody and everything in these books. It's an irony that as I step into this almost cartoon world, I'm able to touch what I consider to be real, ...

this gave me a doorway—a vampire who's able to talk about life and death, and love and loss, and sorrow and misery, and viciousness and grief. (Rice 1996, p. 14)

Rice's enormous cult following has foregrounded the thinking, performative vampire, variously good/bad/demonic/angelic, aligned in diversity and insecurity with the complexities of the postmodern world. Vampires are parasitic on the everyday world but also commentators and translators. They are dandies, flâneurs, delighting in their frock-coated appearances, simultaneously attracting and terrifying the humans on whom they prey. In *Interview with the Vampire* performance is literal: we meet vampires who kill while pretending to be what they are, vampires, in the French fin de siècle Paris Theatre de Vampires, who nightly drain victims onstage in a fantastic self-referential trick.

Rice's *Interview with the Vampire* begins her *Vampire Chronicles* with the adoption of the voice and stance of a gay male vampire and exploration of relationships between male vampires which are largely homoerotic, alternative family groupings rife with jealousy and ritual, rules, pretences, closeness and companionship. But the new vampire grouping breaks laws of humans and vampires alike. Louis turns his own mother, and, in order to rescue her from death when her mother dies of the plague, he also turns an abandoned child, Claudia, Rice's first female vampire. 'The adopted daughter' of Louis and Lestat, Claudia must remain eternally a child, since vampires do not age from the date they are turned. She has a child's emotions, wild energies and selfishness, devouring male twins and burning Lestat in an act of wilful disobedience. The desires Lestat, Louise and Claudia explore highlight and problematise ways in which men infantilise women, and daughters play roles for or react against fathers. Seeking a replacement for her own mother who dies of the plague, Claudia then finds Madeleine (a favourite vampiric name, such as in the online story '2113 the vampires rule'), who has lost her own daughter, and persuades Louis to turn her too. Rice complicates the vampire family and they test vampire lore. While the unity of Madeleine and Claudia signals a return to the Mother's body, as well as a potential lesbian relationship, their existence is condemned by the patriarchal forces of vampire law. Armand and the patriarchal family of the Theatre des Vampires wreak vengeance, burning them together in the sun. While patriarchy and the enforcement of age old lore wins in this instance, the series otherwise tests the boundaries of vampire behaviour and narrative use, so that issues of identity, relationships, mothering, sexuality and power are seen as constructs, and thus questionable.

Rice explores gender and power, women's radical behaviour and patriarchal punishment, and also eroticises the vampire embrace, moving beyond the condemnation, disgust, repulsion and loathing of *Dracula*. Turning others into vampires with a vampire kiss and an exchange of blood is an agonising, erotically charged, homosexual, lesbian or heterosexual exchange, which can be seen to celebrate homoerotic pleasure. Rice uses erotic language to describe Lestat's draining of Louis, Louis of Claudia and others and dramatises the turning of a new vampire in first-person, languorous, intense, hypnotic and ecstatic language. Louis turning Madeleine enables both of them to soar (literally, in the film) to new heights of passion and new life. Intoxicating, rhythmic language enacts vampire eroticism:

> She gasped as I broke the flesh, the warm current coming into me, her breasts crushed against me, her body arching up, helpless, from the couch. And I could see her eyes, even as I shut my own, see that taunting, provocative mouth. I was drawing on her, hard, lifting her, and I could feel her weakening, her hands dropping limp at her sides, 'Tight, tight' I whispered, 'look at it!' Her heart was slowing, stopping and her head dropped back from me on the velvet, her eyes dull to the point of death ... I felt the gentle pressure of her mouth, and then her hands closing tight on the arm as she began to suck. I was rocking her, whispering to her trying desperately to break my swoon; then I felt her powerful pull. Every blood vessel felt it, I was threaded through and through with her pulling, my hand holding fast to the couch now, her heart beating fierce against my heart, her fingers digging deep into my arm, my outstretched palm. (Rice 1976, p. 292)

This is a powerful mutual exchange of near-death swooning, and life giving passions. Madeleine is drained, and then in return takes blood from Louis. But it also reminds us of suckling a child, 'she began to suck. I was rocking her, whispering to her', a maternal, life-giving embrace; a mixed message.

The evil is without, order reigns again. A main trajectory of Gothic horror is from disruption to a calm closure, as Jancovich argues:

> the pleasure offered by the genre is based on the process of narrative closure in which the horrifying or monstrous is destroyed or contained ... the original order is re-established. (Jancovich 1992, p. 9)

However, Gothic horror also offers lack of closure, the promise of the demonic return. Contemporary women's vampire fiction subverts the need for a punitive restorative closure when the vampire figure questions such norms and conventions upon which closure rests.

As Creed suggests, the vampire disrupts polarised systems of thought, undermining Western logic, and hierarchical, oppositional structures:

> driven by her lust for blood, she does not respect the dictates of the laws which set down the rules of proper sexual conduct. Like the male, the female vampire also represents abjection because she crosses the boundary between the living and the dead, the human and the animal. (Creed 1993, p. 110)

While conventionally the vampire's transgression of gender boundaries, life/death, day/night, male/female and its invasion of the sanctity of the body, home, inheritance and blood are elements of its abjection, in its more radical contemporary form, it is celebrated because of its problematising of what seems fixed, because of its Gothic combining of opposites and exposure of restrictive constructions and interpretations. Richard Dyer sees the vampire as a representation of societal fears of women's sexuality: 'the hideous and terrifying form that sexual energies take when they return from being socially and culturally repressed' (Dyer 1988, p. 54). Vampires are particularly terrifying and also delightful, depending on one's conventionality or otherwise, since they offer a promise of eternal love and life: 'the vampire seems especially to represent sexuality ... s/he bites them, with a bite that is just as often described as a kiss' (Dyer 1988, p. 54).

In their work, contemporary women vampire writers embrace the radical challenge this androgynous radical vampire figure enables to dismantle patriarchy's reductive binary thought and behaviour processes. The figure of author Poppy Z. Brite also offers such a challenge. Central to Poppy Z. Brite's 'minoritarian Gothic' is a transgendered subjectivity (Holmes 2007, p. 70). Born Melissa Ann Brite, she became Poppy Z. Brite in 1985, before relinquishing the pseudonym upon becoming Billy Martin in 2011. As detailed in the autobiographical essay 'Enough Rope' (1998b), Brite self-identifies as a queer male—hence the abundance of queer male characters and the marginalisation of women throughout Brite's work—as a challenge to categories of 'male' and 'female', as does 'Dr. Brite', the authorial alter-ego in *Self Made Man* (1998) (published in the United States as *Are You Loathsome Tonight?* 1998), who changes gender with each new story s/he appears in.

The female vampire dramatises an endless potential for alternative, radical behaviour, and for celebrating our Otherness—a powerful contribution to postcolonial and postfeminist awareness and expression. She also represents potential dangers of sexual licence. The terror she evokes peaks when that challengingly abject relationship of woman and woman is involved. The social controls of normative gender roles are so dominant and both enforced by society and embraced by women by choice. In this context, lesbian vampires are seen as even more transgressive than gay males.

LESBIAN GOTHIC AND LESBIAN VAMPIRES

The vampire is the queer in its lesbian mode. (Case 1991a)

Lesbian Gothic is useful in exploring the problematising of convention enabled by both the Gothic in itself and lesbian Gothic in particular. Paulina Palmer sees a clear parallel between the lesbian and outsider in an economy based on gender, power and versions of sexuality, and the figure of the vampire, boundary breaker, who prefers night to day and troubles neat divisions based on gender, ethnicity, culture and power (Palmer 1999).

Vampires are constructions and representations of transgression and the troubling of oversimplistic divisions, categories which constrain and reduce the complexity of perspectives and of behaviours and sexuality. Lesbian vampires are even more transgressive, uniting mother with sexual partner and self, figures of abjection for the conventional, fusing monstrosity with erotic potential disgust and desire. As Gothic figures, their representation of the combination of oppositional categories is disturbing and liberating, depending on whether as a reader one fears the revelations of the Gothic or finds them enabling and empowering, a clear vision. Lesbian vampires are depicted negatively as the ultimate Otherised horror in films such as *The Loves of Count Iorga, Vampire* (1970). But for contemporary women writers, lesbian vampires are reclaimed figures connoting a creative, liberating challenge.

Bonnie Zimmerman suggests that the lesbian, by selecting same-sex lovers, embarks on a 'journey back to the mother'. This equates her with the lesbian vampire causing a blood flow like that in birth. Sue-Ellen Case takes the argument further, explaining the function of the lesbian vampire which can be read using queer theory foregrounding unlabelled same-sex desire. This destabilises gender categories and other categories of life and death, upsetting 'the borders of life and death', refusing 'the organicism which defines the living as the good' (Case 1991a, p. 3). In her argument the queer 'is the taboo-breaker, the monstrous, the uncanny'.

Understood and interpreted by way of queer theory, lesbian vampires undercut the divisions of gender, as well as those of life/death, self/Other, highlighting the performative nature of all gender constructions (cf. Butler, 1990). In the new economy of lesbian vampire fictions, Case's arguments concerning the value of lesbian vampire exchange moves beyond the pre-symbolic re-reading of mother and child relations we find in Anne Rice to project instead an 'in-between' state, as Gelder puts it: 'turning away from the heterosexist fantasy of pre-Oedipal maternal original (life, regeneration) and towards an unoriginal "in-between" state between the familiar and the unfamiliar, the living and the dead, that Freud (and the Slovenian Lacanians) has left relatively untouched' (Gelder 1994, p. 62). Case argues that in seeing no reflection the vampire avoids the symbolic, which can be read as a revaluation of relations refusing the symbolic/pre-symbolic. So 'her proximate vanishing appears as a political strategy; her bite pierces platonic metaphysics and subject/object oppositions; and her fanged kiss brings her, the chosen one, trembling with ontological, orgasmic shifts, into the state of the undead' (Case, quoted in Gelder 1994, p. 62).

As I argued elsewhere, 'The figure of the lesbian vampire deconstructs a fascism of the body and mind, dominant ideologies which project a conformist norm' (Wisker 2012, p. 234). The figure of the gay or lesbian vampire is the ideal icon of a celebratory otherness.

Palmer establishes connections between vampires and lesbians in terms of their lifestyle, pleasures and relationships:

> A key point of affinity between the lesbian and the vampire … is their dual existence both as independent loners and members of a loosely knit network or group. Both figures experience a tension between the need for privacy and anonymity, on the one hand, and interaction with members of 'their own kind' on the other. While concealing their lesbianism/vampirism from the prying eyes of the world, they seek to recognise and be recognised by, a group of like-minded sisters. (Palmer 1999, p. 102)

Lesbian vampires live and love in supportive networks avoiding heterosexual power relationships, sexually exchange like with like, and are also involved in a masquerade, since in many contexts daily life requires performance to 'pass', as it does of the vampire. Elsewhere, I commented, 'Invasion of each other's body spaces inscribes on the body of the loved the lust and adoration, the need of the vampire lover. When there is an exchange between equals the love of each is written on the bodies of both equally' (2012, p. 228). Celebrated for their transgression, they are rewarded with immortality.

The 1990s were a significant decade for lesbian vampire stories and their radical edge, much of which is now more mainstream, perhaps aided by the widespread flowering of lesbian-based and oriented Gothic writing, such as that by Jeanette Winterson and Sarah Waters.

The erotic, conventionally a site for control and prohibition, becomes a site for liberation and exploration in contemporary women's vampire fictions. With an African American lesbian vampire focus, Jewelle Gomez's (1991) *The Gilda Stories* begins with slavery and focuses on racist violence, telling of vampire sisterhood through centuries and engaging with transgression as liberation.

Nite Bites (1996), the first published collection of vampire stories by women, explores a feminist perspective 'reflecting a distinctly female sensibility, and many of the metaphors derive from that definingly female sphere of experience—the domestic' (Brownworth 1996, p. xiv). Like Gomez's work, these also offer political commentary on 'marriage, motherhood, racism, AIDS, drug and gang wars, global destruction'. Socially and ideologically engaged, many tales, as in Poppy Z. Brite's edited collections *Love in Vein* (1995) and *Twice Bitten (Love in Vein 2)* (1996) deal with the erotic, with lesbian vampires and rescript romance. Pat Califia writes the lesbian vampire as invader, and lover, exploring an S&M scene, as does Ruthann Robson's short story (1996), which explores a lesbian relationship between members of a rock band. The death of one, Sammy, from a drug overdose, permeates the lyrics of another who plays within the 'spotlight of safety' in lesbian bars and halls until Sammy returns, changed. Now both vampires, they realise their relationship offers eternal love.

In Judith Katz's short story, 'Anita, Polish Vampire, Holds Forth at the Jewish Cafe of the Dead' (1996), Anita, a wealthy Jewish vampire, frequents expensive restaurants where waiters become increasingly magical. She eats a pulsing heart in front of her companion, the narrator, who literally almost loses her heart to Anita, in an ironic romantic twist, when:

> Anita was about to grab the very heart from out of my breast when, curse him, our waiter appeared, carrying another silver-covered dish. As he placed it before the lovely Anita, she jerked away from me, startled. Immediately I missed the warmth of her beautiful yellow eyes. (Katz 1996, p. 30)

Then Anita offers her own heart (romantically) on a plate. They leave together, having voraciously shared a bloody heart (from the menu). Their relationship escalates, vital with desire, contradictions, crossed boundaries: 'how glad I was for her to touch me—how it chilled me and calmed me, livened and deadened me all at once. I was in her power gladly' (Katz 1996, p. 31).

Victoria Brownworth's own lesbian vampire tale in this collection is set in the traditional home of the vampire, New Orleans. Its intention is ethical and political and it indicts bloody political violence with the example of a woman reporter who covered the genocide of the Tutsis by the Hutu in Rwanda and returns to her friends to share her secrets. These are about initiation into a lesbian love affair with a vampire, Dolores, 'she was everything you thought she was. She was Death itself. She fed me, and then she taught me how to feed' (Brownworth 1996, p. 210). Like Rusty in *Love Bites* (1996) and later, Emily and Frank in Moira Buffini's *A Vampire Story* (2008) and *Byzantium* (2013) (see Chap. 8), the gift of life to the nearly dying is an act of vampire generosity. The children she helps who are dying in the streets survive, but as vampires. The radical vampire has taken on a role as a form of social service, a sister of mercy. Like Anne Rice's Louis, she is a thinking vampire: 'I hate blood, I hate the carnage. But I've learned to use it', 'Remember how angry I used to be? I learned to use my anger for change, I've taught myself how to create change' (Brownworth, 1996, p. 212). Her transgressions lead to positive change and the story has a happy lesbian vampire ending when she finds another companion in the appropriately named Luna (referencing the moon, a female symbol).

Female vampires are frequently feisty, challenging, offering alternative ways of seeing relations of gender and power. In postcolonial contexts, they can be seen to problematise constructions of ageing as entirely negative (*Cereus Blooms at Night*, Mootoo 1996), and individualism and selfishness as rewarding ('Greedy Choke Puppy', Hopkinson 2001a). Whenever we might feel the genre has run its course and become tired, even in its challenge to gendered power, it revitalises itself, because it is ultimately the vehicle we can use to explore, to challenge, to question gendered stereotypes and cultural stereotypes and to dramatise agency.

Conclusion

Lisa Tuttle emphasises the importance of women's perspectives and writing to challenge and change the power of horror, of which the Gothic figure of the vampire is a crucial figure of choice. She argues that:

> If horror is to be more than disposable, 'boy's own' junk, as I think it can be, then it must listen to voices from both sides of the night. (Tuttle 1990, p. 4)

Feminist critics who write about the functions of horror, Gothic and the vampire suggest that gender is crucial to the representation of the female vampire. Recognising that we construct vampires in order to problematise both terrors and complacencies, and that we construct our own vampires, our own Others, is empowering in itself.

David Punter argues that vampire narratives disrupt then close down the new energies they have exposed. Quoting and referring to his earlier work of 1996, he notes:

> The vampire's initial liberation of excess energies and disruption of normality is a very temporary affair. Social order is quickly restored, the cathartic experience nailed down again to the relief of the conformist audience/readership. This has, of course, always been the role of horror, and of much gothic. (Punter 2012, p. 228)

But I wonder whether this is the case with the more radical feminist vampire fictions?

> Vampirism springs from not only paranoia, xenophobia, or immortal longings, but from generosity and shared enthusiasm. (Auerbach 1995, p. vii)

Grown from the mythic, legendary and historical vampires, fictional vampires are used as metaphors, ciphers for the desires and fears of their cultural contexts. The vampire myth is reconfigured in different cultural contexts to embody what is feared and desired, and in many cases feared just because it is desired. Vampires are popular figures in contemporary women's horror, not merely because of their promise of eternal youth, but also because of their naturally transgressive and potentially revolutionary nature. In the twenty-first century, the vampire has metamorphosed even beyond the radicalism of the late twentieth century. As we see in Chap. 8, contemporary vampire writers rescript romance, either replaying its forms with vampire lovers (in YA vampire romance and *Twilight*, 2005) or through troubling romance with the problems of early death, where instead, eternity is offered through the vampire kiss. On the one hand the vampire has become quite a conventional figure in much YA writing, a figure inviting romantic fantasies, reinforcing heterosexual relationships based on undying love. Simultaneously, it is a figure used to explore and enact imaginative, radical critique of restrictive, oppressive cultural regimes.

Vampires are the ultimate shape-shifters and indices of different times. Their potential for metamorphosis enables us to identify and dramatise concerns, and to break boundaries which restrict thought and action. Vampires can reinvest the erotic with energy, rejecting the demonising of women's sexuality and power. Much radical critique expresses itself through transgression of gender boundaries and the celebration of homosexual and lesbian relations. Vampire fictions and the vampire myth in the hands of many contemporary women writers explore and enact practices based in queer theory, defying boundaries, refusing categories and destructively oriented definitions of difference, expressing the carnivalesque. Nina Auerbach reminds us 'the best vampires are companions' (Auerbach 1995, p. vii). They are our others, ourselves, and in contemporary women's writing and feminist reincarnations they afford us a wealth of insights on what it means to be human.

Contemporary women's radical vampire fictions move beyond oppositional readings and refuse binaries, boundaries and divisions. They explore and embrace the conventionally abject: the mother's body, gay and lesbian sexuality, the erotic. This chapter looks at the more dangerous radical feminist vampires, the next chapter at the revival of the everyday and the Gothic vampire conventions, albeit with fangs and blood. In case we become too fascinated with their challenges to convention, however, it is useful to remember as Moira Buffini's vampires acknowledge: 'I freely confess that I have stayed alive for all these years by drinking human blood' (Buffini 2008, p. 485). And, as Caitlín R. Kiernan comments, 'vampires are, by definition, serial killers' (Brite 1999, p. 177).

Bibliography

Auerbach, N. (1995) *Our Vampires, Ourselves* (Chicago: University of Chicago Press).
Brite, P. Z. (1993b) *Lost Souls* (New York: Dell).
Brite, P. Z. (1994) *Love in Vein* (New York: Harper Voyager).
Brite, P. Z. (1999) *The Lazarus Heart* (Colorado Springs, CO: Gauntlet Press).
Brownworth, V. A. (ed.) (1996) *Night Bites* (Washington: Seal Press).
Buffini, M. (2008) *A Vampire Story* (London: Faber and Faber).
Butler, J. (1990) *Gender Trouble: Feminism and the Subversion of Identity* (New York: Routledge).
Campbell, J. (2013) 'Brite, Poppy Z.', in *The Encyclopedia of the Gothic*, W. Hughes, D. Punter and A. Smith (eds.) (Oxford: Blackwell), http://www.literatureencyclopedia.com/subscriber/tocnode.html?id=g9781405182904_chunk_g97814051829044_ss1-10

Carter, A. (1979c) 'The Lady of the House of Love', in *The Bloody Chamber and Other Stories* (London: Gollancz).
Case, S.-E. (1991a) 'Tracking the Vampire', *Differences: A Journal of Feminist Cultural Studies*, Vol. 3, No. 2.
Creed, B. (1993) *The Monstrous Feminine: Film, Feminism and Psychoanalysis* (London: Routledge).
Dyer, R. (1988) 'Children of the Night: Vampirism as Homosexuality, Homosexuality as Vampirism', in *Sweet Dreams: Sexuality, Gender and Popular Fiction*, S. Radstone (ed.) (London: Lawrence & Wishart).
Friedman, J. K. (2007) '"Ah am Witness to its Authenticity": Goth Style in Postmodern Southern Writing', in *Goth: Undead Subculture*, L. M. E. Goodlad and M. Bibby (eds.) (Durham, NC: Duke University Press).
Gelder, K. (1994) *Reading the Vampire* (London: Routledge).
Gomez, J. (1991) *The Gilda Stories* (New York: Firebrand Books).
Hitchcock, A. (1996) Quotation from Exhibition: 'Phantasmagoria: Pre-Cinema to Virtuality', Museum of Contemporary Art, Sydney, 27 March–30 June.
Holmes, T. (2007) '(Un) becoming Goth: Poppy Z. Brite, Courtney Love and Gothic Biography', *Gothic Studies*, Vol. 9, No. 1.
Hopkinson, N. (2001a) 'Greedy Choke Puppy', in *Skin Folk* (New York: Aspect).
Jancovich, M. (1992) *Horror* (London: Batsford).
Joshi, S. T. (2004) *The Evolution of the Weird Tale* (New York: Hippocampus Press).
Kalogridis, J. (1995–1997) *The Diaries of the Family Dracul series* (New York: Dell).
Katz, J. (1996) 'Anita, Polish Vampire, Holds Forth at the Jewish Cafe of the Dead', in *Night Bites*, V. A. Brownworth (ed.) (Seattle, WA: Seal Press).
Kristeva, J. (1982) *The Powers of Horror: An Essay on Abjection*, L. Roudiez (trans.) (New York: Columbia University Press).
Mootoo, S. (1996) *Cereus Blooms at Night* (New York: Avon Books).
Palmer, P. (1999) *Lesbian Gothic: Transgressive Fictions* (London: Cassell).
Punter, D. (1996) *The Literature of Terror: Volume 2: The Modern Gothic* (London: Longman).
Punter, D. (2012) *A New Companion to the Gothic* (London: Blackwells).
Rice, A. (1976) *Interview with the Vampire* (St. Ives: Futura).
Rice, A. (1996) Quoted in M. Riley, *Interview with Anne Rice* (London: Chatto & Windus).
Schlobin, R. C. (1989) 'The Femivore: An Undiscovered Archetype', *Journal of the Fantastic in the Arts*, Spring.
Siegel, C. (2005) *Goth's Dark Empire* (Bloomington: Indiana University Press).
Smith, S. (1994) 'When the Red Storm Comes', in *Shudder Again*, M. Slung (ed.) (New York: Penguin).
Stallybrass, P. and White, A. (1986) *The Politics and Poetics of Transgression* (Ithaca, NY: Cornell University Press).

Stoker, B. [1897] (1979) *Dracula* (London: Penguin Books).
Swenson, K. (2003) 'The Menopausal Vampire: Arabella Kenealy and the Boundaries of True Womanhood', *Women's Writing*, Vol. 10, No. 1.
Tuttle, L. (1990) *Skin of the Soul* (London: Women's Press).
Wisker, G. (1998) 'If Looks Could Kill: Contemporary Women's Vampire Fictions', in *Fatal Attractions:Rescripting Romance in Contemporary Literature and Film Hardcover*, L. Pearce and G. Wisker (eds.) (London: Pluto Press).
Wisker, G. (2012) 'Love Bites: Contemporary Women's Vampire Fictions', in A New Companion to the Gothic (2nd edn.), D. Punter (ed.) (Oxford: Blackwell).
Wisker, G. (2014) 'Contemporary Women's Gothic: From *Lost Souls* to *Twilight*', in *A Companion to the American Gothic*, C. L. Crow (ed.) (Chichester: Wiley-Blackwell).

CHAPTER 8

Vampire Kisses

The second part of this exploration of the fascination with the vampire looks at the popular fictional vampire of the twenty-first century—Stephenie Meyer's and Charlaine Harris' conservative use of a radical figure—*Twilight* vampire lovers, return of the vampire romance and management of cultural values, power of the family and social normativity. It also revives the figure with Moira Buffini's *A Vampire Story* (2008) and *Byzantium* (2013).

Nina Auerbach comments on her personal journey from a need to challenge conformity, to recognising the figure of the vampire as offering escape and alternative ways of seeing and being:

> Vampires were supposed to menace women, but to me at least, they promised protection against a destiny of girdles, spike heels and approval. (Auerbach 1995, p. 4)

However, while alternatives might be exciting, they also might be rather too popular, and popularised which, in many instances, is what has happened to this once edgy creature of the night and its radical energies. Vampires have become everyday familiars. Sanitised and figuratively de-fanged, many twentieth- and twenty-first-century vampires are just like the boy or girl next door. Even Poppy Brite (now Billy Collins) turned to writing novels about food, and using cooking metaphors, rejecting both the exciting edginess, the amorality of Gothic vampires and the critique of society they enable, arguing that the metaphor is now tired. She says:

> You can only maintain an intensely Gothic frame of mind for so long before either killing yourself or starting to feel like a bit of a poser, and neither alternative appealed to me. (Brite 1995, pp. viii–ix)

The vampire is a very mutable creature, which befits one whose role is to operate as a kind of demonic wind-vane of cultural censors and both problems and investments in values. The variously damaged, contested and conservative body is at the heart of the issues which the figure of the vampire negotiates. The title and substance of Nina Auerbach's book, *Our Vampires Ourselves* (1995), suggest ways in which we produce and read the vampire, since as Moira Buffini's Ella notes, 'True vampires live and move in society just like everyone else' (Buffini 2008, p. 488). Auerbach also normalises the vampire when she says: 'the best vampires are companions' (Auerbach 1995, p. vii.)

This self-identification has a more conformist side, one which has flourished in much vampire writing by women since the radical heyday of the late twentieth century. As I noted elsewhere, 'The vampire is no longer a creature of social radicalism and imaginative exploration but rather either an alternative revisioning of the familiar texts whose vampire like tendencies were somewhat suspected rather than stated, or a tortured romantic lead who will be rescuable with the love of a good woman' (Wisker 2012, p. 234).

In the twentieth century, vampires represented sexual energies and alternative ways of being, and they offered both critique and exploration of difference with regard to conventional roles, such as mothering, being a wife, a daughter, a sexual partner. They enabled exploration of the negative trends in mothers, for example, the power games of Akasha Queen of the Damned in Anne Rice's novel (1988), and the dominating life-sucking mother in Melanie Tem's 'Mama' (1995). They also broke out of the stale old confines of heterosexuality and inevitable conformity, since the trajectories of vampire narratives in the hands of women writers often reward lesbian love, S&M sex and alternative families, and are set in rocket ships, bars and clubs. The mean streets which threatened women are turned into vampire hunting grounds, so women vampires seek the opportunity to turn the tables on conventional predators, or become sexual hunters themselves when seeking partners. Vampires were appropriated for the dark side, the transgressive. While seen as deviant and to be punished in more conventional times, instead, the alternative sexual desires and energies they exhibit were celebrated. It is perhaps with some dismay that we see the ways in which vampires have again been reappropriated for conventionality (romantic bliss, heteronormativity) in late twentieth-, early twenty-first-century writing. Luckily, some of these conventional responses are also tinged with parody.

Vampire Romance, YA Fiction and Mash-Ups

In much Young Adult (YA) fiction, the vampire returns as a romantic lead, a tall, dark, dangerous, handsome stranger who can rescue the rather passive woman from herself and perhaps devour her but more frequently somehow satisfy her romantic dreams. His dangerous energies produce frissons of desire which are then rewarded in conventional ways. There are a number of YA vampire romances which follow this trajectory, although by far the most popular is Stephenie Meyer's *Twilight* (2005–2008) series in which the classically handsome outsider, Edward, the male vampire romantic lead, is a sexy, dangerous lover. Edward might have vampire strength and aggression but, a throwback, protective and passionate, he is dependable and wants to marry the heroine, Bella.

Twilight opened up a YA audience and added a mature female audience, all eager for tall, dark, handsome, isolated strangers who could sweep them off their feet, with a little danger and some sexual frisson, but ultimately into marriage. Bella is rescued by Edward both into marriage and motherhood, albeit via some angst and pain and the expectation that she herself must become a vampire to survive childbirth. As I remarked earlier, the 'anodyne Gothic often lurks beneath the violence and erotica of young adult vampire romance' (Wisker 2014, p. 422). There are other YA fictions which depend on the vampire. L. J. Smith's *Vampire Diaries: The Awakening* (1991) seems to be the start of YA vampire romance. In this novel, the heroine is torn (only metaphorically and romantically) between a vampire lover and his brother. Smith produced four novels and a TV series in 2009. In her *Night World* series, starting in 1996 with *The Secret Vampire*, she used vampirism to focus on rescue from a deadly illness, a common theme in vampire romance, whether adult or YA (*Love Bite* by Sherry Gottlieb 1994, uses this). Both Katie MacAlister's (writing as Katie Maxwell) *Got Fangs?* (2005) and Vivian Van de Velde's *Companions of the Night* (1995) are vampire romances. Romance and vampire fiction work well together but, as Margaret C. Carter, author of both vampire romances and criticism, points out, they tend to reinforce conservative values, including frowning on mixed-race and mixed mortal/vampire couples (see Carter's online *The Vampires' Crypt*, discontinued 2002). Carter (2010) notes that in YA vampire romances the men resemble Gothic male romantic leads, while vampire women have merely conventional roles as high school buddies, jealous bitches, or troubled misfits with a mission. Carter's *Different Blood: The Vampire As Alien* (2004) is an excellent guide to trends in vampire fictions, as is S. T. Joshi's *Encyclopaedia of the Vampire* (2010).

Much earlier, the critically game-changing Gilbert and Gubar's *The Madwoman in the Attic* (1979) identified Gothic figures and the power of the Gothic as offering a critique of relationships based on the disempowerment, conformity and silencing of women: patriarchy all dressed up as conventional behaviour. Their critical explorations, discussed earlier, also underlie current comic mash-ups which interrupt familiar tales with the monsters lurking in the minds of readers, splattering corpses on the eighteenth- and nineteenth-century lawns of the literary canon. The presence of vampires in such texts (which also feature sea monsters, zombies and a variety of shape-shifting creatures) offers some critical undercutting of the conformity to which they eventually and necessarily return their characters and readers. In works by the Brontës and Jane Austen, romance and marriage might be questioned, but are ultimately rewarded. In contemporary mashed-up versions, post-second-wave feminism, Hammer films and the explosion of interest in the Gothic as a mix of parody and horror, the devious unlicensed sexual energies of a vampire (or sea monster, zombie, werewolf) offer a temporary comic intrusion, a wry parallel world and reading for these original tales which critiqued contemporary values but necessarily ended with conventional resolutions. This indicates on the one hand some of the critiques we might bring to such texts and to their ultimate conventionality, but on the other a spoof, along the lines of *Young Frankenstein* (1974) and *Carry on Screaming* (1966). A splicing of the vampire (or werewolf, or sea monster, etc.) tale, in which the familiar text opens out its now rather spurious comfort, renders the serious amusing. Jane Austen's *Pride and Prejudice* (1813) is a favourite, with Seth Grahame-Smith's *Pride and Prejudice and Zombies* (2009) and Amanda Grange's *Mr Darcy, Vampyre* (2009), two such versions of a twenty-first-century sequel, or monster mash-up (a mash-up intermixes the original text with a new text springing from some of its hidden tendencies, and our latter-day insights about subversive problematic behaviours, made tangible, so that zombies or vampires, for example, roam and intrude on the rather straitlaced ways and byways of a Jane Austen or Charlotte Brontë novel). However, the power of this particular romance is overwhelming despite the zombies or vampires. While mash-ups or sequels rewrite canonical texts, exposing their subtexts, they actually also repeat the myth of undying love because they involve conventional romantic heroes, and encourage both erotic fantasies and yearning. Some end with these norms a little undermined, a little edgy, but most end with the reward of love, marriage, inheritance and a comfortable family life, as they always did.

Twilight for Vampires

The *Twilight* saga (2005–2008), unfortunately, has neither the edginess nor the parodic qualities of the mash-ups. Vampire romance and YA fiction have re-revived the vampire for the twenty-first century, acting as a vehicle for a range of meta-narratives about romance, eternal love, friendship and family values. Enjoying the *Twilight* series might feel a little daring to anyone committed to pulp romantic fiction because there are vampires centre stage, but actually the novels just recycle familiar figures and very conservative values, in fantasy form. *Twilight*'s less than subtle narrative and effects can appeal to readers and audiences who are used to fantasy, shape-shifting, vampires and werewolves and who might like to embrace a frisson of familiar excitement in the service of conservatism. The *Twilight* series, like other Gothic fictions, articulates a sense of unease at a variety of social concerns. However, concerns, as norms, are culturally constructed, and the concerns dealt with in *Twilight* are largely generated by conservative unease. For lesbian vampire writers, such a sense of unease was directed at homophobia, patriarchal power and repression, and at the otherising of those variously different from the mainstream, whatever that happened to be. *Twilight*, however, directs a conservative unease at an America suffering broken homes, political rivalries and sex before marriage. In doing so it reminds us that 'Gothic was, from its very inception, a form that related very closely to issues of national assertion and social organisation, and which even on occasion, could "take the stage" in foregrounding social issues and in forming social consciousness' (Punter 2000a, p. 4). What is lauded, what deplored, depends on what the issues and social consciousness appear to be. Even contemporary vampire fictions can be essentially conservative, which Marie Mulvey Roberts notes, is keying into the cult of celibacy before marriage, which has an American inflection tied to Christian religion (correspondence, December 2015).

It is hardly surprising that *Twilight* has proved so popular. It is a very familiar romance fulfilling fantasies of teenage girls, older readers or audiences seeking dashing, romantic heroes and eternal love. The teen story is riddled with the discomfort of Bella's identity as an outsider, neither beautiful nor sporty. This is probably a universal theme but has a particularly American nuance. Bella does gain some popularity despite her wimpish, relatively unattractive personality and behaviour, because she is new and has the advantage of having covered much of the syllabus at school already. Her teenage angst drives her into isolation, a sense of worthlessness and boredom.

Her enervated behaviour reminds us of the fairytale Sleeping Beauty. Bella is in stasis, waiting for something to happen to her, which it does, in the form of a sullen, arrogant, extraordinarily beautiful Edward Cullen, who resembles Darcy in *Pride and Prejudice*, with his family history, large house and his designer clothing, ultimately offering to take the girl 'away from all this'. Edward also reminds us of Superman, another romantic superhero with secrets. At times of crisis he swoops in, faster than a speeding bird, and prevents Bella from being crushed by a car. Cullen literally sweeps Bella off her feet into his strong arms and they fly through the air, soaring above trees and the oppressive small-mindedness of the endless expanse of small town Forks, eventually into his home, and his powerful vampire family, who find ways to accept and protect her.

The love story, dressed up with vampires and werewolves, is every teenage girl's romantic fictional fantasy come true (Grossman 2008, 2009). *Twilight* offers eternal love, rescuing the reader from herself, as does romance more generally. Even for the most ridiculously fantastic events, suspension of disbelief adds to its popularity. Writing for the conservative Clare Boothe Luce Policy Institute, Miriam Grossman comments on *Twilight*'s chaste romance: 'a girl should be encouraged to wait until her own Edward Cullen comes along, a man who has waited for her as she has for him' (2008, n.p.). Edward is a 'throwback' to romantic figures of conventional romance, inviting longing, promising eternity and some vampire chivalry.

The trilogy's second meta-narrative is one of family values, based in Meyer's religious Mormon background. The Cullen family last forever, adopt and manage troubled teenagers, and live in a big house which stands for success and family values. Whatever secrets they have between them they keep to themselves, and their family bonds, just like the romantic bonds, are for eternity. Their teenagers are under control. Carlisle, who rescued Esme to be a vampire and also his wife (one family secret kept from outsiders), is recognised by Bella's law enforcement official father, Charlie, as a strong, professional parent. Elsewhere I noted that 'Bringing Bella into that family is essential for their future and the message of the novel, which reinforces heteronormativity, coupledom, and law and order' (Wisker, 2014, p. 443). Silver comments that 'Meyer has not written solely a romance novel about Edward and Bella. She has written, instead, a romance about family and the human need for connection and community' (Silver 2010, p. 135).

As humans, Bella's parents struggle more than the Cullens do, and suffer from marital breakup, selfishness, and problems with communication. Bella's mother Renee left her father, Charlie, for a new life in the sunshine and partying of California, but the vampire family have stayed together for hundreds of years, and Edward, born in 1901, maintains old-fashioned family and courtship values. His withdrawal from Bella in the second volume is largely for her own protection; a gentlemanly act, possibly because he knows that sex with him could kill her, or that he intends to save her from the vulnerability of being a human and potential victim to other vampires in the wider, more dangerous circle. But Bella is reading a romantic fiction script of her own life, and can only see loss, disillusionment and pointlessness. She also sees the loss of her lover, her reason for living at this point, and also that of his family with whom she has found some peace and welcome. It 'had been more than just losing the truest of true loves … It was also losing a whole future, a whole family' (*New Moon*, 2006, p. 398). Their acceptance gives Bella an identity and impetus to live a good life. They act as a model, cohesive, religious (of sorts) family although the cross in the house denotes more than a conventional Christian commitment, since as vampires, that is a little contradictory. The aim of the cross as symbol is one of protecting the family, including the new members whose human blood makes them more vulnerable to vampire purists. Bella's future is sealed when she and Edward have Renesmee—a half human, half vampire child. This is a relatively new character for women's vampire fictions, where children such as Anne Rice's Claudia are usually 'turned' when young and kept that away, unageing. However, this birth is entirely in keeping with the family and community cohesion meta-narrative. Bella is also turned into a vampire for her own survival. It could also be argued that she would expect Edward to turn her in order to preserve her and that she is collusive in this act, seeking the power and beauty which comes with being more completely a member of the vampire family. Silver sees this new version of life as one of agency and empowerment, focused on the role of motherhood, and notes that 'In the final book of the series, *Breaking Dawn* (2008), Meyer allows Bella to become the kind of mother that she never had, the apotheosis of the self-sacrificial, selfless mother, who is willing to die for the good of her unborn vampire child, and the warrior-mother who successfully protects the integrity and survival of her family' (Silver 2010, p. 123). When Bella develops a vampire nature she also develops special powers. This could either be an indication of her changing utterly from her earlier human character or, on the other hand, represent an opportunity to draw out a strong maternal self, the latent warrior mother, a characteristic lacking in her own more hedonistic, self-oriented (California-based) mother, now marvellously enabled by her revitalisation through developing into a vampire mother, member of the Cullen clan. I would argue that this makes the *Twilight* trilogy more of a historical Gothic saga, since heredity and inheritance are key concerns in eighteenth-and nineteenth-century Gothic novels, whether romance or Gothic horror. It also makes it a moralistic tale lauding stoicism, resilience, family values and motherly strength.

The other clan who disrupt, but live alongside, the vampire family, are the Native American werewolves, mostly male, including Jacob, Bella's second love interest, especially during the middle book when Edward has left her alone. In her work on the *Twilight* saga, Silver researched the Native American myth of the third wife of Taha Aki, a Quileute chief. When attacked by a vampire, the wife sacrificed herself for tribe and family and Bella identifies with her not only when she risks her life to preserve Renesmee, but in developing a womblike shield to protect the whole family. Native American werewolves might look like a threat, but they are also examples of different models of cohesion. Strong clan behaviours regulate them and the eventual imprinting of Renesmee on Jacob draws these families and clans together, which is useful when attacked by the dark, violent, trendily dressed and clearly more Gothic-influenced vampires (more familiar in popular culture). Against this invasion, the family values-loving, religious Cullens are under threat and made to seem an unwanted development in a dominant version of the vampire world. Meyer has neatly twisted and reformed the vampire myth to suit her own, essentially conservative, religious, family-orientated Mormon-based purposes: what is radical and new, is stable, caring, conforming. Bella has her family: 'I looked around the room at their faces—Jasper, Alice, Emmett, Rose, Esme, Carlisle … Edward—the faces of my family' (Meyer 2007, p. 309).

Talking to a *USA Today* interviewer, Meyer reveals her intentions to emphasise the family values above the romance: 'I guess there's a conditioning from fairy tales that the wedding is the end of the story, but I think most of us know that it's another kind of beginning' (Memmott 2008). She negotiates some of the questions we all have about vampires—Can they have children? Will Bella have to become one?—and by doing so reduces their strangeness. Meyer takes this familiar fantasy metaphor figure to reinforce romantic love, heteronormativity, coupledom, family values and the importance of social coherence in small town America. Unlike the more radical Sookie Stackhouse novels (2001–2013) and *Buffy the Vampire Slayer* (1997–2003), which in many ways also reinforce social norms and romantic fictions, Meyer's work fails to offer any trace of the radicalism of racial differences (except for vampire or werewolf) or homosexuality. In Forks, growing up normal is expected, and even being a member of the established vampire family is a version of normal. This is by no means a radical fiction; the vampire fantasy is being used to teach conformity.

Interestingly, family values are also the focus of Tananarive Due's series of vampire novels, which splice vampire fiction with another fictional form, the thriller. Due's work is not as conventional as *Twilight*, and has some elements in common with Charlaine Harris in its recognition of ethnicity, neighbourhood or village values and social harmony. It also emphasises the difficult negotiation with patriarchal power when established over hundreds or thousands of years, and here reminds us of the theatre of the vampires, the vampire estate, and the deadly forces used against the two women in Moira Buffini's *A Vampire Story/Byzantium*, discussed later in this chapter.

Respectability—Tananarive Due's African Vampires

> I needed to address my fear that I would not be respected if I wrote about the supernatural. (Tananarive Due in interview 17 March 2002, at http://www.tananarivedue.com/interview.htm)

'It takes a village to raise a child', says Due's character Jessica Wolde in *The Living Blood* (2001), commenting on Fana, the hybrid, vampire/human child at the centre of the 'African Immortals' series. One reading of this series is that of its intention to remind the father and the wider family of their responsibilities to those more vulnerable. *My Soul to Keep* (1997), *The Living Blood* (2001), *Blood Colony* (2008) and *My Soul to Take* (2011) explore a relationship between immortals, a vampiric African race, and humans, using Gothic tropes of boundary crossing, liminality and hybridity to engage issues of race and gender. An African American tale with some of the range of Anne Rice's family sagas, Due's is a complex, extended myth-based saga spanning continents, involving South and central Africa and the USA, focusing on Black communities and their experiences. The search for roots, family, equality and change underpins each text.

In narratives authored by middle-class white males, for example, those more vulnerable are likely to be women and ethnic Others (Black, Latin American, Native American, indigenous populations, Asian, Irish, whoever is considered Other by the dominant group). We find contemporary women writers intervening on gender, ethnicity and power imbalances, and Due's work provides a very good example of this. Dawit or David is one of a race of immortal vampire men who live underground in Africa. Although he has had a loving relationship with a woman, Jessica, and they have a child, Fana, he cannot live with her as she is neither vampire nor immortal, and his group, the life brothers, behave like racist slave owners. They treat women and white people like a subclass of being and kill them off without compunction, maintaining a certain sense of moral superiority as they do so. Their underlying myth is intermixed with Christianity since David/Dawit's Immortal Brothers were chosen by their leader and spiritual adviser Kaldun to receive the 'Living Blood', originally stolen from Christ upon the cross.

Jessica Wolde brings Fana to meet her father because she knows the child must learn to manage her own hybridity, not merely because David and the life brothers must take responsibility for one who is partly their own, but also because her powers will grow to such strength that she needs the controls of moral choice, curtailment and decision-making, which are only possible from the wiser of the brothers. Kaldun, known to Fana as 'The Man', appears in visions guiding her to make moral choices, since with her great powers she could be a force either for good or destructive evil. She is certainly random, careless and easily causes harm. A familiar, rewritten version of a blood and ethnicity-related elitism in *The Living Blood* and the 'African Immortals' series indicates that such exclusive elitism can only lead to selfishness, disaster and the end of the race. Jessica, wife of David/Dawit, was herself made an immortal through a process by which David shared the Living Blood. The novel, Due acknowledges, springs from her management of her own fears; it is 'a lesson on overcoming loss' (http://maxinethompson.com/Tananarive.html, p. 2). What seems initially to be a vampire tale because of the eternal life-giving properties of 'the Blood' develops into a religious, mystical saga.

Elsewhere, in an essay considering Due, Hopkinson and other African American/Caribbean women writers of vampire fictions I note that, 'The novel questions gender inequalities and the oppressive power of withholding knowledge—the ritual history, myth and above all the blood of the immortal life brothers. It also concerns the duty of care we all have to the next generation' (Wisker 2005, p. 86). Due's reversal of power is based on gender and ethnicity and the value of family and moving forward. It also celebrates recognition of the creative value of ethnic and religious diversity, which might be called a version of cosmopolitanism (Bhabha 2002) as, at the end of the novel, above ground, a new settlement is formed where great international thinkers come together to seek positive ways forward for the diverse, hybrid civilisation which is in a state of becoming.

'It takes a village to raise a child, Jessica thought suddenly, remembering the African proverb that was one of her favourites. Fana needed everyone she could get' (Due 2001, p. 324). This is Gothic speculative fiction, and fiction about community, harmony and celebration of difference.

NEIGHBORHOOD VAMPIRE GOTHIC

Buffy the Vampire Slayer (1997–2003, WP and UPN), the TV series written by Joss Whedon, took vampires into high school, then college, and mixed homework and supper time demands with those of defeating the vampire hordes by staking them. Buffy maintained romantic connections with Angel and Spike while combating whatever was appearing from the Hellmouth over which the school was built. Contemporary women's vampire Gothic focuses on relationships and neighbourhood values, and, as is the case with Buffy, how to get along with some rather diverse neighbours. Vampire romantic love offers the potential for eternal and undying love, domestic security, family values with grandmothers and siblings, and stability. But at the same time, these values are undermined, and, in the Sookie Stackhouse novels and *True Blood* TV series, grandmothers can be murdered by unexpected paranormal visitors, while romance with vampires who live forever offers a series of undying yet changing relationships, involving investment and inheritance.

Charlaine Harris' Sookie Stackhouse novels, the first of which is *Dead Until Dark* (2001), update Southern Gothic with vampires, shape-shifting, romance, family values, community, neighbourhood, and a regular neighbourhood-based soap, with crime. The novel series was turned into a TV series *True Blood* (2008–2014, HBO) which, like other TV series and home town-based soaps, brought the characters' lives into our living rooms, making their vampire-nuanced themes and complications of failed relationships, neighbourly quarrels and problematic family histories both unfamiliar (because vampire-themed) and yet familiar. Bon Temps is a small town with diners, local history groups focusing on the civil war, relationships, trailer parks, bars (Melots), spite, a lot of memories and some strange goings on. Sookie's job in the diner as a waitress in a small town means she overhears a lot, a problem for someone with what she terms a disability, an ability to read minds. In a small town anything slightly different could be considered a disability but Sookie is also unusual, an outsider, and her gift/disability both enables her to hear plots of attacks on her or her friends, and to reveal men's intentions. This is difficult to manage, since much of what she hears is inchoate and overladen sound with sound, unformed thoughts falling over each other. Her parents are dead; her brother is suspected in the murder of two local girls who seem to have been fang bangers, as bites on their legs show. Fang bangers are mortals who have relationships with the local vampires, who comprise large numbers of the everyday population of Bon Temps, along with other shape-shifters, and the gay Black cook, Lafayette, who has his share of relationships with the variety of different characters in Bon Temps. Sookie's boss, Sam, has designs upon her but she is a restrained, modest person because of her telepathic intrusions, somewhat resigned to a dull life, until the arrival of 'her' vampire, Bill Compton, who lived through the civil war, in which he lost his wife and family. Bill resettles back into his old Louisiana estate home, lecturing on the civil war. Vampires in Bon Temps have a virus, which keeps them out of the light, so they use the power of Glamour to overwhelm the minds of others, persuade people to do what they want, and erase any unwanted memories or doubts about them. Because of their ability to Glamour those they wish to manipulate or on whom they might prey, vampires are attractive to many humans. The series both normalises and explains vampires without losing the thrill of the outsider and the threat which small town ways present to anything or anyone representing difference. While some residents adapt and welcome these different beings so that bars serve them fake blood and they intermix relatively easily, nonetheless there are many humans who hate them, just as some people are alarmed by and hate any kind of difference, however that might be constituted. In relation to these varying responses, we can see this is a series which deals with difference, ethnicity, vampirism, sexuality and disability, each seen as fascinating but as a threat to some form of normativity, a threat leading to violence from the uneasy majority who find it difficult to admit that their similarities are greater than their differences and their histories have been intertwined for centuries. Harris engages with the issues of Othering, abjection and the construction of strangers (Kristeva 1988) and the variability and narrative nature of tolerance. While this is like a soap in that we find out about relationships, families, histories, lives and deaths, there is rather more violence than in *East Enders* or *Coronation Street*, and the antisocial habits of the locals can be more threatening and deadly, involving staking and ex-sanguination. There are trailer and house fires, mob violence and reprisals, and the love interest is various given the shape-shifting. Sookie avoids Sam, but when she finds out he is a shape-shifter she is relieved, somewhat ironically stating that 'I felt I had truly connected with another human' (Harris 2001, p. 94). Her relationship with Bill is extraordinary, however, since looking into his mind 'was like being plunged into a pit of snakes, cold snakes, lethal snakes' (p. 225). This is a soap opera with values, disputes, crimes to uncover and a general desire to live and let live, enabling difference and neighbourliness to triumph. However, the tolerance is stretched because of the difficulties of living alongside vampires and the more violent vampiric others who enter the town. Charlaine Harris' work concerns love, family values, inheritance, stability and coping with diversity, and it focuses on the everyday, even on dress codes, so on one occasion, about to go out and socialise with vampires, Sookie remarks:

> I had no idea what constituted appropriate dress for visiting a vampire bar. (p. 110)

THE EDGES OF ENGLAND: SEASIDE TOWNS AND VAMPIRE SISTERHOOD: MOIRA BUFFINI'S *A VAMPIRE STORY* (2008) AND *BYZANTIUM* (2013)

The best vampires are companions. (Auerbach 1995, p. vii)

After *Twilight* there had to be a revival of the vampire who questions social conventions and complacencies, rather than reinforces many of them. Moira Buffini provides this, and gives us vampires who are outsiders, vulnerable, homeless and struggling to survive. Buffini's main vampires are two women, mother and daughter, playing sisters, who appear first in *A Vampire Story* (2008), a play for young adults, then the script of the Neil Jordan directed film, *Byzantium* (2013). The latter is set in Hastings, an arty, but run-down seaside town which has bohemians mixing with foreign students and refugees, and a faded grandeur about its seaside buildings, a kind of less opulent version of its sisters Eastbourne and Brighton. Both play and film explore what it might be like to be women without economic stability or a home, in two time frames, pre-nineteenth century through the nineteenth century, and the twenty-first century, often in the same geographical location (much changed). While they are clearly abused, silenced and powerless in the earlier period, the natural entrepreneurial abilities which saved them hundreds of years ago enable the mother and daughter vampires in the contemporary world, since at least for a while various social loopholes let Ella go to college and Clara to operate a successful seaside brothel.

A Vampire Story is based in a nameless twenty-first-century run-down British town where two sisters (or rather, mother and daughter) who have different names in different centuries—Eleanor/Ella and Claire/Clara—have decided to settle briefly, since theirs is a transient life. We first meet them in a railway compartment deciding where to go. On the side of the stage throughout is Eleanor, who wrote the play which spans both periods of the nineteenth century and twenty-first century. The characters Clara (nineteenth century) and Claire (twenty-first century) are sometimes on stage together and sometimes apart but are essentially the same person in the same way as Ella (nineteenth century) and Eleanor (twenty-first century) are also the same person. Eleanor has to go to school since, like Claudia in Anne Rice's novel and Neil Jordan's first vampire film, *Interview with a Vampire*, and also Edward in *Twilight*, she never ages, she is always 16. Unsurprisingly, it is very difficult to be socially accepted as a real vampire and the weight of the British social services and education system closes around the sisters/mother and daughter when the pressures of disclosure mixed with teenage revolt lead Eleanor to inadvertently let this slip. On entering a drama class, her admission that she is a vampire is treated as a psychological and social problem, both part of her 'hilarious sense of fun' and a kind of acting out because of her other traumatic history. However, eventually she does drink pig's blood in the food technology class, to everyone's disgust.

Eleanor is friends with Frank Stein (an allusion to Frankenstein), whose parents cosset him and have him home schooled. He is rebellious, also an outsider, and they get on well, but his plan to escape and protest for a variety of causes while living in a tent in London are scotched by Claire, Eleanor's sister/mother. The scenes of the school and the play alternate with the nineteenth-century scenes of Ella in an orphanage in bed with two other girls, and scenes in the nineteenth-century whorehouse, where her mother meets Ruthven (named after Polidori's Lord Ruthven), who tells her a tale which saves her, but fails to save him. In the nineteenth-century time span, Clara goes to a cave in a lofty mountain, rises from a grave, becomes a vampire, and therefore does not die of either syphilis or tuberculosis. In one sense, she takes eternal revenge on men, but mainly in the twenty-first century we find her just working behind a bar, occasionally removing the odd abusive or dangerous man. The situation deteriorates when one of the students, Briggs, goes missing and another man wants to go off with Eleanor. Claire has to step in to rescue them both from prying eyes.

The play ends with Eleanor being congratulated for writing a play. It is a complex interweaving of two sets of characters and time frames, allowing leakage between their past and present, always on the outskirts of life, always vulnerable. Their only strength is their vampire curse, which in the end gives them a strange way of fighting back. But they always have to move on because even when one tells the whole truth, they are, of course, never believed.

Transferred to film, the tale is racier, more obviously about vampires and more engaged with the mythic, although there are new versions of the mythic at work. Neil Jordan's film of Moira Buffini's script captures the seediness of their transient existence in poorly furnished tower block flats, one night in a field, then a run-down hotel which is owned by the bereaved son of a recently deceased mother, a hotel which Claire turns into a brothel reminiscent of the brothel in which she lived and worked 200 years ago. Eleanor writes her story, rips up the pages and throws them to the wind, but this brings in an old man who recognises her as able to save him from the pains of his life. In a seaside town for the retired elderly and the sick, each taking some last benefit from the sun and sea (or hoping to), there are many people who are happy recipients of Eleanor's ministrations. An angel, a deliverer, Eleanor only kills when elderly people see her as a way of relief, a way out. In a society where death is to be avoided at all costs, Eleanor the teenage vampire suddenly has a social purpose. She can relieve the pain of unwanted longevity. Meanwhile Clara/Claire cleans up in Hastings by removing pimps and those who abuse their positions of power. She extends this to a further education teacher who intends to bring in the police and social services when he reads the tale Eleanor wrote for a class assignment, the truth about who 'I am'.

The women's story is portrayed in two time frames, and gender and economic abuse are at its core. Historically, they suffered because of their gender and poverty which make them vulnerable victims to abusive men. Clara is very entrepreneurial. Removed from clam picking to the whorehouse by an unscrupulous Captain, Clara kept her daughter Ella alive against the rules and whored to enable her to grow up in a fee-paying orphanage. She takes the abusive Captain's place, travelling to a cave on a distant island shore, joining the bats and being visited by a Soucriant and turned, so gaining eternal life as a vampire, at which point the waterfall over the island's rocks runs red. The Captain takes revenge upon her, infecting her daughter Ella, whom Clara turns in order to rescue her from the pox. Their lives 200 years ago are retold/replayed to explain why they live on the run, how their initial position as victims was transformed by their own energies so that they could either live a peaceful life, or take appropriate revenge. What the film emphasises is the immense inequality between men and women. Not only do human men abuse them, and the powers of the social services hound them as they do not fit in, but there are worse problems. There are guardians of vampire lore chasing them, men in black. The patriarchal clan of vampires refuse any recognition of women, and seek these two women out in Hastings in the modern day. Eleanor meanwhile befriends a young writer with leukaemia, and the final sequence has her rescuing him through turning him into a vampire in the cave on the island. Since he has a disease of the blood and is dying, this is a celebratory and just ending. We have two sets of vampire pairs walking off into the future together, a romantic ending of sorts, so that *Byzantium* confirms many of the tropes of eternal love. However, it is also a feminist film and interpretation. This is a modern vampire tale of gender and power, it exposes inequalities over two hundred years and emphasises the driving force of Claire/Clara's determination to keep herself and her daughter Eleanor/Ella safe and alive through moving on. *Byzantium* combines vampire romance with maternal love, and a strong woman who revalues and alters the victim role of abused prostitute into one of power, economic independence and occasional necessary justice, in order to do more than just survive, but gain and maintain individual and economic power. The tale ends with the sisters/mother/daughter and partners surviving and moving on, so it is both traditional and, in its enabling of women's sexual and economic power, also radical. In the next section we see how Ana Lily Amirpour's film (she is both author and director), shot in black and white and using Farsi dialogue, similarly overturns the social tradition of women's vulnerability, putting in its place the vampire's managed predatory violence.

Ana Lily Amirpour, *A Girl Walks Home Alone at Night* (2013)

Women might seem vulnerable, on the streets, at night, and in many social contexts walking the streets, even to get home safely, is itself seen as 'asking for trouble'. We are reminded of Lisa Tuttle's comments in *Skin of the Soul* (1990) that locations are differently dangerous for men and for women, place and space experienced as variously safe or not. Shot in black and white (actually in a rather derelict US suburb, standing for Iran) and set in Iran, Amirpour's film challenges such limitations and curtailments with a female vampire, wearing a Chadur (like an Iranian abayah) fearlessly skateboarding through the streets, who becomes embroiled in a little love interest, and acts as a small-scale social avenger rather than a victim. She might be quite diminutive but shots of her walking parallel to those she intends to punish and drain are terrifying because of her ability to shift between her culturally constructed, seeming vulnerable innocence and actual managed savagery.

The film has an eternally youthful energy in the blackened, run down, industrial wasteland where the industrial cranes against the flat roofs of the town splice and score the sky and turn the night into something dangerous, at least for those who do wrong, or do wrong to the central character.

Conclusion

The more energetic and deviant energies, the S&M vampires, the radical feminist warrior vampires, and Poppy Z. Brite's disaffected youth fundamentally challenged conventional behaviours and complacencies in the twentieth century. Some of these energies remain in other vampire narratives and films including *The Vampire Diaries* (Smith 1991) and *Vampyre Nation* (2012). Nonetheless, the vampire has been mainstreamed and some of the energies used earlier to critique the conventional are now, in YA fiction in particular, also used to reinforce it. Cultural unease is rife in Charlaine Harris' novels, and neighbourliness preserved at a cost, but the plotlines also resemble those of soaps, with fangs. Twenty-first-century vampires are our neighbours, they live amongst us and offer the opportunity to critique or reinforce certain beliefs about conformity, education, romance, families, sisterhood and neighbourliness.

Moira Buffini's vampires represent a new turn, however. Patriarchal violence is experienced by Anne Rice's Madeline and Claudia, who are burned up in the sun, victims of the exclusive rules of an age-old male vampire history and refusal of new vampires, and by mortal women in Tananarive Due's 'African Immortals' series. For Moira Buffini's vampires, the mother and daughter posing as sisters tracked down to Hastings in the film *Byzantium*, and another small town in *A Vampire Story* (2008), a kind of border control conservatism is replayed through the patriarchal forces which left each abused and brutalised, thrown into prostitution, then punished when they showed individual energy and agency, and became vampires. However, they have the last word. They escape; they are resilient, devious and entrepreneurial even when faced with the stranglehold of the neoliberalism and remnants of the welfare state. They survive. With Buffini's women, as with Ana Lily Amirpour's Iranian skateboarding night stalker, vampires are again edgy, radical and free, critiquing complacencies and oppressive behaviours which differ with time, place and culture.

Bibliography

Auerbach, N. (1995) *Our Vampires, Ourselves* (Chicago: University of Chicago Press).
Bhabha, H. (2002) in *Cosmopolitanism*, C.A. Breckenridge, S. Pollock, H.K. Bhabha, and D. Chakrabarty (eds.) (Durham, NC: Duke University Press).
Breckenridge, C.A., S. Pollock, H.K. Bhabha, and D. Chakrabarty (eds.) *Cosmopolitanism* (Durham, NC: Duke University Press).
Brite, P. Z. (1995) *Love in Vein* (New York: Harper Voyager).
Buffini, M. (2008) *A Vampire Story* (London: Faber and Faber).
Carter, M. L. (2010) 'Vampire Romance', in *Encyclopedia of the Vampire: The Living Dead in Myth, Legend and Popular Culture*, S. T. Joshi (ed.) (Westport, CT: Greenwood Press).
Due, T. (2001) *The Living Blood* (New York: Washington Square Press).
Gottlieb, S. (1994) *Love Bite* (New York: Warner).

Grossman, L. (2009) 'It's Twilight in America: The Vampire Saga', *Time Magazine*, 23 November.
Grossman, M. (2008) 'What Girls Want: An Edward Cullen to Love Them', Clare Boothe Luce Policy Institute, 12 August.
Kristeva, J. (1988)*Strangers to Ourselves* (New York: Columbia University Press).
Memmott, C. (2008) '"Twilight" Author Stephenie Meyer Unfazed as Fame Dawns', *USA Today*, 30 July, p. D1.
Punter, D. (2000a) *A Companion to the Gothic* (2nd edn.) (Oxford: Blackwell).
Silver, A. (2010) 'Twilight is Not Good for Maidens: Gender, Sexuality, and the Family in Stephenie Meyer's Twilight Series', *Studies in the Novel*, Vol. 42.
Smith, L. J. (1991) *The Vampire Diaries: The Awakening* (New York: Harper).
Wisker, G. (2000) 'Love Bites', in *A Companion to the Gothic*, D. Punter (ed.) (Oxford: Blackwell).
Wisker, G. (2005) '"Your Buried Ghosts Have A Way of Tripping You Up": Revisioning and Mothering in African American and Afro-Caribbean Womens Speculative Horror', *Femspec*, Vol. 6, Issue 1.
Wisker, G. (2012) 'Love Bites: Contemporary Women's Vampire Fictions', in A New Companion to the Gothic (2nd edn.), D. Punter (ed.) (Oxford: Blackwell).
Wisker, G. (2014) 'Contemporary Women's Gothic: From *Lost Souls* to *Twilight*', in *A Companion to the American Gothic*, C. L. Crow (ed.) (Chichester: Wiley-Blackwell).

CHAPTER 9

Ghostings and Hauntings: Splintering the Fabric of Domestic Gothic

Susan Hill's revival of the British ghost story, *The Woman in Black* (1983), suddenly reawoke many readers to the power of the Gothic through the ghost story to reveal the horrible secrets of the past and their deadly legacy in the present. At the same time, Angela Carter, Margaret Atwood, Fay Weldon, Emma Tennant, Michele Roberts, Sara Maitland and Joyce Carol Oates, among others, were revitalising the Gothic and fleshing it out with the nuances of a gendered perspective, revealing from women's and feminist perspectives the oppressive representations of women's lives in popular narratives, as well as their perpetuation in traditional, established Gothic texts. They were all breaking silences, speaking from the shadows and revealing some of the contradictions and everyday horrors of families, domestic situations, romance and relationships. Ghost stories are a well-established vehicle for such revelations and reinterpretations.

As Avery Gordon reminds us, 'To write stories concerning exclusions and invisibilities … is to write ghost stories' (Gordon 1997, p. 17). A major role of the ghost is to reveal what lies beneath, revisit what has been neatly hidden away in both present situations and tales of the past. The figure of the ghost puts spectral flesh on those hidden, repressed stories, versions, perspectives and lives, inviting us to look again and understand differently. This is not always a friendly invitation, and although revenants are frequently familiar figures, their familiarity can be unsettling; their anger at previous silencing and marginalising is as likely to return through the settling of old scores, or specific revenge, as it is in rewriting misleading or silenced narratives. Essentially, contemporary women's ghost stories are also rich examples of domestic Gothic, in which the promise and security of the home, hearth and family are revealed as oppressive nightmare. Edgar Allen Poe's 'The Fall of the House of Usher' (1839) is a model here, where the house seems demonic, the family and its heritage cursed, crumbling. In contemporary women's domestic Gothic ghost stories, the complex histories of troubled families, the incarceration of the domestic space and domestic roles are expressed and enacted in uncanny returns, in homes which explode or implode. Destructive family scenarios, relationships, children and loved ones are deadly, and succour and nurturance are replaced by a kind of social cannibalism.

This chapter focuses on twentieth and twenty-first-century women's ghost stories, briefly exploring characteristics inherited from the traditional women's ghost story and examining how contemporary writers have rediscovered, replayed and reframed the ghostly spectral presence, the haunted past, and to what ends. Disinterring these characteristics, these traces, is essential or everything seems new, when in fact it is itself a revenant, returning to focus on new or occluded issues. It is important to set the context and see how contemporary writers reconsider nineteenth and twentieth-century histories, so I do so by looking at hidden histories explored through ghostings in the work of a range of women writers, particularly focusing on Susan Hill's *The Woman in Black* and *The Small Hand* (2010), Kate Mosse's *The Winter Ghosts* (2010), Sarah Waters' *The Little Stranger* (2009), and Helen Dunmore's *The Greatcoat* (2012), and, in passing, other ghost stories or spectral presences used for a variety of purposes are mentioned here and in the final chapter, including Audrey Niffenegger's *Her Fearful Symmetry* (2009) and Sara Maitland's *Three Times Table* (1991). In the contemporary period, women's ghost stories can be used to dig up hidden histories and reveal oppression and silencing, expose domestic bliss and family values as performance and construction, and indict oppressive narratives, through rewriting the past and its constraining versions of gendered roles for women.

Julia Briggs (2012) was the first of the feminist critics to really explore the roles of women's ghost stories. In the early days of the late twentieth-century Gothic revival, she recuperated and emphasised their importance as ways of reading the hidden lives of women in periods where they had no property, had little education, and were expected to marry and be silent, or just be silent, marginalised because they are unmarried. Briggs is clear about the ways in which ghost stories intersect with, and grow from, the Gothic. Their ambivalence is one of their most effective characteristics, luring the reader into a liminal space of uncertainty, offering an 'ambivalence or tension', 'between certainty and doubt, between the familiar and the feared, between rational occurrence and the inexplicable' (Briggs 2012, pp. 176). Part of the fascination with the ghost is its role as the returned, revenant, reminder of unfinished business, and another its liminal state, neither living nor dead, its story not closed down, as it seeks revenge, completion and rest. Hélène Cixous (1976) emphasises this fascination:

> What is intolerable is that the Ghost erases the limit which exists between states, neither alive nor dead.

Ghosts appear alive, but are not; they belong to the past, but reappear in the present, and remind us that the neatness of binary distinctions between alive and dead, good and bad, male and female, dark and light, are often tenuous impositions on history and lived experience. This is also a characteristic which disturbs our logical hold on interpretations of events, and the comfort of imposed securities, a feature common to the Gothic. Ghost stories also evidence the importance of the supernatural as a way of expressing the insights offered by the imagination.

Many Gothic tales use the trappings of dungeons, corridors, castles, monks and damsels in distress. Ultimately, wrong can be righted and though frequently used, the supernatural is not always an essential item. However, in ghost stories, the explanation for returns, distress, dispossession and disturbance is ultimately always supernatural. The ghost represents returned memories and reminders, there is a spectral presence; something otherworldly alerts the protagonist, characters and readers to unfinished business, murder, hidden secrets, loss and silencing. The source of this is most often supernatural rather than realistic and everyday, though some of the greatest effects are achieved because the supernatural enters the realistic everyday, taps on windows, upsets your kitchen, sits down and has a cup of coffee or a goblet of wine, calls your name. Briggs says: 'the supernatural events remain unexplained' (2012, p. 177). We take the supernatural as actual, our initial sense of defamiliarisation enacted in front of us by the protagonist, then confirmed as actual because of their responses, but the answers, the living skeleton, the disinterred airman, the walled-up ancestor are presented as logical explanations. A supernatural discovery such as a hidden murder or secret is offered as the solution to the problem; however, this ostensibly logical proof, this closure, is something supernatural. The disturbance in Dunmore's *The Greatcoat* is a circular return of a dead airman, lover of the protagonist, Isobel's landlady, who fathers Isobel's child. Nicely explained, the offering of resolution is one which leaves a particular kind of unease. You accept the supernatural as logical and rational in the narrative; however, 'The ghost story's "explanations" do not operate to rationalise or demystify the supernatural events, but rather to set them outside a kind of imaginative logic' (Briggs 2012, p. 178). Cause and effect are suspended and Freud's 'animalistic' ways of thinking (Briggs 2012, p. 178) operate: we believe in this because we are locked in the story, told usually by someone dependable (also fictional) and layers of the certification of the events somehow are meant to reassure us they're verifiable, rather like the instances of witness statements or references for plumbers. We rely on the veracity of the evidence offered by others, building on their reputation where evidence is in place, and in this case, the others and their evidence are all part of a fiction anyway.

Talking of American texts, Jeffrey Weinstock links ghost stories with our desire to rediscover truths, as well as to confirm the notion of an afterlife, which can be comforting (or not, depending on what kind of an afterlife):

> It needs to be acknowledged that our ghosts are also comforting to us. They represent our desires for truth and justice (not to mention the American way) and validate religious faith and the ideas of heaven and hell. They speak to our desire to be remembered and to our longings for a coherent and 'correct' narrative of history. (Weinstock 2004, p. 6)

Their role in rebalancing cultural historical and personal histories is important:

> We value our ghosts, particularly in moments of cultural transition, because the alternative to their presence is even more frightening: if ghosts do not return to correct history, then privileged narratives of history are not open to contestation. If ghosts do not return to reveal crimes that have gone unpunished, the evil acts may in fact go unredressed. If ghosts do not appear to validate faith then faith remains just that. (Weinstock 2004, p. 6)

Traditionally, the form of the ghost story has been one popular with women writers, perhaps because of the histories of hidden and silenced lives, the denials and the guilt, the repressions and the marginalisation, the domestic incarceration and the lack and loss of identity and power which have accompanied the roles of women, differently played out in different times and places. Ghost stories allow the repressed, hidden histories to be seen and heard, and the incarcerated to break out. The walls of the Gothic enclosures of castles, mansions and everyday homes are cracked and undermined; fear and oppression exposed. Many women's ghost stories from the nineteenth century speak to the late twentieth century and today: a revival.

Women's ghost stories offer the opportunity for the obliterated to reappear like the SSsss (shhhh) writing on the wall in Sarah Waters' *The Little Stranger* (2009), and the long dead Cathar community who reappear to enable the visitor, Freddie, to help their story be found, their bodies discovered, in Kate Mosse's *The Winter Ghosts* (2010). Traditional Gothic ghost stories by women often focused on entrapment, being walled in, hidden in castles, or physical danger, such as being threatened by ghost dogs, by revengeful predecessors and demon lovers. Contemporary women's ghost stories recover the past and offer the opportunity to speak to those silenced by history, some of whom are representative of the ways in which societies outcast people who do not or cannot conform. The nineteenth century is riddled with tales of fallen women sent away and never spoken of for bringing shame on the family, mad women in attics, colonial women deemed mad (Charlotte Brontë's *Jane Eyre*, 1847), inheriting madness as a result of colonial intrusion, and women locked up, murdered and put away so others can steal their fortunes (Wilkie Collins, *The Woman in White*, 1859).

Daphne du Maurier's *Rebecca* (1938) is a missing link in the early to middle twentieth century when the Gothic was somewhat discredited and silent. *Rebecca* does not have an actual ghost but instead a constant haunting presence, reminding the second, nameless wife of what she believes to be her secondary position in the home and heart of Max de Winter, the charismatic, wealthy, romantic hero with a hidden secret: the (semi-accidental) murder of his wife, Rebecca, who was unfaithful and transgressive. The scenario in which the second Mrs de Winter finds herself once they are married, as lady of the grand house Manderley, is one in which she feels always out of place, oppressed by Rebecca's lingering presence. Secrets, betrayal and guilt haunt the house and her but she can only (mis) read the signs as evidence of her inability to live up to Rebecca's energy and presence. Du Maurier's novel undercuts narratives of romance as the ultimate reward for women, even as it simultaneously disturbs and destroys the notion of the solid dependability of wealth, heredity and inheritance expressed in the English country house as a sign for the stability of English identity, economy and politics (Wisker 2003b; Horner and Zlosnik 1998), values disturbed but reinstated in Emily Brontë's *Wuthering Heights* (1847). It does this through using many of the strategies of the ghost story, places that are out of bounds, traces through writing pictures and stories, the revelation of a death, but without the supernatural presence. Séances revealed the past in the late nineteenth/early twentieth century, and figure in Sarah Maitland's *Three Times Table* (1991). Here women's lives in three time periods layer over each other and a nineteenth-century medium, Flora, parallels and ghosts the life of her twentieth-century counterpart.

Neo-Victorianism, a popular, recently developed genre, can enable novelists to bring hidden histories to life through fictions which have no hauntings, as we find in Sarah Waters' *Fingersmith* (2002) (see Chap. 10), *Tipping the Velvet* (1998) and *Affinity* (1999), which concerns a false medium, for example. These texts too can be seen to rewrite versions of previous narratives, and are laced with silent, hidden histories, and so are, to some extent, inevitably ghost stories. A kind of ghosting without a ghost is also a way of expressing the situation and experience of those whose lives have been hidden, invisible. Lesbian histories are explored by Sarah Waters in her own neo-Victorian texts, and in terms of critical writing, both Paulina Palmer in *Lesbian Gothic* (1999) and Terry Castle in *The Apparitional Lesbian* (1995) find in fiction images of the spectral to reinvigorate and reveal lesbian history. David Punter emphasises that postcolonial contexts and postcolonial texts inevitably express the ghostings of versions of the past which have been largely unexpressed but which are all around us, in a form of cultural haunting (Punter 2000b, chaps. 5 and 6). Toni Morrison's *Beloved* (1987) (see Chap. 4 in the present volume) uses cultural haunting, the legacy of a history of pain and silencing written onto the homes, bodies and landscapes, and a ghost, Beloved. The ghost represents the hidden torturous legacy of slavery written on the body of Sethe, whose back is covered with a tree of life cut from the slave owner's brutal whipping. The daughter she sacrifices to save the family from slavery returns full grown to haunt, dominate and impress upon her, the community and readers how revenants and the past must be come to terms with, so that those in the present have some chance of moving on.

Domestic entombment and entrapment in romantic fictions are common scenarios in contemporary women's ghost stories when they deal with the condition and lives of women, replaying issues of constrained lives, confined spaces, domestic enclosure and silenced histories. Women's ghost stories tend to deal with issues of identity, incarceration, conformity, patriarchal norms, family history and the ways in which one can perceive, deal with and move on from the utterly limiting versions of lives in societies which offer freedom, financial and social, mainly to men and then to married women. Conforming is a bigger threat even than patriarchy, since women and men collude to ensure compliance both in the way of behaviour and of interrelations of work and identity. In women's Gothic the social constructions of ideal shape, identity, self-worth and achievement are also questioned by ghostly returns and domestic turbulences.

Some of the strategies in contemporary women's ghost stories replay and revisit those we find in earlier works, but they also revisit past moments and reinterpret them, placing silenced, absent, ghosted figures at their centre: the domestic prisoner, the women left behind, the women whose lives strain to change but cannot, given social norms. These figures include those long ago who were outsiders, unmarried mothers, or members of groups who suffered genocide (such as the Cathars in Mosse's trilogy and *The Winter Ghosts*). Women writers recover and rewrite the experiences of other women in previous periods when their stories were left untold. Contemporary women's ghost stories scrutinise women's current situations, focusing on women incarcerated in domestic roles, between the wars, after the Second World War, their lives constrained by the power of popular narratives limiting aspirations to family and domesticity, linking these to femininity and 'proper', secondary, supportive roles for women. And they look at romantic narratives, showing them to be dreams which turn into recurring nightmares, as in Helen Dunmore's *The Greatcoat*.

Mark Jancovich emphasises the everyday domestic quality of horror, which we also see in women's ghost stories:

> Throughout its history, horror has been concerned with forces that threaten individuals, groups, or even 'life as we know it'. It has been concerned with the workings of power and repression in relationship to the body, the personality, or to social life in general. (Jancovich 1992, p. 118)

Alfred Hitchcock (1996) also suggests that we should 'put horror back where it belongs, in the family'). What is hidden and suppressed in what is familiar is most horrifying. Gothic horror is domestic, whether in ghost stories or more generally, because Gothic undermines the complacencies of the deceptively cosy familiar. The ghost story is a branch of Gothic horror, and much of this is both domestic and focused, as is so much women's writing, on the body, the community, the space and places where we live, and the conventional narratives we tell ourselves in order to remain comfortable. Like subversive Gothic horror which is spatialised and quite literally looks beneath the surface, into the cracks, below the floorboards, up in the attic, and in the corners, often threatening or enacting violence, the Gothic ghost story opens the door to expose that of which we are afraid, that which is hidden, the door to a hidden room we would rather ignore. As Stephen King insists: 'The good horror tale will dance its way to the center of your life and find the secret door to the room you believed no one but you knew of' (King 1981, p. 149).

Susan Hill reveals silenced histories, figures lost in stories or paintings which trap them (*The Man in the Picture*, 2007), and hidden abuse (*The Mist in the Mirror*, 1992). Her Gothic invades our view of Englishness and her ghost stories prevent any comfort.

The Woman in Black (1983)—Susan Hill

Susan Hill is well known as an accomplished author of contemporary ghost stories: *The Woman in Black*, *The Mist in the Mirror*, several short stories, and also of crime fictions. Both her tales of the strange living and the dead impinging on the living depict individual feelings and the confusions of relationships and hidden family secrets. She creates social microcosms with delicacy and a sense of threat, of vulnerability.

In *The Woman in Black* Hill explores social and family cruelties which lead to a curse, the death of children. The woman in black wreaks deadly revenge on a society whose short-sighted gendered bigotry separated her from her own child, who died in a tragedy, ensuring that all children who come under her gaze are violently, permanently, fatally separated from their own parents. Here the return of the repressed not only haunts but fatally disrupts the lives of those unlucky enough to come into the range and consciousness of the revengeful dead. Hill's most famous novel has a traditional ghost story formula, that of the first-person narration of Arthur Kipps, a solicitor, to authenticate the strange tale which is his own reluctant contribution to a traditional fireside Christmas Eve ghost story session with his second family. The popular Gothic quality of the children's ghost tale is sent up for its excess, which further bolsters the father's tale to come. Kipps first refuses to tell us the tale then succumbs to the compulsion to do so, emphasising the truth of his experience and the very real terror of repeating it to listeners, who might somehow be tainted by what they hear. It is 'a true story, a story of haunting and evil, fear and confusion, horror and tragedy. But it was not a story to be told for casual entertainment, around the fireside upon Christmas Eve' (Hill, 1983, p. 21). Kipps' tale begins in his past, when he was sent to the remote village of Crythin Gifford by the rather dour, and blunt Mr Bentley, head of his small London firm, to sort through the will and papers of a reclusive client, Mrs Drablow. This reminds us of the procrastination and complex configurations of the law ensnaring everyone in Dickens' *Bleak House* (1853), in which inheritance, fog and contagion also play a deadly role, as they do in Hill's novel. Kipps is informed there are no children, no heirs to Eel Marsh House, an isolated estate in a remote part of Lincolnshire, cut off from the mainland daily by the tide, and from society by the behaviour of those in the house. However, when Kipps asks directly if Mrs Drablow had any children, Bentley is very cautious about his answer, rubbing at the window pane as if trying to clear it, and his response, '"According to everything we've been told about Mrs Drablow," he said carefully, "no, there were no children"'(p. 29), makes both the reader and Kipps suspicious. In *Great Expectations* (Dickens 1860), the narrator (Pip in Dickens' narrative) already knows the horrors in the story we will hear, the importance both of the lack of children and of the hesitancy of mentioning their lack. Whilst he is being told, however, young Mr Kipps is as naïve and ignorant as the reader, and probably less suspicious. But outside a bell tolls, yellow fog surrounds the office: there's clearly a mystery. A solicitor's clerk sent to sort things out, he and the systems of order he represents can offer only an ostensible, legal closing down, a tidying of papers, names and property and of the stories of this dysfunctional family.

Kipps heads off on an interminable journey to the Lincolnshire village. He does not find out much more on arrival and meets only hints and whispers of losses in the village, when he attends Mrs Drablow's funeral. However, the village seems somewhat lacking in children, and looking around at the funeral, which takes place next to a school, Kipps notices children silently watching the burial: 'They were all of them quite silent, quite motionless' (p. 51). Since everyone is determined to reveal nothing to this stranger, Kipps cannot begin to imagine what, if any, the connection is between the air of isolation and silence surrounding the family history and the isolated house, and a similar air emanating from the village and the children. Although he receives numerous warnings about going to

Eel Marsh House and staying there, like Stoker's Jonathan Harker, Kipps is a dutiful worker, so he dismisses it all until events take his life over.

The Woman in Black uses many strategies of the conventional ghost story: spectral visits, sounds in the night, empty rooms with the movements of the past continuing beyond the deaths of those who lived there, and an overwhelming, unidentifiable atmosphere of dread. It also reminds us of the narratives of the nineteenth century in which much of the plot is set, the emphasis on inheritance, houses, heredity, propriety. It interlaces references to *Great Expectations* and *Bleak House* both of which deal with the hauntings of the past on the present, damage done to young lives and potential, indicting the destructive effects of nineteenth-century society's contradictory values regarding innocence, wealth and morality. Comparisons between Mrs Drablow's house and Miss Havisham's in *Great Expectations* add to the Gothic, threatening atmosphere and hint at thwarted, misdirected expectations, lies and artifice (though no actual ghosts are present). In Hill's novel we have a ghost story with a dead child and mother. This is also a tale with a feminist message. Unlike most nineteenth-century novels, which often remain silent about fallen women, inappropriate romantic entanglements (unusually central to Elizabeth Gaskell's *Mary Barton*, 1848 and Charles Dickens' *Oliver Twist*, 1837), it immediately focuses on Mrs Drablow's disgraced sister, the young woman Jennet Humfrye, whose child was born out of wedlock, her outsider status as an unmarried mother disenfranchising her and allowing her no identity, no power, no status. Jennet cannot live in the big house and she cannot support her own child. She was first sent away to Scotland, then condemned to wander, her son Nathaniel adopted by her moneyed, isolated sister and brought up out at Eel Marsh House, with all the comforts of a home, but none of the connections to the real world or to his mother. Jennet Humfrye is a product of a bigoted age which banished, silenced and incarcerated unmarried mothers (until at least the 1950s, and more recently in the Republic of Ireland; during Margaret Thatcher's leadership, many such children of working-class mothers, not merely those who were unmarried, were taken into care). The cruelty meted out to such powerless women was one characteristic of a patriarchal society which rewarded those willing and able to conform. The fate of Jennet and her son are an indictment against the cruel, destructive behaviour of the age. She experiences personal sacrifice to support the survival of her child, but her sister rations her access and, in the end, Jennet's isolation and marginalisation disempowers, silences and maddens her.

Isolation is spatially represented by the landline, the narrow spit which links and divides the house, and its wealth, from the village. Similarly, it divides life and death. When the pony and trap carrying the boy and his nursemaid cross the spit to Eel Marsh House they are engulfed in the mist, miss their footing, and fall to their deaths in the water, drowned by the mud and the rising tide. Jennet loses everything, goes mad and dies. But she returns and wanders as a ghost, haunting the area, particularly the graveyard, emphasising the liminal space between acceptability and her marginal status, life and death. Jennet is not just the ghost of a mother who lost her son, but also represents haunting repercussions of the cruelties of an unjust society. This is specific revenge for a widespread evil in the name of conformity and social order. A society which condemned women to the status of outsider considers her better off dead, and Jennet's haunting is a response to the Otherising, silencing and early deaths of thousands of women whose worth as living human beings was denied because they didn't fit society's formulae and norms. However, her revenge is taken not merely on Mrs Drablow, the sister who raised but kept her from her child, but ranges widely over anyone who has children and so who fits the norms of family structures of the time. The woman in black, Jennet, is seen haunting the graveyard and the village, and the children begin to die, one by one.

On his first visit to Eel Marsh House, across the marshes, Kipps is somewhat traumatised. Amidst the entrapping mist, repetitive ghostly returns, the isolated house with its secrets taken to death, he hears the terrifying sound of a pony and trap crashing and the crying of a child:

> Baffled, I stood and waited, straining to listen through the mist. What I heard next chilled and horrified me, even though I could neither understand nor account for it. The noise of the pony trap grew fainter and then stopped abruptly and away on the marsh was a curious draining, sucking, churning sound, which went on, together with the shrill neighing and whinnying of a horse in panic, and then I heard another cry, a shout, a terrified sobbing—it was hard to decipher—but with horror I realised that it came from a child, a young child. I stood absolutely helpless in the mist that clouded me and everything from my sight. (p. 74)

The immediacy of the ghostly horror terrifies and paralyses him, and the cause is only revealed to us latterly, such is the convincing quality of the experience. The young Drablow child Nathaniel and his nurse Rose Judd caught in the mist, drowned in the marshes, were watched helplessly by Jennet Humfrye and are condemned to repeat the deadly accident over and over again, after death. The ghostly presence of the young child never moves beyond the spit, and at night, beyond the nursery, when he cries out in his loneliness. Kipps repeatedly hears both the child's cries and the sounds of the crash and drowning, locked in the moment. But the true haunting is not of little Nathaniel but rather of his wronged mother Jennet. Mullan points out that 'The ghost in *The Woman in Black* is in fact given a kind of voice' (2012). This happens initially because Kipps finds her letters begging to see her son. The house is not merely a reminder of Mrs Drablow's death, which Kipps would be used to as a solicitor, but preserves the presence of the dead child in the empty nursery where there are neat, ordered, unused toys. His sudden sense of empathy, 'a desolation, a grief in my own heart' (p.121), is actually auspicious given his own future loss, caught up in the malevolent revenge cycle of the woman in black, which encompasses any and all children, each a victim to Jennet Humfrye, so their parents can feel her loss as their own.

When Kipps encounters the woman in black first, in the cemetery, what he sees is not only a vision but a threat, hinted at in the description filled with negatives:

> the thinnest layer of flesh was tautly stretched and strained across her bones so that it gleamed with a curious, blue-white sheen, and her eyes seemed sunken back in her head ... Nor did she look old. (p. 49)

She only reveals her ghostly self to those whose life she will haunt and persecute. Later, too late, he recognises her stare as malevolence, a passionate wish to direct her evil at someone, which terrifies him.

Many of the elements of the novel are familiar in ghost stories more generally. Eel Marsh House is isolated; the natural surroundings are deceptive, threatening; the unsettled nature of rules, order and reality are expressed spatially; the misty English marshes make the land and sea, order and safety tenuous, untrustworthy. The spit is safe one moment when the tide is low, the next suddenly treacherous as the tide encroaches, overwhelms and drowns anyone crossing it. The certainties of land and water, sight, sound, life and death are undermined, and in this liminal space the ghostly figure appears and curses all who see her. The tale is fuelled with tension, suspense and characteristic Gothic details of wills and dusty papers, nineteenth-century settings of cobbles, pony and trap, shuttered windows, threatening spaces, an isolated village, a cut-off house haunted by the dead child and the sadness which it contained, a cemetery where the figure in black waits for her next cursed victim, and the sudden deaths of children. *The Woman in Black* rewrites the domestic ghost story, indicting the cruel conformities which condemned Jennet, the spectral *femme fatale*, the outsider status of her and her lost child, dramatised in his drowning, her unending revenge on 'respectable' others. The climactic point is when Kipps' wife and son go for a spin in a pony trap and notice, all too late, the woman in black standing malevolently at one side—the trap crashes, killing his son, and fatally wounding his wife (who dies ten months later). Based in domestic tragedy, Jennet's curse overwhelms helpless parents. They cannot prevent the deaths of their families, and neither can the protagonist, Arthur Kipps.

Wilhelms (2012) considers this novel to be a ghost index of concerns about women's lives, particularly concerning women's social position and threats to families in the time *about* which it was written, the nineteenth century, and the time *in* which it was written, the 1980s. It also speaks to more recent times, because its concerns seem to change alongside our own, so latterly it is also an index of responses to women's position and hidden histories in the times of the adaptations, including the play from 1987 (Mallatratt), the first film in 1989, and then the 2012 film version. Wilhelms notes that: 'As a novel, *The Woman in Black* (1983) both repeats and revises the gothic genre, revealing which themes and concerns were still relevant in 1983. The theatrical adaptation of *The Woman in Black* (1987) by Stephen Mallatratt shows how these motifs and anxieties have evolved from the early 1980s to the late 1980s. Finally, James Watkins' 2012 film adaptation of *The Woman in Black* further emphasises the importance and timelessness of Hill's original subject, the question of what it means to be a good parent' (Wilhelms 2012).

There are also echoes of *The Turn of the Screw* (James 1898), as noted by John Mullan (2012), where he focuses on the special role of children in ghost stories. In Henry James' tale, the girl and boy are vulnerable either because of the evil influence of Peter Quint or perhaps more from the interpretations or misinterpretations of the new governess, whose ability to recognise the truth, though doubted, is given veracity through the formula of the ghost story.

Jennet Humfrye and her child are victims of the bigger story of the time, but her revenge is greater than a single loss: timeless, specific, endlessly terrible, and aimed at every example of a conventional family, at every family with a child.

There are several other ghost stories which focus on dead children and past guilts, such as Susan Hill's *The Small Hand* (2010) and both Sarah Waters' *The Little Stranger* and Helen Dunmore's *The Greatcoat* have ghostly children/the children of ghosts at their heart. Although societal norms further our beliefs that children are innocent and to be cared for, demonic children rage through the films of the 1980s onwards. Damien in *The Omen* (1976) is the most obvious example: son of the devil, he murders his own mother and anyone who tries to resist him; while the teenage girl possessed in *The Exorcist* filled then emptied cinemas in the 1970s (1973), as her head cycled round, green vomit and lewd words spewed from her mouth, and she exhibited demonic possession way beyond the powers of priest or parent, leading to riotous behaviour, violent sexual suggestiveness and self-violation. *The Exorcist* has been seen as demonising the sexuality of adolescent girls, a metaphor, a restraint narrative supporting order and compliance.

POST-WAR GHOSTS: SARAH WATERS, *THE LITTLE STRANGER* (2009) AND HELEN DUNMORE, *THE GREATCOAT* (2012)

The Little Stranger is about conflict and waste. (Waters 2010)

Both Sarah Waters' *The Little Stranger* and Helen Dunmore's *The Greatcoat* are novels born of the losses and stagnations resulting from the end of the Second World War, a transitional moment in the lives of both women and men. For some women, the new-found freedoms of wartime Britain, where they were expected to work outside the home, translated post-war into independence, jobs and their own incomes. However, for many others, the pressure was to wholeheartedly re-embrace a return to the safety and restrictions of home. At such transitional moments, people clamour for some continuity of presence, which can be seen in the form of ghosts, hauntings of what was lost, and a refusal of change. Both *The Little Stranger* and *The Greatcoat* centre on narratives of romance and home, and both also have a child at their centre, one a ghost, the other the child of a ghost. For Waters' Carolyn Ayres (echoing *Jane Eyre*), daughter of the great house, Hundreds Hall, uneasy in her outdated home which rots around her and refuses change, and for Dunmore's Isabel, wife of the local doctor, displaced, settling into a rented house and investing in domestic bliss only to find disruptive passions intervening on her compliant boredom, ghostly returns hold them back, entrap them and refuse their agency. Gothic representations of incarcerating spaces, the oppression of the domestic, indicated in clothing, interiors and domestic behaviours, enact the overwhelming stranglehold of the past, and of narratives which prevent any escape into a new way of being, particularly for the women in each novel.

The opening scene of *The Little Stranger* offers us the setting of a long summer, immaculate lawns, imperial splendour and social hierarchies, through the eyes of the fallible narrator, the aspirational, grammar school educated Dr Faraday:

> I first saw Hundreds Hall when I was ten years old. It was the summer after the war, and the Ayreses still had most of their money then, were still big people in the district. The event was an Empire day fete: I stood with the line of other village children making a Boy Scout salute while Mrs Ayres and the Colonel went past us, handing out commemorative medals; afterwards we sat to tea with our parents at long tables on what I suppose was the south lawn. Mrs Ayres would have been twenty-four or five, her husband a few years older; their little girl, Susan, would have been about six. They must have made a very handsome family, but my memory of them is vague. I recall most vividly the house itself, which struck me as an absolute mansion. I remember its lovely ageing details: the worn red brick, the cockled window glass, the weathered sandstone edgings. They made it look blurred and slightly uncertain—like an ice, I thought, just beginning to melt in the sun. There were no trips inside, of course. (p. 1)

Hundreds Hall at its best is an English country house in the tradition established prior to Jane Austen's Pemberley in *Pride and Prejudice* (1813) and undermined latterly by Kazuo Ishiguro's *Remains of the Day* (1989) and by Julian Fellowes' *Gosford Park* (2001). The sunny days of imperial splendour, the line-up, the indoor and outdoor hierarchies remind Faraday of a past glory which actually would exclude him as son of a servant, while his memory of the theft of a small piece of the fabric of the hall is read as a promise that he will be able to move in eventually. A grammar school boy made good, scientist and doctor, he is drawn back to the house and a need to own the past and the version of Englishness which it represents. The ghost of that past reacts against change, against the threat of usurpation, the council houses, the new build represented in the property developer Baker-Hyde (reminding us of Mr Hyde in Stevenson's novel), and of Faraday possessing Caroline, daughter of the house, the land and the house itself. As Hilary Mantel comments, describing in Gothic terms a decayed past embodied in a decayed house, split selves, hidden secrets, family blights and paralysis:

> Sarah Waters' masterly novel is a perverse hymn to decay, to the corrosive power of class resentment as well as the damage wrought by war. Hundreds Hall is crawling with blights and moulds, crumbling from subsidence and water damage. Beetles knock behind panelling. Weeds force themselves through stone. The window panes are dim and warped; they reflect nothing truly. Its corridors are dark, light spilling unexpectedly from open doors and the great dome above. The psyches of the inhabitants are riddled with ambivalence, holed by self-doubt, worn away by genteel, stifled frustration. They speak the soothing language of upper-class good manners, but all are unable to face their damaged selves, or contemplate their capacity for doing damage in their turn. (Mantel 2009)

Post-war, the return to normality, the beginning of the welfare state, education for all and the NHS enabled many women to find jobs and freedom from domestic roles, not least because many escaped those roles, as marriage was not always an option. Others were seduced by the cult of romance and domesticity perpetuated in fictions and the media, which kept them at home at a point when men returning from war needed to find employment. In the popular media, adverts show adoring females wearing high heels and flared skirts embracing washing machines and fridges, their clothing no longer curtailed by ration books, but also changed into something which would be awkward for work. Many women after the Second World War married and stayed at home, seeking domestic bliss which often turned into domestic incarceration, as characterised in Hannah Gavron's *The Captive Wife* (1966). Some, whose lifestyles had been destroyed by the war and post-war changes, found themselves in a limbo space between old expectations and new possibilities.

Caroline Ayres is someone whose energies are curtailed by her class and her context. Trapped in her class, the family's past and its representation in their decaying home, both Caroline and Mrs Ayres would have found it impossible to develop roles outside the house. Although Caroline is frequently seen working in the grounds and walking the lanes, she is hemmed in by space, opportunity and expectation. Her future is set to be one of entrapment, maintaining the house, guarding against a tide of expenses, loss and rot.

Arifa Akbar (2009) comments that:

> Their country pile, like the rural gentry of the time, is in a state of irreversible decay; the imperious Mrs Ayres is mourning her loss of social standing; her mannish daughter, Caroline, is a bundle of unfulfilled desires; Roderick, her son, a survivor of war who is still haunted by its savagery; and Susan, the long dead daughter whose memories linger like a purgatorial spirit … Their anxiety in a fast transforming Britain, with its Labour government and upwardly mobile working class, is reflected by a sense of growing menace felt in the mildewed corridors of their home.

The house is decaying around them and they can neither maintain it and their past lifestyle, nor move forward satisfactorily into a new way of life. Waters marks a change in lifestyle, class behaviour, and at the same time the opportunities or lack of them for women. Betty the housemaid is ready to run off; she hates being stuck out in the country while her friends make more money in factories, and, plagued by the nagging spirit of the house which attacks her and upsets what she carries, she is eventually forced to move out and on. The family suffer from lack of money to maintain the house as it was in imperial days and its decay seems actively aided both by stray airs which tug at the rotting wallpaper, and by relentless active attacks on lone individuals.

As Monica Germana (2013) has noted, clothes play a part in the novel in emphasising decay, change, class, gender and power. Mrs Ayres retains a fascination with mantillas, lace and impractical, shiny, elegantly crafted shoes amidst the rotting, decayed wallpaper and furnishings. She is not unlikeable; she is part of a bygone era, and a sad figure of loss and confusion. Waters doesn't seem to me to particularly dislike this family stuck in a time warp and hoping to move or at least survive. Neither does the narrative support the longing and loathing of the prosaic narrator, Dr Faraday, who is insensitive to anyone else's interpretations of feelings, enforcing his own reading of events. In this reading, within which we too are trapped, the women appear to be increasingly crazed in their response to the interventions of the ghostly intruder, who scrawls SSsss on the walls, calls terrifyingly down the servants' speaking tubes, rings the phone at night, and flings the war-damaged son, Roderick's (possibly named after the brother in Edgar Allen Poe's 'The Fall of the House of Usher', 1839) things round his room in a personalised attack. Waters places these women in a liminal time of change: Mrs Ayres cannot move on, Caroline might, but is prevented from doing so by the house and its burdens, and by the extant narratives which have no place for her, and only Betty does escape, into the working world and independence. Waters depicts their entrapment and incarceration and for Caroline, as an example of a woman of a certain class, she shows the difficulties of moving or constructing any other kind of narrative than that of being married off to a male relative (a brash unsuitable one) or perhaps a professional such as Dr Faraday. Finding their own future in marriage is the only story available to such women. Like a Sleeping Beauty without either sleeping or conventional beauty, Caroline Ayres is trapped in the prison of her family, class and gender.

We are also trapped, in Faraday's narrative. Faraday is an obtuse fallible narrator who misreads as nonsense the hectic Gothic attacks, intrusions and refusals of the house. Reader response to him surprised Waters at first but Mantel recognises his function:

> Every ghost story needs a Dr Faraday, a blunt literalist with a sturdy sense of self. Such a figure begins as the reader's surrogate, the voice of scepticism. We've been told ghost stories before, and we're not going to fall for the author's wiles and tricks; our narrator is determined, on our behalf, to avoid melodrama. Then as the story progresses, our representative comes up with ever more tortured 'rational explanations' for bizarre events, explanations that require us to be more imaginative and gullible than we would be if we simply accepted the supernatural. 'I see what's in front of me,' Faraday claims stoutly. For the love of God, the reader cries: wake up man, look behind you! The author has worked a spell. We now see that our guide and mentor is dull-witted, complacent, perhaps self-deceiving. (Mantel 2009)

Emma Parker (2013) sees the intrusive power which is enacted in the ghost as that of Faraday, since we have his limited, biased narrative perspective to rely on. I have commented further on this and on the ghost in the novel elsewhere (Wisker 2016). The fabric of the past and of the house lure Faraday as they entrap Caroline, offering him, as he sees it, a chance to gain the house and status through marrying the woman, a kind of reverse nineteenth-century romantic fiction. Meanwhile, the ghostly presence refuses any suggestions of change. The poltergeist nags at the curtain, lifts the wallpaper, annoys Gyp the lovely old friendly Labrador until he bites Gillian, the annoyingly precocious daughter of the local planner. A ghostly unseen hand scrawls the words of silence, SSssss, across the walls, suggesting the dead daughter Susan as well as malevolence, repression and restraint. An evil spirit intends to keep the family locked away in the house, in stasis. It resents progress and change, and it resents intrusions from Faraday who would upset heredity and hierarchy should he win Caroline. The poltergeist or spirit of the house throws Roderick's shaving gear around, attacks him, upsets the servant Betty and entraps Mrs Ayres in the haunted nursery until she commits suicide. Its energies are determined to prevent change.

Arifa Akbar (2009) comments that the novel 'combines the Gothic gloom of Henry James' *The Turn of the Screw*, with the generic reference points of Agatha Christie's country-house mysteries, with each character being "picked off" one by one, and every survivor falling under suspicion'. In *The Little Stranger* the illness of Betty, the servant, is the reason for the first call to Faraday, the regular doctor not being available. As a character, Betty is developed from a real servant girl whose case came before Henry Fielding, a JP as well as a novelist and the author of *Tom Jones* (1749). Betty, the historical servant, was accused of lying about being kidnapped, trapped and abused. In *The Franchise Affair* (1948), historical fiction author Josephine Tey wrote of her times, story and trial, illustrating how she stands for the culpable misinterpretation of silenced, economically dependent women, in this instance of servants. Although Betty resembles Faraday's mother, he treats her fears of the poltergeist as one would an attention-seeking child. Betty escapes, Mrs Ayres and Caroline cannot. Their entrapment is as much a problem of their class status and the oppression of the past as embodied in the house as it is of any ghost representing reluctance to let the past go or allow change. Class riddles *The Little Stranger* and oppresses the stories the women and the men tell themselves.

Everyone is caught in the trap of a liminal state, a limbo between the old and the new, post-war welfare state and the promises of a future of equality that grammar schools, housing and social freedoms seem to offer. But while this might seem available to Betty, it is denied to Caroline. The house sucks her back, wallpaper peels, hands grab, fires start, phones ring and mumble of their own accord. Both the old fabric and the relatively new technology refuse change and the intrusion of outsiders. The Ayres are incarcerated in time and space in a version of Englishness, one which the nineteenth-century novel (and Hundreds Hall) burns up but never quite replaces, always returning the novels' endings to romance and restoration of order. There is no order post-Second World War; everything is in turmoil and this is represented in a ghost disturbed and threatened, a version of the past upset, tugged and trammelled, a past which emphasises empire, wealth, family, solidarity, hierarchy and the fabric of Englishness, all embodied in the house. Caroline's mother lives the remnants of a dream of the decayed aristocracy, the rotting fabric of her house falling about her and the memories of the lost daughter, Susan, and reminder of lost hopes as well as a child. This family is on the brink of the disaster of the upper-class landed gentry, the loss of funding, and of any real meaning to their positions. This is a ghost story based on hidden cruelties of the period: decaying landed families and their homes; the physical and mental destruction of war embodied in Roderick's physical injuries, and the mental injuries which lead to his incarceration; the restricted lives of servants whose well-being is irrelevant, whose loneliness and ailments are considered lies. Women who resist the roles in which they are cast are seen as hysterical. Both Mrs Ayres, locked in the nursery, suicidal, and Caroline, represented by Faraday as unstable, remind us of those wealthy, powerful male doctors' removal of rights and denouncements of hysteria on the incarcerated women of a number of novels. In *Jane Eyre* (from which the name Ayres is derived, in addition to the sense of 'airs and spirits'), Caribbean Bertha Mason, the mad woman in the attic, was brought back as a trophy from the British Empire (reflecting theft and the denigration of those it controlled), so that impoverished second son Rochester could gain her inherited wealth, then she was lost in the upper reaches of a strange house, victim to inherited mental illness and marginalisation. Mrs Ayres is drawn upstairs, to the nursery. The yellow paper of the room in which the damaging party takes place reminds us of the designation of madness in women (particularly with postnatal depression), against which Charlotte Perkins Gilman rails in *The Yellow Wallpaper* (1892). Women in this novel are incarcerated, silenced, prevented from moving on by a mixture of class, location and narratives of domesticity and romance. Waters' novel is a hymn to the past, a particular period in English history, and it is also a dirge on the loss of women's freedom and opportunities.

The dreadful party is a catalytic moment. In Faraday's dazed eyes there is an oscillation between fairytale/horror and the decay and disorder revealed as the reality behind ostensible grandeur and beauty of the house, as if by a trick of changing light. The saloon is gorgeous, antique furniture appearing from beneath dust covers, 'light was caught and returned by touches of gold on various ornaments and mirrors'(p. 81), yet Caroline sticks drawing-pins, 'fixing down the edges of yellow paper that were dropping or bulging from the walls' (p. 82). This damage presages the full onslaught of decay after the events of the party, in which the poltergeist attacks the dog who bites, scarring the spoiled wealthy Gillian, reducing her value on a future marriage market. To Faraday, Caroline is more attractive in workaday clothes. He comments more generally on her unfeminine, hairy, thick legs and how her décolletage reveals her as unsexy and ungainly: 'The low neckline showed her prominent collarbones and the tendons of her throat', and 'her mouth, red with lipstick, was almost startlingly full and large' (p. 82). The latter comment reveals his alarmed disgust at the sexuality she suddenly represents. Though they briefly become engaged, the attempt at sex in the car is merely an awkward, confused tussle. Meanwhile Roderick cannot even get to the party, such are the increased attacks on his surroundings, things, body. At night his furniture moves around him, scorch marks appear on his body and the room: 'It was as if the house were developing scars of its own' (p. 147), defined as 'creepy' by Caroline. His collar studs disappear, as do his cufflinks and then 'in the very second of drawing back his hand he saw, through the dressing-table mirror, and from the corner of his eye, something small and dark dropping down in the room behind him—like a spider dropping from the ceiling' (p. 160), things crash and break, he is attacked. The house has malevolent designs against him and although others define this as epilepsy, Roderick feels attacked and is safer in a care home. The ghost story re-enacts wartime attacks on the body of Roderick, and the attacks of time on the house with invasions, spirits, marks and violence. In the main, it is a ghost story of the suppressed silenced lives of women: Betty, the maid, marginalised and thought hysterical; the mother, Mrs Ayres, also thought hysterical; Caroline, whose story should include a wealthy suitor if she were in a Jane Austen or a Brontë novel, but whose new story, equally constructed for others by her, would be to marry the doctor, a grammar school boy, a member of the working class come good.

The prosaic narrative voice of the new part of the century, the voice of one such as Faraday, could never credit as fantastic and genuine the spectral reminders of the past, the haunted histories invading the present, the threats to hanging on to false hopes and dated stories about the family and its future. The ghost warns of the decay and the change, it insists that they see the changes and make changes. It threatens total dissolution, which befalls Mrs Ayres, Roderick, and eventually Caroline.

Critics are divided, as some see it as a more light hearted, less insidious and threatening ghost story than others. McCrum defines it as a:

> light-footed foray into the ghost story genre, a format only half-followed. Its conclusion suggests it is a haunted house tale without a ghost, a country-home murder with no actual victim, and Waters mischievously gives us an open-ending in a genre that demands explanations. (McCrum 2009)

While for Kate Mosse:

> It's a gripping story, with beguiling characters … As well as being a supernatural tale, it is a meditation on the nature of the British and class, and how things are rarely what they seem. Chilling. (Mosse 2009)

Significantly, one of the novel characteristics of *The Little Stranger* is to play with the ghost story formula and its troubling narratives of great house romances and continuity. The novel is characterised by its refusal of the familiar formulae of the final revelation of the source of the ghost, and ideally the laying to rest of its ultimately revealed secret or grudge. We never really know who or what the ghost is, the tale never finally lays its real or supernatural presence to rest. To some extent Faraday does inherit the house. At the end he's the haunter, the pretend owner (he has the keys), maintenance man and cleaner (like his mother) of Hundreds Hall, which is unsellable and rotting (not even suitable as a teacher training college), a crumbling relic of the outdated values of aristocracy and imperialism (the Colonel, Empire day).

As contemporary women's Gothic, *The Little Stranger* questions, exposes and problematises established roles for women—mothers, wives, daughters, servants, nurturers—and queries views of women's proper place as the home, undercutting and devaluing narratives which promise romance as the resolution to everything, and which both reinforce domesticity and trap women in the house, in subordinate roles. Sarah Waters uses the strategies of the literary Gothic, a ghost story, interlaced with the social change novel, D. H. Lawrence's *Lady Chatterley's Lover* (1928) without the sex, Daphne du Maurier's *Rebecca* without the marriage, manslaughter/murder and collusion.

The Greatcoat (2012)—Helen Dunmore

Ghosts are obsessives. Whatever the wrong to be righted, the events to be remembered, the problems to be replayed over and over again, the ghost is stuck in an obsessive-compulsive loop, wandering about, returning, reminding and insisting, until whatever it was that betrayed them, killed them, overwhelmed them and caught them in their life and their usually untimely death, is settled. Whoever they need to take revenge on, directly or indirectly, or who needs to notice and to respond in order to settle their compulsive, stuck, unsolved problem, their need to return over and over until the thing, the person, the problem, the mystery are all solved and sorted, acts for them, because often they cannot take much direct action themselves. Once they are let into your life they won't let go, they dominate thought and action, insisting on a compulsive return to unsolvable problems, locking both parties into a cycle of repetition which can only be damaging and inescapable, until something is resolved, peace descends and the haunting stops. And their insistence, their circling and reminding, is so like an eternally compulsive romantic love scenario, often one from which one partner at least wishes to break out but can't.

In *The Greatcoat*, Helen Dunmore ranges across the obsessions of romantic love and those of ghostly returns and in so doing also revives the culturally haunting stories of war. The Second World War haunts the Western world still because of the European front, and the eastern world because of the Japanese invasion of Malaysia, of Singapore, and the destruction of Pearl Harbor. The Second World War, like the first, is unavoidable in cultural memory even as the survivors die out, and whole cities have been rebuilt, covering over the damage. Jokes about cultural difference mask lingering fears of tales told about horrors committed, while most of those horrors closer to our own culture (whatever that might be) tend to be still hidden, so it is more straightforward still to always indict the 'enemy'. The return of memories of those lost is unavoidable in areas of Britain where one can still see the overgrown, semi- or completely deserted windswept aerodromes, the decayed barracks and living quarters, the disused landscapes. The family memories of bereavements hover at roadside memorials, lurk in letters neatly hidden away, reappear in photographs of the lost, black and white or sepia tinged. The effects of war are everywhere, ghosting the landscape and people's lives, the relationships which accompanied war's displacements and its emotional upheavals, the liminal space between life and death, all truly the stuff of ghost stories and of Gothic horror. While many of these stories are put on display, like a poppy worn publicly on Remembrance Day, there will always be relationships and events held more secretively. These are the alternative lives people led, the hidden attachments, the parallel stories which were not destroyed and publicly mourned, as legitimate relationships could be, but must be hidden, remaining permanently covert, known only to a few. These latter are popularly the stuff of potential ghost stories.

Dunmore's tale unites ghost story, the hidden illicit history of relationship secrets, damage and cultural catastrophes. They all appear as the promise or threat of eternal love, where too easily obsessional relationships can turn from desire and passion to devouring destruction. These tensions are held in the liminal space of the ghostly return, where the invited, embraced lover becomes a demon lover. In *The Greatcoat*, this demon lover is a young officer whose ghostly greatcoat precedes him and whose returns are ironically the result of the calling of the bereaved landlady, his illicit wartime lover. The landlady is stuck in a circuit of guilt, compulsively circling her room, calling him back. During the war, in pursuit of her affair, she left her husband and child for fair-haired Alec, her pilot lover, only to have her farmhouse home obliterated, her husband and son killed when Alec's plane returned from its final mission and crashed onto the house. Denied death, her compulsive wandering overhead calls Alec back and up and out of his wartime sleep, but he returns to the younger, lonely, vulnerable Isabel, wife of Philip, the ambitious, hardworking, new doctor. Isabel is forced to act as a surrogate for the landlady, vulnerable because lonely, her life an empty vessel not fully filled with housekeeping, domestic chores, shopping and just being the doctor's wife. The empty lives of intelligent women, post-war, refused the opportunity of work, condemned them to mere domestic roles because of the social construction of women and work as one layered with paternalistic assumptions about husbands as providers, and because the men needed the jobs. Isabel is wide open for the entrance of Alec, tapping at her window late one night like Cathy at Lockwood's window in *Wuthering Heights*, expecting to be let in, recognising her where she can't recognise him, taking her life, love and body over. The link across the liminal space is the greatcoat, initially kept as a bed cover, calling the dead pilot out of his unsettled slumbers.

> She could still hear the tapping sound that had woken her. It must be her dream still turning, like a record after the needle had been lifted off. Tap, tap, tap. Soft, insistent, determined. It was a real sound. It was coming from the living room. It sounded like someone tapping on glass ... on a window.... Isabel snatched the greatcoat and pulled it around her. Thank heavens he was back. She'd make some tea and he'd tell her about his case and everything would be fine. She ran over the cold lino, into the living room and across to the window, without switching on the light. She drew back the curtain. (2012, pp. 55–56)

Isabel initially believes it is Philip returning, but the greatcoat takes her over, transferring her into a liminal space/time which Alec can enter. What seems terrifying, a strange man outside, is rendered relatively comforting because he is identified as an officer and so probably honourable, signs which indicate reassuring everyday reality and its values. The ghostly visitation is normalised for Isabel and the reader.

> There was a man outside the window, she saw the pallor of his face first, as it seemed to bob against the glass, too high up to belong to a man who had his feet on the ground. The street lamp hit him from the side, throwing the sharp shadow of his cap over his face. He was too close, inside the railings that separated the house from the pavement. Of course, the level of the ground there was higher than the level of the floor inside. That was why he seemed to float in midair. An RAF greatcoat, exactly like the one on her bed: she couldn't mistake it. An officer. There, he was an everyday figure, safe as houses, but her heart clenched in fear. It was the look on his face: recognition, a familiarity so deep he didn't have to say a word. But she had never seen him before in her life.
> He gave her the thumbs up as if to say, 'Good show. I wasn't sure if you'd heard me tapping.' (p. 56)

Alec hovers between the ground and the window, he knocks on the window with a familiarity which confuses Isabel but which she somehow accepts as natural; the defamiliarised rendered familiar to her. She invites him in on his next visit as if they were used to each other. And Alec's manner suggests a long-term intimate relationship, into which she falls, their embraces passionate, their bike rides to the suddenly fully peopled, suddenly deserted and ghostly wartime airbase emphasising for the reader that he slips out of his own and into her time, she out of her own and into his.

Their passionate love affair fills the gap left by Isabel's husband's absence. Philip is compulsively devoted to being an attentive and successful local doctor, caring for his wife in a cursory way, unaware that she is totally isolated, undermined and likely to become depressed in the pointless mundanity of a post-war housewife's role. He is right when he feels that once she has a child her life will be filled up; the surrogate life of caring for another will dominate. However, he has no idea that this will be more than the usual surrogacy of living vicariously through a child, of devoting everything to a child and husband, since as the story develops, Isabel actually becomes the surrogate for the landlady's and Alec's child. Her fair-haired, placid, smiling boy is at home on the suddenly newly reappeared, repaired greatcoat. The boy is recognised as his own by the equally suddenly reappearing Alec. Then the passionate, illicit love affair turns to a deadly replay. Historically, Alec visited the landlady, and now Isabel, in the liminal space before his last fatal bombing mission. Alec died on the mission's return, between the 26th and 27th of a nameless winter month, his Lancaster smashing into the farmhouse, killing the landlady's husband and child. But his ghost cannot lie down and Alec is continually returned to Isabel, stuck in the grooves of the moments before he set off on that final mission, and he re-returns and re-returns until following the birth of the child, the time shifts on beyond that of moments before the final fatal mission, to the moment after the mission, the time of the night crash.

Hearing and seeing the sky and buildings around her shift through the years to the war, the noise of aircraft returning, Isabel refuses and escapes the moment of the related crash which would kill her son and smash the farmhouse in which they now live. However, the cruel catch of this story is that the obsessive love affair, the obsessive return of the ghost, the obsessive return to the moment of the enactment of some cosmic punishment for the landlady's adulterous relationship with Alec, must haunt Isabel forever. The landlady dying in hospital passed to Isabel her compulsive-obsessive link with the ghostly, dead, demon lover and his shattered aircraft. The novel ends with our awareness that Isabel is going to fear for the life of her child from a potentially burning, smashed farmhouse for as long as she lives. The greatcoat will never move on and neither will the moment until and if the ghost of Alec and the ghost of the war have been laid to rest.

The Greatcoat is romantic fiction, a cultural history and a twisted tale of the ways in which eternal love will never just lie down. The obsession of the ghostly Alec stuck in his moment, called up and out by the landlady, can never rest until the cycle is repeated, Isabel's child killed.

As a feminist ghost story, it focuses on the compulsion and damage of obsessional romantic love, and on the depleted lives of women just after the war, sent back to embrace domesticity when they or their mothers had had active roles in the war years. It hits a particularly important liminal moment of change for women's development and their awakened sense of being trapped, denied, silenced and marginalised, which led eventually to the growth of second-wave feminism. In repeating the traditional romantic love tale with a twist—the ghost, the re-enactment of someone else's illicit affair in Isabel's own—Dunmore links love and passion, domesticity and child rearing, the popular cultural reasons for women's lives, with haunting obsession, entrapment and a kind of death sentence.

Conclusion

Contemporary women writers of ghost stories use familiar tropes and characteristics of the Gothic—haunted spaces and places, troubled haunted minds, revenants, the return of problematic events and people—but they also uncover hidden histories of limitations on women's lives, constrained by time and place. In *The Little Stranger*, after the Second World War, the women in the Ayres family enact the limited roles available to women locked into narratives preventing escape from the past or the house: the mother haunted by her dead daughter Susan, whose ghost (possibly) refuses change in the decaying house and lifestyles of the impoverished landed gentry; Caroline, who cannot fulfil the role of heiress, nor that of a married or independent woman; and Betty the maid, who actually escapes to a living wage and a job outside the great house.

Women experience oppression, whether shunned by society because of illegitimacy, designated mad because of failing to conform (Jennet Humfrye in *The Woman in Black*) or incarcerated in limited, constrained domestic contexts, such as Isabel in Dunmore's *The Greatcoat*. They also trouble neat romantic trajectories. Caroline in *The Little Stranger* resists the narrative of others who would force her into a marriage, whether to a relative or Faraday. Isabel's Alec is a demon lover whose role as revenant is to lock her into his perpetual circling destructive returns, his replay of the damage of war. Love and marriage are no way out in these tales of women's oppressive narratives and debated histories of place and role.

Ghost stories refuse to let histories and constraining cultural or personal narratives remain hidden, emphasising the damage they do to perceptions and behaviours. They reveal alternative truths which, like the ghost embodying the revelation, need facing, their damage exorcising, their troublesomeness settled, lives changed so that people can move on. The haunting is manifest in the figure of the ghost, who reminds the living of unsolved problems and hidden secrets, intrigues, deaths, deceits and guilt, whether it is a cultural or individual issue. In contemporary women's ghost stories, the hidden problem or secret is often domestic, often hierarchical, caught up in broader cultural power relations and inequalities, injustices and domination. The ghost reveals loss, deceit, silence, alternatives, damage, a horrible past hidden by those in power, dominating and paralysing the living. In their reconfiguration of the formulae, contemporary women's ghost stories expose the silencing and social constraints on women, and equally, they challenge the trajectory of the ghost story itself, one which seeks catharsis, resolution and rest.

Bibliography

Akbar, A. (2009) 'Sarah Waters: "Is There a Poltergeist Within Me?"', 29 May, http://www.independent.co.uk/arts-entertainment/books/features/sarah-waters-is-there-a-poltergeist-within-me-1692335.html

Briggs, J. (2012) 'The Ghost Story', in *A New Companion to the Gothic*, D. Punter (ed.) (Oxford: Blackwell).
Dickens, C. (1860) *Great Expectations* (London: Chapman and Hall).
Germana, M. (2013) 'The Death of the Lady: Haunted Garments and (Re-) Possession in *The Little Stranger*', in *Sarah Waters (Contemporary Critical Perspectives)*, K. Mitchell (ed.) (London: Bloomsbury).
Gordon, A. (1997) *Ghostly Matters: Haunting and the Sociological Imagination* (Minneapolis, MN: University of Minnesota Press).
Hill, S. (1983) *The Woman in Black* (London: Vintage).
Hill, S. (2007) *The Man in the Picture* (London: Profile Books).
Hitchcock, A. (1996) Quotation from Exhibition: 'Phantasmagoria: Pre-Cinema to Virtuality', Museum of Contemporary Art, Sydney, 27 March–30 June.
Horner, A. and Zlosnik, S. (1998) *Daphne du Maurier: Writing, Identity and the Gothic Imagination* (Basingstoke: Macmillan).
James, H. (1898) *The Turn of the Screw* (London: William Heinemann).
Jancovich, M. (1992) *Horror* (London: Batsford).
King, S. (1981) *Danse Macabre* (Nashville, TN: Everest House).
Mantel, H. (2009) 'Review *The Little Stranger*', *The Guardian*, 23 May.
McCrum, R. (2009) 'What Lies Beneath', 10 May, http://www.guardian.co.uk/books/2009/may/10/books-sarah-waters
Mosse, K. (2009) *The Times*, Summer Read, Women's Gothic.
Mullan, J. (2012) '*The Woman in Black* by Susan Hill', 10 February, http://www.guardian.co.uk/books/2012/feb/10/woman-in-black-susan-hill-book-club
Parker, E. (2013) 'The Country House Revisited: Sarah Waters' *The Little Stranger*', in *Sarah Waters: Contemporary Critical Perspectives*, K. Mitchell (ed.) (London: Bloomsbury).
Punter, D. (2000b) *Postcolonial Imaginings: Fictions of a New World Order* (Edinburgh: Edinburgh University Press).
Waters, S. (2010) '*The Little Stranger* by Sarah Waters; Week three: Sarah Waters on writing her supernatural thriller', 7 August, http://www.theguardian.com/books/2010/aug/07/bookclub-sarah-waters-little-stranger
Weinstock, J. (ed.) (2004) *Spectral America: Phantoms and the National Imagination* (Madison, WI: Popular Press).
Wilhelms, L. (2012) 'Mediums Change, Fears Stay the Same', Thesis, http://digitalcommons.colby.edu/honorstheses/627/
Wisker, G. (2003b) 'Dangerous Borders: Daphne du Maurier's *Rebecca*: Shaking the Foundations of the Romance of Privilege, Partying and Place', *Journal of Gender Studies*, Vol. 12, No. 2.
Wisker, G. (2016) 'The Feminist Gothic in The Little Stranger: Troubling Narratives of Continuity and Change', in *Sarah Waters and Contemporary Feminisms*, A. Jones and C. O'Callaghan (eds.) (London: Palgrave Macmillan).

CHAPTER 10

Opening the Gates to Darkness: Gothic Diversity

Despite threats of its imminent exhaustion and demise, the several branches of contemporary women's Gothic flourish and diversify. Meanwhile, the Gothic continues to be the only mode which even approaches a way of representing the contemporary world when life and art are sometimes indistinguishable in their horror and bizarre qualities. One such example currently unfolding this summer of 2015, as I finish this book, is the political and media references to those refugees fleeing oppression as cockroaches, pests, hordes and swarms, as if they are otherworldly mutants, inhuman parasites, zombies, instead of people seeking safety from the horrors of war and terror. We can still agree with Angela Carter that we do indeed live in Gothic times (Carter, *Fireworks*, 1974). The extraordinary horrors of the everyday might threaten to overwhelm our sensibilities and abilities to cope, imagine and act, but having a Gothic mindset helps put some of this into perspective so that we use our imaginations for vision and agency, without underestimating the threats and horrors. Gothic is a cultural connection and critical comment, essentially political and personal. Speaking from a similar perspective, Catherine Spooner (2006) and Johan Höglund (2014) both suggest that American imperialism leads to the revival of nineteenth-century Gothic motifs in contemporary film and is 'a mode capable of infecting and informing a number of media and genres' (Hoglund 2014, p. 5), 'so it can engage us in a scholarly way with a range of genres from slaughter films to nineteenth-century novels and other forms of public and political discourse' (p. 5). While Höglund identifies American and other imperial gothic as shoring up imperial values and behaviours, we can also see that postcolonial Gothic dismantles them along with 'Massa's house' (Hopkinson and Mehan 2004). Spooner wrote her contemporary Gothic in the wake of 9/11, which she felt might end the taste for the kind of Gothic popular at that time but mentions Patrick McGrath's work as finding in the Gothic 'a language with which to discuss the pain and suffering caused by 9/11: a language of haunting, of guilt, of mental instability, of dereliction' (Spooner 2006, p. 165). The Gothic enables us to recover and rewrite the past, reinterpret and even try and understand it. We are ever haunted by its discordant complexities while fully aware of how the exclusions and silences of events and people are both disinterred and reimagined, revived. The alternative stories and perspectives which a Gothic revival offers also enable us to see more clearly, in more varied ways, the shortcomings of the orthodoxies and propaganda around us, the dangers of limited worldviews. This final chapter is not a conclusion. It would seem an act of hubris to assert that everything has been said about contemporary women's Gothic, and limiting to say that I have nothing more to add. Instead, this chapter looks briefly at the ubiquity of the Gothic, at claims of its exhaustion and demise, then opens the 'daylight gate' (to steal Jeanette Winterson's Hammer title *The Daylight Gate*, 2012) to some (more) of its sprawling, spawning, rich diversity, offering only a taste, a sample of what else is out there.

Everyday Gothic Horror

Much of our contemporary world seems to be or rather is represented as Gothic, and more particularly as a form of postcolonial Gothic, in an everyday, insidious sense. The world seems to have turned into something from Gothic horror, upsetting our complacencies at every turn, and this intrusion, invasion and undermining, destabilising and defamiliarising of the everyday, is also both sensationalised and normalised. The horror of wars, diseases, terror, natural calamity and disaster are on screen and in our newspapers on a daily basis, as are the headlines of contagious diseases creeping, seeping camouflaged across borders in Africa (Ebola, AIDS), Asia (bird flu, swine flu), entering the seeming safety of Western, Northern countries (because more ostensibly comfortable, well fed). AIDS and HIV are worldwide. Ebola was ignored for too long, its terrors, like those of

SARS and various other diseases before and alongside it, terrible because of its ability to cross borders and travel with the wealthy on international flights. The diseases of the poor and of 'Other' countries (anywhere that is not your small spot in your country becomes 'Other' when there is an epidemic) might, it seems, even be able to get you as you pass through Heathrow Terminal 5 buying duty free goods. Horrors of body invasion through disease, death from explosions in the streets, the beheading of ordinary people (in a far-off place) by those who were once at school with our children are everywhere in our media and our lives. Constructions of the foreign 'Other' as dangerous, wrong, are products of global inequalities and historical, morphed, entrenched, rejuvenated fears and dislikes of the different.

For women, these are indeed dangerous times, when across (in particular) the Middle East, Iran, Iraq, Pakistan and India, women are subject to rape, brutality at the hands of their fathers and partners, silencing, lack of education and total disempowerment. The relative liberation of the1960s and 1970s has given way to curtailment of dress, education and every freedom. Kristeva (1988) as a Gothic theorist of all that is culturally inflected and gendered, reminds us that these oppressions based on race and gender are indeed constructions, interpretations, so it could be argued that (at least in and through fiction), once aware these are constructions and projections, it might be possible to deploy the imaginative energies of the Gothic to upset complacency and bigotry, and to use imagination and empathy to speculate how behaviours might be different, to reverse the destructive beliefs and behaviours which such dangerous Otherising produces.

The Gothic challenges all those constructions by which we live our lives: time, space, identity, body, family, nation, language, wholeness and progression, and shows each of these to be more tentative than we might have thought. While this is terrifying on the one hand, on the other, if you have been constrained by such constructions, deemed Other in terms of culture, gender, sexuality, bodily form, age, health and so on, when the Gothic is deployed to expose the artifice, and to enact and celebrate alternatives, it can be seen as liberating. It opens minds, and can feed into changed behaviour.

Our tendencies to revisit and re-read the past, to uncover events and alternative readings, and our mixture of discomfort and excitement at difference, culturally and imaginatively, which enables new understandings, are each responses encouraged by the Gothic. In much contemporary women's Gothic we find gendered fears of bodily harm, imprisonment, denial, silencing, damaging lies. We also find exposés of the damaging behaviours which are considered normal, put in place to preserve order. In much women's Gothic the exposés and revelations are followed by reversals, celebrations of the liberation of alternative ways of seeing the world and of being and what has been constructed and represented as deviant, dangerous and to be destroyed if it cannot be controlled. Space and place resonate differently for men and women and these are also culturally inflected. Gothic strategies emphasise and reveal such differences, and the contradictions of places considered safe and nurturing for women, which are felt as threatening, silencing, endangering freedom of thought, action and being. Gothic as a genre offers ways of exposing, and articulating, some of the horrors and fears, enabling us to face them, imagine our way through them without ignoring them, dismissing them or panicking. This it does through theorising and enacting, engaging us using literary strategies, representation, context and forms of expression.

This chapter deals with two main issues: the self-aware use of Gothic by contemporary women writers to revisit or rewrite periods in history and established texts, and the ways in which Gothic has been mainstreamed in some women's writing and is therefore often either the genre of choice, or effectively spliced in alongside other genres. Some contemporary texts are full blown Gothic, with updated settings reminding readers of castles and tombs, dungeons and attics, scenarios of duplicitous invasive lovers, threatening patriarchal figures, split selves, scientific experimentation based on hubris and a demonic desire to create and alter what it means to be human. Metamorphosis reveals the otherness beneath the mundane and the everyday, the construction and projection of what we fear onto an Other, bursting out from, seeping out from, our seemingly well-maintained constraints of body, home and identity. Much contemporary women's Gothic writing also uses Gothic characteristics and tropes spliced with other familiar genres—crime, historical fiction, romance, science fiction, comedy, chick lit—to deal with a range of issues such as solving crimes (*The Lovely Bones*, Alice Sebold 2002; *Case Histories*, Kate Atkinson 2004), love and loss (*The Time Traveller's Wife*, Audrey Niffenegger 2003) and exposing cultural incarceration and danger (*Eight Months on Ghazzah Street*, Hilary Mantel 1988).

Gothic influenced by postmodernism and neo-Victorianism revisits the past, rewrites, replays, re-stories familiar figures such as Dracula (*The Historian*, Elizabeth Kostova 2005) or fictionalised Victorian poets (*Possession*, A. S. Byatt 1990). It explores and reimagines historical moments (*Fingersmith*, Sarah Waters 2002; *The Swan Thieves*, Elizabeth Kostova 2010) and uses psycho-geography to reinterpret and replace the history of haunted spaces places and events (*Labyrinth*, Kate Mosse 2005; *The Winter Ghosts*, Kate Meosse 2010). Jeanette Winterson's Hammer Horror novel, *The Daylight Gate* (2012), is a particularly powerful version of revisiting history, indicting the really duplicitous and sinister, letting the silenced speak, exposing hypocrisy, abuse and violence against women, without losing any of the inflection of the demonic and the powerful otherness, in fact revealing and celebrating its synergies.

Neo-Victorian Gothic

Does Neo-Victorian Gothic merely revive the Gothic of the period? Rewrite it? Explore and critique it? Andrew Smith suggests, 'In its more radical formations the Gothic provides a way of looking at identity that helps draw out the covert symbolism that inhabits Victorian texts' (2012, p. 52), seeing it as a way of revisiting and exposing the subtexts of values and beliefs explicitly about those formations under social control, identity, gender, sexuality, language and modes of power. Jean Rhys' *Wide Sargasso Sea* (1966) is a form of neo-Victorian text which revisits the colonial disenfranchisement, disempowerment and patriarchal silencing which undermined subaltern subjects, depicting them as mad and dangerous because they fundamentally undercut the established values. The dark secrets of Victorian times are exposed to a critique which encompasses the underlying value systems which produced them—crime and poverty, gender and power. In her neo-Victorian *Possession* (1990), A. S. Byatt produces twin tales of then and now, showing how Victorian writers gained inspiration from place, relationships considered illicit and from mutual literary influence, hidden secrets, hints of which are sometimes seen in reading texts in parallel. The novel also enacts the ways in which in researching, reading and writing about Gothic texts we are obliged to repeat them. In Byatt's novel, invented Victorian poet R. A. Ash is the subject of intense scholarship ranging from an American collector's fascination with any vaguely related item of his property or life, stored in a remote desert showroom, to a devotion to the minutiae of the everyday writing of Ash's wife, to the forensic foraging and detailed annotating of contemporary academic researchers: Roland Michell, who has devoted his life to Ash scholarship, and Maud Bailey, who has devoted her life to the work of the poet

Christabel la Motte. The practices of academic research are revealed as riddled with secrets, hidden information and potential for misrepresentation, and in the trajectory of this novel, opportunities to live lives parasitic upon the academic subject, vicariously treading in their footprints (literally) and mirroring their lives in one's own. Spaces, places, projects and re-read events resonate with alternative readings and wrong turns. The tendrils of the vast poisonous plant of the Gothic (see Marie Mulvey Roberts' comment noted in Chap. 1 of this book) reach out from the past and entwine the present, and the fictional entwines the real until telling the difference is impossible, itself an act of invention. The twentieth-century parallel of two critics, Randall Michell and Maud Bailey, seeking out and uncovering the past of their objects/subjects of study is an example of a Gothic trope—the 'truths' of their interactions which the twentieth-century pair discover causes them to re-read anew the poetry of both Ash and his lover/fellow writer, Christabel la Motte, while their own intertwined relationship also affects their writing, and re-reading. Nothing is as it seems; more is always revealed and read into anything which seems fixed, and for Gothic literature in particular, the repetition and reinterpretation of what is returned through the text is a major cause of both disturbance and defamiliarisation, potentially leading to a host of new perceptions.

Sarah Waters' *Fingersmith* (2002) is a treasure-trove of neo-Victorian lesbian Gothic. Darker than *Tipping the Velvet* (1998), it exposes ways in which structures of gender, power and economics play out in people's lives through their experiences of theft, murder, lies and disempowerment, and through language and education seen as warped power. But while it is in many ways a dark novel exposing the cruelties and deceits of the period, it is also a celebratory and radical, liberating novel, since it enacts new ways of interpreting and seeing hidden moments in history, uncovering women's lives and loves hitherto ignored and denied. That uncovering and revealing is vehicled through a text based on twinning and parallels, imagining and celebrating alternative ways of being, alternative relationships, and fundamentally rewriting the experiences of the time, using the structural form of parallels and exchanges played out through twinned lives and twinned readings. Its focus on lesbian histories of the nineteenth century recalls Paulina Palmer's comments about the essential similarity between the vampire and the lesbian (Chap. 7). A lesbian in the nineteenth century was an outsider in the heart of the everyday, a Gothic figure of doubleness. Waters imagines lesbian lives at historical moments when they were absent in fiction and in polite conversation, yet living lives both merged with those of others, and parallel, secretive, because they were so unimaginable that they did not even have a name. Lesbians were hidden in plain sight, forever on the outskirts of conventional society, in a constant masquerade of normality, involved in close-knit relationships operating unnoticed right at the centre of conventional society. Paradoxically, if you cannot imagine same-sex love and desire, how can you even suspect, see and recognise that your close relatives and friends could be part of this otherised set of beings? The notion of the parallel, disruptive existence is at the heart of *Fingersmith*, which is based on expressing and dramatising a fundamental unease with the narratives and deceits of romantic love, male intellectual superiority and power, and paternalistic care of and idealisation of women who, as a norm, were rendered childlike, physically, mentally and economically distressed and disempowered.

The subterfuge of the female characters in Sarah Waters' lesbian Gothic neo-Victorian fictions is one which is often like an empowering game played in the midst of and against the naïveties of others, and sometimes it seems played against themselves because they too, her lesbian protagonist and other characters, are often initially unaware of their own sexuality or their right to express it. In *Fingersmith*, the two girls, Susan Trinder and Maud Lilly, are swapped at birth, their lives confusingly twinned since Susan, illegitimate child of wealth, the one born to inherit, actually grows up poor (though nurtured) in a criminal family, with Mrs Sugsby and Mr Ibbs. The girl who is actually born poor, daughter of a murderess, is named for the wealthy girl, Maud Lilly, and adopted into a rich uncle's abusive power in an isolated grand house. Here her reading and rewriting of salacious sadomasochistic pornography initially disempowers her, making her ostensibly the victim, especially when an object on display, observed reading these texts by Lilly's prurient friends. Ironically, her skill ultimately renders her empowered as a woman author herself, expressing these written secrets by using her education to write saleable pornography. Nothing is at it seems in *Fingersmith*, everything is paralleled, twinned, hidden, deceitful, buttoned up. Sarah Waters plays with readers' expectations as the characters play with the expectations of those around them. There are several Gothic settings, including Lilly's own grand, isolated house with labyrinthine rooms, forbidden texts, locked doors and curtailed spaces. Similarly threatening and even more entrapping is the asylum where Susan is incarcerated, when tricked into being recognised as Maud, part of a complex plan to ruin both young women because of the inheritance of one of them. The city of London is also dark, a dangerous labyrinth of mean streets, poverty, crime, lack of any safe place, murders and hangings, into which Maud eventually escapes but can find no safety, her shoes broken, and her gender rendering her vulnerable, homeless, without either rights or money. Everything constrains and hides in this world. Clothes, stays, corsets, buttons and confining clothes, people, including false suitors are all confining and artificial. Nothing is as it seems. Hidden histories infiltrate and warp the present. Madness, hysteria, misrepresentation, death, deceit, theft, corruption, pursuit and hypocrisy dominate in the novel, and because of the twinning and the mistakes over their identity, the two women seem to share the ghostly returns of the stories of their mothers (one mad, one a murderess who was hanged). The text itself would be Gothic even without these settings and trappings because of its revelations, its overturning of the otherising, which in the conventional Victorian novel would inscribe these women as non-existent, mad, bad or dead.

Fingersmith replays, reminds and reopens to new scrutiny many familiar nineteenth-century narratives for women, exposing ways in which women were economically, physically and emotionally trapped, seduced, fleeced of any inheritance and incarcerated as hysterical or mad to finally disempower them. Characters might seem to be replaying *Great Expectations* (Dickens 1860), with the cruel trickery of Estella at its heart, stalled inheritance, but ultimately hope; however, the novel also references *Oliver Twist* (Dickens 1837) for the links between thieves, poverty, crime and London, and *Bleak House* (Dickens 1853) for the excessive complexities of inheritances, an isolated grand house and the permeation throughout society of a rot founded in inequalities. Wilkie Collins' *The Woman in White* (1859) is also revisited, in which Anne, a woman with money, is tricked into marriage then incarcerated in a lunatic asylum, from which she is rescued largely by the actions of her stronger sister, Marion, thus exposing the marriage narrative as one unlikely to always have a happy ending, and, unusually, constructing a female character with power, energy and good connections, all characteristics developed further in Waters' novel.

Many of the elements of nineteenth-century Gothic novels are replayed in *Fingersmith* in a highly self-conscious manner, highlighting the artifice, producing at times a performative pantomime of Gothic, but one which is dark, chilling, brutal in intention rather than played for laughs. A particular example is the entrance of a gentleman, called Gentleman (Richard Rivers), whose arrival reminds us of the knocking of death or the police, and whose name signals a thief, and a rake. Actually he is both, a duplicitous, violent thief who intends to trick everyone, raping Maud's maid, replacing her with Susan, who is trained to deceive Maud, while Maud plays the part of the vulnerable isolated woman, wooed in secret by 'Gentleman', who pretends to be an art teacher. Maud's elopement with 'Gentleman' is perceived by each young woman to be part of *their* plot with him: Susan to trick Maud, and win some of the inheritance; Maud to trick Susan by swapping clothes and names, and having her locked up as mad, so that she and Gentleman can escape with the inheritance. The dark heart of the novel is the Gothic marriage of Maud and 'Gentleman', at night, with neither love nor flowers, in an atmosphere resembling a funeral rather than a wedding. 'One of the dark birds started up from between the stones' (p. 122). The black chapel 'was shut up with a rusting chain and a padlock, but above it was a porch of rotted wood' (p. 123). The rain falls like arrows, the sky is dark, this marriage is deadly, as the tombstones surrounding the chapel suggest.

Waters' tale exposes disempowerment, the hypocrisy, prurience and violence against women, and the deceit of the romantic narrative at the core of nineteenth-century Gothic novels. In a triumph of reimagining an era, *Fingersmith* enables the two women to love and live happily ever after, their relationship never suspected because it is unnameable, their skills acquired from now defunct controlling males, living in the house to which they have joint ownership.

Cultural Imprisonment: Hilary Mantel's *Eight Months on Ghazzah Street* (1988)

In Hilary Mantel's *Eight Months on Ghazzah Street*, there are no castles, ghosts or clanking chains, no vampires or werewolves or performative creatures of the Gothic. However, the characteristics of feminist Gothic are used throughout in an otherwise seemingly realist text, which is the story of a young woman brought out to join her husband and live in Saudi Arabia.

Frances and Andrew have lived abroad on tenuous contracts but each with their own freedoms, although endangered and poor in Africa and forever having to move because of the temporary nature of contemporary life for ex-pats. Andrew, the husband, gets a job in Saudi Arabia, paid more than anyone might ever imagine. For some, Saudi Arabia is the stuff dreams are made of since it offers money, servants, sunshine and a life of ease, where the constraints of class, culture and religion can to some extent be circumnavigated if you know the right people. What Frances actually finds is an updated, culturally switched version of entombment. Frances is a cartographer, in Jeddah, a city where streets have been reclaimed from the sea, so changed at will, dead-ends and half built roads are suddenly cut off, you are easily lost, and routes are always devious, or jammed with traffic, so you cannot move if you do go out. Her going out is utterly dependent on her husband. She has no freedom of movement, a form of normality culturally constructed but otherwise unimaginable in its extreme forms. Space is particularly gendered here. The strictness of the rules in Saudi Arabia incarcerate her in a ground floor flat in a house where every window opens on to a wall, the main entrance has been boarded up, and everyone scuttles into their own flats so the women in particular cannot be seen. If the women do move about or between flats, and certainly if they are taken out by drivers, they are fully veiled, secretive, hidden, shuttered and silenced, and with nowhere to go. Frances feels walled up alive—time loses its sense and there is nothing to talk about. The setting is culturally contextualised modern-day Gothic, and she's a Gothic victim, silenced, incarcerated, disempowered and disenfranchised. There seems to be no bodily danger except to visitors, who are driven off the road (attacked because their presence and behaviour are seen as at odds with the rules of the Kingdom), or those who disobey complex rules about relationships, politics and power, and end up dead. Frances is not quite a woman in an attic as she loses sense of time but fails to succumb to the disorientation common in 1960s and 1970s novels about women breaking down/breaking through (*The Summer Before the Dark* by Doris Lessing 1973), underpinned by the writings of R. D. Laing. But she then suspects a mystery, so there is a Gothic plot, reminiscent of *Northanger Abbey* (Austen 1817). Boxes are thumped upstairs, left on balconies, unexplained, the feet of unseen people walk to and fro in a supposedly empty flat, rumours abound about adultery, punishable by death. The interruption with home invasions and the smashing of their illicit and rather poor wine-making attempts, trashing their flat, followed by the murder of a visiting business colleague and then the revelation of a crime, would probably lead in conventional Gothic to escape and a new life. However, contemporary women's Gothic refuses the narrative closure that would suggest that such culturally paralysing, disempowering situations can be changed overnight. Andrew and Frances merely move into the compound with the other ex-pats, and now out of her window instead of walls, she sees highways. She can't get to them, however, as she cannot walk in the street, and can only move, act, exit, if taken by her husband (or a driver). Mantel's contemporary, culturally inflected Gothic transposes the traditional into the foreign, and there are no ways out and no resolutions.

THE SWAN THIEVES: ELIZABETH KOSTOVA (2010)

Kostova's *The Historian* (2005) revives *Dracula* for contemporary times, and links family relationships, travel, academic research and the constant revival in the present of influential Gothic tales and their warnings. *The Swan Thieves* (2010) recovers a moment in time, in the history of art and artists, and parallels this with the life of a contemporary artist, reminding us of the ways in which possession works to recover the past through the lives of the contemporary on whom it has an influence. It also adds to the Gothic literature which focuses on the obsessive behaviours of those who work with the past and bring it into their lives: artists, librarians, historians, academics. *The Swan Thieves* is crucially about obsessions and possession, the ways in which artists, like writers, historians and researchers, become utterly obsessed by those who influence them, their lives, ideas or messages. At the centre of the narrative is a contemporary painter and teacher, Robert Oliver, who saw a painting of Beatrice de Cerval, an Impressionist, then hunted down work by and information about her, becoming obsessed by painting and drawing his vision of her—sometimes at rest, sometimes choosing a dying woman, sometimes holding back rage. Elements of the life of this other hidden twentieth-century woman artist took him over so completely that he painted her obsessively even while holding down a normal job, wife and family and encouraging the work of others. The novel details the obsession of art and its intrusion on one's personal life when being produced. Art and artistic talent reveal themselves as kinds of Gothic predator and preserver. Art captures one timeless and utterly time-bound fleeting moment in time and place, such as people together or night-light leaving the bay, the moment after figures have walked on. Researchers and creative people will recognise the ways such moments engage and influence, and how such artistic products capture and force a return in each re-viewing, and in Oliver's case each repeated painting on the same topic, Beatrice de Cerval. For Robert, this obsession which is a part of his talent leads to life in a sanatorium (mental health facility), a ruined marriage and relationship.

Some of this novel is also about the haunting of the present by hidden women artists of the past, women whose lives have been off record and whose works linger in basements and attics (or were never painted) or were passed off as someone else's, or appeared only under pseudonyms because of the dangerous scandals that seemed to accompany being an artist, as if they were somehow members of the Folies Bergère. The upset to the stability of family life comes from the time, commitment and the public scrutiny of being an artist or writer (one recalls Lily Briscoe in To The Lighthouse, Woolf 1927), forever hearing in her subconscious Charles Tansley's taunt, product of his own chip on his shoulder, 'women can't write, women can't paint.' Olivier Vingot, Beatrice's husband's uncle, briefly becomes her lover and supports her art. Beatrice stops painting when she has her daughter and forever believes she has just dedicated herself to being a mother and wife, a conventional choice. Any revelation of her identity that could have followed from the success of showing her painting under the pseudonym Madame Revere would have ruined her. Instead, her work is passed off as someone else's. Robert Thomas, unscrupulous and less talented, adopted and showed her work as his own. This causes us to wonder about ownership, identity swaps, and the hiding of women's talent. How many women artists have hidden behind the threat of scandal, the shock of their being anything other than domestic, the disempowerment of lack of investment, and lack of power to expose those who stole their publicity and greatness? Beatrice's tale is an example of what was probably common: artists were often anonymous. Anonymous was a woman, hidden from view. Robert Oliver's obsession with Beatrice as a subject for his work, and the discovery of the letters held by her daughter, left to her lover Henri in Paris, stolen by Robert, reveals her story. In familiar Gothic fashion, letters, research, piecing stories and images together, the paralleling of two times, the mirrors to more than two sets of events and relationships, the haunting of the lives of others, of the past in the present, as muse, all emphasise Gothic haunting of past histories and art, in the work of the present.

The Daylight Gate: Jeanette Winterson (2012)

The Daylight Gate, Jeanette Winterson's short Hammer novel, is a brilliant Gothic piece capturing a transitional moment in history (1612) and the borderline of truth/fiction, right/wrong, natural and supernatural. In the liminal space between day and night, whether dusk or dawn, nothing is fixed and all transmutable, it is possible to open up a vivid moment for the Pendle witches and the dullness of prosecution and detail in the name of regulation. Potts, who spends his life on the detail, claims he writes plays (unheard of) and eventually provides the official record, and Shakespeare makes a small cameo appearance, resembling his famous image, intrigued by the version of *The Tempest*, his magical play in favour of King James. Alice Nutter, Winterson's invented witch, is at the heart of the tale, while the historical Pendle witches are depicted as impoverished, famished and embittered, a community reliant on their alternative powers, with the herbalists on the acceptable end of that continuum and the varied tribe at the other end. The straitlaced powers of Protestantism which James I represented conflated witchery and popery with heresy—remnants of and acts of Catholicism as satanic lore and craft—what is particularly unpalatable is seen as both constructed to fit the times, and also construed as satanic witchcraft by those who believe this nonsense (Potts, in the novel), and those whose time-serving need to preserve their own lives causes them to buy into it (Nowell, in the novel). The construction of witches and witchcraft is represented as both a political product of a moment of transition between Protestantism and Catholicism, where Catholicism is seen as dubiously evil, as *Macbeth*'s witches with their pilots thumb in the north, guiding people astray—but on the other hand it is also in this novelette more than a metaphor for political incorrigibles and popery. It is also an experience on the cusp of that marvellous moment which in Shakespeare is captured in *A Midsummer Night's Dream* as well as *The Tempest*, when the darkness of the fairy world, the alternative parallel world, shows us something of ourselves.

Beaten and famished the local families are incarcerated in a dungeon, awaiting trial for being part of a coven, a familiar community turned into the filth they are seen as. The women sell their bodies to the gaolers for a crust of bread, and eat the rats who would otherwise gnaw their feet. Deprived of heat, water, food and air, they fester. From such a cauldron it is not surprising that they seize any opportunity to boil a head, sew in a tongue, stick a poppet with pins, attacking their enemies with their own witchcraft. Witchcraft runs throughout this novel. The Pendle witches themselves are in the tale, part of history although Alice Nutter, a rich local woman inventor of magenta dye, is a constructed character and occupies a liminal space between wealth and her vulnerability as a woman. Disempowered she can be flayed and caged, and ultimately nearly hung. When powerful, her reputation and wealth preserve her and her ability to deny accusations as nonsense, hiding behind the logic and realism which her very being and seemingly everlasting youth deny. Another liminal space or daylight gate is that of truth and construction—the representation of evil is seen as mostly a construction perpetuated on the poor by the rich, on the papists by the Protestants, on the politically disempowered and valueless (because of gender and poverty) by those in power.

With some devilish help from Dee (based on Dr John Dee, the magician), Alice Nutter invents magenta dye, and in this moment achieves also her wealth, status and so safety. With her female lover Elizabeth Southern (latterly the aged crone the demdyke), she initially engaged in a relationship with John Dee and historical necromancers, procurers or seekers, who dabbled in alchemy, making gold. Elizabeth seems to have sold her soul to the devil, but Alice is the one who profits and survives. Alice's youthful appearance is enabled by the vial of elixir produced by Dee. She can look beautiful forever, and beauty and wealth have their power. Alice is the real hero of the novel—she is scrupulous, caring, intelligent and able to manage her world so that no one is accused and no one incriminated, but eventually she is overcome by the social and political drive to incriminate her. She is not outwitted; she is the victim of bureaucracy, pedantry mixed with starvation. Potts seeks her, and the community led by Jem and Jennet, expose her. The tour de force of all of this is that while most of these women are merely victims of poverty and accusations of witchcraft, Alice actually is in league with the powers of otherness, not always seen as darkness. She has truly crossed through a daylight gate into the liminal space between acceptability, denying pompous pedantry, charting and fixing. Her ways deny political conformity, and the brutal treatment of any outsider, woman, child, the poor. Into a historical story of persecution and death for witchcraft, which was most likely condemnation of women, age, alternative religion and belief and poverty, Winterson inserts someone who is truly powerful, eternally beautiful, social, just maintaining her own land, and also marvellously, other. Alice's first love was a woman, her secret of youth and beauty an elixir from John Dee. She really is someone who transcends the bounds of history and reality. When the going gets tough and she cannot save her community and her hope over her papist lover Christopher Southworth, Alice can summon dark forces, and the force of her familiar, the hawk, who finally slits her throat so that she can evade the noose and die at her own command. Alice remains in control in an increasingly unsafe contest. Christopher also finds a way to take his own life, cutting his wrists, and so like Alice acts as an agent, gains control. The novel indicts political and religious powers which denigrate people who refuse, resist and think otherwise—for reasons of religion, gender or power. Alice is part of an alternative way of life and time; ultimately she and the novel celebrate that liminal space, that daylight gate, which is a way through into seeing things differently and seeing through the bureaucratic lying nonsense which twists and demands.

A dark, energetic novel, its Gothic qualities are in spaces, dungeons, castles, secret rooms, hidden bedchambers, lonely hilltops, the moor Alice haunts, and the mists and the trees. Dominant dimensions of power are revealed as based on lies and ignorance, bought into by those who have to collude to survive. The novel's power is in its revelation of contradictions in terms of values, economics, and the dimensions of space and light and day, realised in myth.

Winterson's marvellous novel/novella exposes the demonising of anyone whose religious, political or sexual activities countered those of the wealthy and powerful. Lies are easily bought, bodies broken, poverty a curse and love in the main a temporary refuge and lasting loss. But the liminal space offered by the tale is that of Alice and her lovers. Alice Nutter actually is a woman with supernatural powers, a fictional figure existing on the cusp of a moment when superstition and fairy lore were being forced into a deadening, denied, locked down, worldview—when the binary divisions between rich and poor, men and women, right and wrong, natural and supernatural were both rigorously enforced and yet utterly tenuous, a moment of liminality, a daylight gate, shut by history but opened by Winterson's retelling.

Only a Contemporary Obsession?

Different moments find their reflection in different genres, so just after the Second World War, westerns and science fiction became the modes of choice with which to deal with challenges, fear and hopes, while romantic fictions dominated in the interwar years. Superficially, this could explain the current obsession with Gothicising everything from true love eternal romances to T-shirt sales. Dissipation and trivialising can happen with a genre which becomes the genre of popular choice. In my mind this would be a problem and one to be avoided while we might still enjoy the popular. Not only can the radical edgy disturbing energies and forms of expression in the Gothic become trivial and watered down when so thinly spread, so superficial, but we are perhaps in danger of forgetting the role of the Gothic beyond entertainment. It certainly is often darkly, amusingly entertaining just because it destabilises in order to cause us to rethink, to move beyond blinkered complacencies. But beyond entertainment and edginess, the Gothic does have designs upon us as readers, and those designs are not just to entertain. The very ways in which Gothic texts reveal, reverse, revisit, and re-read versions of our established histories of periods and place, as well as of self and others, throw the reader into a state of questioning and reinterpretation. Gothic narratives challenge the strategies of fiction itself, and of grand narratives, emphasising their plottedness and the ways in which we make and inhabit story, so that the placid comfort of repeating narratives without questioning their intentions and their deviations is no longer open to us. The Gothic is a daylight gate, a gap into otherness, a mirror that reflects back history, story, self and others with new perspectives and edges. With the deliberate exception of just a few texts considered in this book on contemporary women's Gothic fiction, everything explored and discussed holds up a cracked mirror to a seemingly smoothed-over set of ways of seeing, behaving and retelling, and with the emphasis on parallels and twinning, it also shows that we can read, see and be from many different perspectives. Gothic reading does not merely entertain, it enables agency, and causes us to see, think and to act in radical, new and varied ways.

BIBLIOGRAPHY

Atkinson, K. (2004) *Case Histories* (New York: Doubleday).
Austen, J. (1817) *Northanger Abbey* (London: John Murray).
Dickens, C. (1837) *Oliver Twist* (London: Richard Bentley).
Dickens, C. (1853) *Bleak House* (London: Bradbury & Evans).
Dickens, C. (1860) *Great Expectations* (London: Chapman and Hall).
Höglund, J. (2014) *The American Imperial Gothic: Popular Culture, Empire, Violence* (Farnham: Ashgate Publishing).
Hopkinson, N. and Mehan, U. (2004) *So Long Been Dreaming: Postcolonial Science Fiction & Fantasy* (Vancouver: Arsenal Pulp Press).
Kostova, E. (2005) *The Historian* (New York: Little, Brown).
Kostova, E. (2010) *The Swan Thieves* (New York: Little, Brown).
Kristeva, J. (1988) *Strangers to Ourselves* (New York: Columbia University Press).
Lessing, D. (1973) *The Summer Before the Dark* (New York: Alfred A. Knopf).
Mantel, H. (1988) *Eight Months on Ghazzah Street* (New York: Viking Press).

Niffenegger, A. (2003) *The Time Traveller's Wife* (San Francisco: MacAdam/Cage).
Sebold, A. (2002) *The Lovely Bones* (New York: Little, Brown).
Smith, A. (2012) 'The Limits of Neo-Victorian History: Elizabeth Kostova's *The Historian and the Swan Thieves*', in *Neo Victorian Gothic: Horror, Violence and Degeneration in the Re-imagined Nineteenth Century*, M.-L. Kohlke and C. Gutleben (eds.), p. 52.
Spooner, C. (2006) *Contemporary Gothic* (London: Reaktion Books).
Waters, S. (2002) *Fingersmith* (London: Virago).
Winterson, J. (2012) *The Daylight Gate* (London: Hammer).
Woolf, V. (1927) *To the Lighthouse* (London: Hogarth Press).

Bibliography

Atwood, M. (1983) *Bluebeard's Egg and Other Stories* (Toronto: McClelland & Stewart).
Atwood, M. (1988) *Cat's Eye* (Toronto: McClelland & Stewart).
Atwood, M. (1992) *Good Bones* (Toronto: Coach House Press).
Atwood, M. (1995a) 'Concerning Franklin and his Gallant Crew', in *Strange Things: The Malevolent North in Canadian Literature* (Oxford: Oxford University Press).
Atwood, M. (1995b) *Strange Things: The Malevolent North in Canadian Literature* (Oxford: Oxford University Press).
Atwood, M. (2000) *The Blind Assassin* (Toronto: McClelland & Stewart).
Atwood, M. (2003) *Oryx and Crake* (New York: Nan A. Talese).
Atwood, M. (2014a) 'I Dream of Zenia with the Bright Red Teeth', in *Stone Mattress* (Toronto: McClelland & Stewart).
Atwood, M. (2014b) *Stone Mattress* (Toronto: McClelland & Stewart).
Baring-Gould, S. [1865] (1995) *The Book of Werewolves* (Guernsey: Studio Editions).
Barker, M. (1984) *A Haunt of Fears:The Strange History of the British Horror Comics Campaign* (London: Pluto Press).
Barker, P. (1991) *Regeneration* (New York: Viking Press).
Barker, P. (1995) *The Ghost Road* (New York: Viking Press).
Barnes, D. [1936] (1963) *Nightwood* (London: Faber and Faber).
Brite, P. Z. (1993a) *Drawing Blood* (London: Penguin Books).
Brite, P. Z. (1993b) *Lost Souls* (New York: Dell).
Brite, P. Z. (1994b) *Swamp Foetus* (Harmondsworth: Penguin).
Brite, P. Z. (1996a) *Exquisite Corpse* (New York: Touchstone Books).
Brite, P. Z. (1996b) *Twice Bitten (Love in Vein 2)* (New York: Harper Prism).

Brite, P. Z. (1996c) *Wormwood* (formally published as *Swamp Foetus*, 1994) (New York: Bantam Doubleday/Dell Publishing Group).
Brite, P. Z. (1998a) *Are You Loathsome Tonight? A Collection of Short Stories* (Colorado Springs, CO: Gauntlet Press).
Brite, P. Z. (1998c) *Self-Made Man* (formerly published as *Are You Loathsome Tonight?*) (London: Orion).
Brite, P. Z. (1999) *The Lazarus Heart* (Colorado Springs, CO: Gauntlet Press).
British Council (2011) *Alice Munro*. http://literature.britishcouncil.org/alice-munro
Brontë, C.[1847] (2003) *Jane Eyre* (Harmondsworth: Penguin).
Brontë, E. (1847) *Wuthering Heights* (London: Thomas Cautley Newby).
Cagney Watts, H. (1985) 'Interview with Angela Carter', *Bête Noire*, August, p. 170.
Califia, P. (1993) 'The Vampire', in *Daughters of Darkness: Lesbian Vampire Stories*, P. Keesey (ed.) (San Francisco: Cleis Press).
Carter, A. (1966) *Shadow Dance* (London: Heinemann).
Carter, A. [1967] (1981) *The Magic Toyshop* (London: Virago).
Carter, A. (1968) *Several Perceptions* (London: Heinemann).
Carter, A. [1968] (1998) *Shaking a Leg: Collected Journalism and Writings* (London: Vintage).
Carter, A. (1971) *Love* (London: Virago).
Carter, A. (1972) *The Infernal Desire Machine of Dr Hoffman* (London: Rupert Hart-Davis).
Carter, A. (1974a) 'Afterword', in *Fireworks: Nine Profane Pieces* (London: Virago).
Carter, A. (1974b) 'The Executioner's Beautiful Daughter', in *Fireworks: Nine Profane Pieces* (London: Virago).
Carter, A. (1974c) *Fireworks: Nine Profane Pieces* (London: Virago).
Carter, A. (1974d) 'Flesh and the Mirror', in *Fireworks: Nine Profane Pieces* (London: Virago).
Carter, A. (1974e) 'The Loves of Lady Purple', in *Fireworks: Nine Profane Pieces* (London: Virago).
Carter, A.(1974f) 'Master', in *Fireworks: Nine Profane Pieces* (London: Virago).
Carter, A. (1977) *The Passion of New Eve* (New York: Harcourt Brace Jovanovich).
Carter, A. (1979a) 'The Bloody Chamber', in *The Bloody Chamber and Other Stories* (London: Gollancz).
Carter, A. (1979b) 'The Company of Wolves', in *The Bloody Chamber and Other Stories* (London: Gollancz).
Carter, A. (1979c) 'The Lady of the House of Love', in *The Bloody Chamber and Other Stories* (London: Gollancz).
Carter, A. (1979d) *The Sadeian Woman: An Exercise in Cultural History* (London: Virago).

Carter, A. (1979e) 'Wolf Alice', in *The Bloody Chamber and Other Stories* (London: Gollancz).
Carter, A. (1983) 'Notes from the Front Line', in *On Gender and Writing*, M. Wandor (ed.) (London: Pandora).
Carter, A. (1985a) 'The Cabinet of Edgar Allan Poe', in *Black Venus* (London: Chatto & Windus).
Carter, A. (1985b) 'The Fall River Axe Murders', in *Black Venus* (London: Chatto & Windus).
Carter, A. [1974] (1986) 'The Loves of Lady Purple', in *Wayward Girls and Wicked Women* (London: Virago).
Carter, A. (1987) *Nights at the Circus* (London: Chatto & Windus).
Carter, A. (1991) *Wise Children* (London: Chatto & Windus).
Carter, A. (1993) *American Ghosts and Old World Wonders* (London: Chatto & Windus).
Carter, A. (1994) 'John Ford's Tis Pity She's a Whore', in *American Ghosts and Old World Wonders* (London: Vintage).
Carter, M. (n.d.) *The Vampire's Crypt* (discontinued 2002), http://www.margaretlcarter.com/home/index.php?option=com_content&task=view&id=53&Itemid=32
Carter, M. L. (2004) *Different Blood: The Vampire as Alien* (Indian Hills, CO: Amber Quill Press).
Carter, M. L. (2010) 'Vampire Romance', in *Encyclopedia of the Vampire: The Living Dead in Myth, Legend and Popular Culture*, S. T Joshi (ed.) (Westport, CT: Greenwood Press).
Case, S. E. (1991a) 'Tracking the Vampire', *Differences: A Journal of Feminist Cultural Studies*, Vol. 3, No. 2.
Case, S. E.(1991b) 'Tracking the Vampire', in *Reading the Vampire*, K. Gelder (ed.) (1994) (London: Routledge).
Cixous, H. (1976b) 'Fiction and Its Phantoms: A Reading of Freud's Das Unheimliche (The "Uncanny")', *New Literary History*, Vol. 7, No. 3.
Collins, M. (1985) 'Crick Crack Monkey', in *Because the Dawn Breaks: Poems Dedicated to the Grenadian People* (London: Women's Press).
Dickens, C. (1854) *Hard Times* (London: Bradbury & Evans).
Du Maurier, D. (1938) *Rebecca* (London: Victor Gollancz).
Due, T.(2002a) http://maxinethompson.com/Tananarive.html, Maxine Thompson's Literary Services, Black Butterfly Press.
Due, T. (2002b) Interview 17 March, http://www.tananarivedue.com/interview.htm
Eaglestone, R. (2000) 'Undoing English', *CCUE News*, Issue 13, p. 22.
Evans, M. (1985) *Black Women Writers: Arguments and Interviews* (London: Pluto Press).
Fiedler, L. (1960) *Love and Death in the American Novel* (New York: Dalkey Archive Press).

Freud, S. [1919] (1953) 'The Uncanny', in *The Standard Edition of the Complete Psychological Works of Sigmund Freud*, Vol. XVII, J. Strachey (ed. and trans.) (London: Hogarth).
Gamble, S. (1994) *Angela Carter: Writing from the Front Line* (Edinburgh: Edinburgh University Press).
Gamble, S. (ed.) (2001a) *The Fiction of Angela Carter: A Reader's Guide to Essential Criticism* (Basingstoke: Palgrave Macmillan).
Gamble, S. (2001b) 'Postfeminism', in *The Routledge Companion to Feminism and Postfeminism*, S. Gamble (ed.) (London: Routledge).
Gaskell, E. (1848) *Mary Barton* (London: Chapman & Hall).
Grahame-Smith, S. (2009) *Pride and Prejudice and Zombies* (Philadelphia: Quirk Books).
Hamilton, L. K. (1993–2010) *Anita Blake, Vampire Hunter* series (19 novels) (New York: Ace Books).
Harris, C. (2001) *Dead Until Dark* (New York: Ace Books).
Hill, D. R. (2007) *Caribbean Folklore: A Handbook* (Newport, CT: Greenwood Press).
Hill, S. (2007) *The Man in the Picture* (London: Profile Books).
Hoffman, M. (1992) *The Cabinet of Dr Caligari* (Monster Comics).
Hogg, J. (1970) *Confessions of a Justified Sinner* (London: Panther).
Hopkinson, N. (1998) *Brown Girl in the Ring* (New York: Time Warner International).
Hopkinson, N. (2001b) 'A Habit of Waste', in *Skin Folk* (New York: Aspect).
Hopkinson, N. (2001c) 'Precious', in *Skin Folk* (New York: Aspect).
Hughes, W. (2012) 'Sexuality and the Twentieth-Century American Vampire', in *A Companion to American Gothic*, C. L. Crow (ed.) (Oxford: Wiley-Blackwell).
Jackson, R. (1981) *Fantasy: The Literature of Subversion* (London: Routledge).
Kemp, P. (1993) 'Bewitched, Bothered and Bewildered', *The Sunday Times*, 17 October, p. 44.
Kiernan, C. R. (1998) *Silk* (New York: Penguin Putnam).
King, F. (1993) 'Ruthless Charm of a Monster', *London Evening Standard*, 14 October, p. 44.
Laing, R. D. (1960) *The Divided Self: An Existential Study in Sanity and Madness* (Harmondsworth: Penguin).
Laing, R. D. (1967) *The Politics of Experience and The Bird of Paradise* (Harmondsworth: Penguin).
Le Fanu, S. (1872) 'Carmilla', in *In a Glass Darkly* (London: R. Bentley and Son).
Lim, C. (1976a) 'The Ghost Child', in *Little Ironies: Stories of Singapore* (Singapore: Heinemann Asia).
Lim, C. (1976b) 'Paper', in *Little Ironies:Stories of Singapore* (Singapore: Heinemann Asia).

Lim, C. (1982) *The Serpent's Tooth* (Singapore: Times Books International).
Lovecraft, H. P. [1928] (1973) *Supernatural Horror in Literature* (Mineola, NY: Dover Publications).
Marryat, F. (1897) *The Blood of the Vampire*(London: Hutchinson).
Martin, S. (1993) 'Playing with Razor Blades', *Quill and Quire*, 25 August, p. 94.
Mew, C. (1903) 'A White Night', *Temple Bar CXXVII*, pp. 625–639.
Meyer, J. H. F. and Land, R. (eds.) (2003) *Overcoming Barriers to Student Understanding: Threshold Concepts and Troublesome Knowledge* (London and New York: Routledge).
Meyer, S. (2005) *Twilight* (New York: Little, Brown).
Modleski, T. (1982) 'The Female Uncanny: Gothic Novels for Women', in *Loving with a Vengeance* (London: Routledge).
Moers, E. [1976] (1978) *Literary Women* (London: Women's Press).
Mosse, K. (2008) *Sepulchre* (London: Orion).
Mulvey-Roberts, M. (2015) 'Correspondence with Gina Wisker', December.
Munro, A. (1968a) *Dance of the Happy Shades* (Toronto: Ryerson Press).
Munro, A. (1968b) 'Images', in *Dance of the Happy Shades* (Toronto: Ryerson Press).
Munro, A. (2012a) 'Amundsen', in *The New Yorker*, 27 August.
Munro, A. (2012b) 'Haven', in *The New Yorker*, 5 March.
Munro, A. (2013a) *Dear Life* (Toronto: McClelland & Stewart).
Munro, A. (2013b) 'To Reach Japan', in *Dear Life* (Toronto: McClelland & Stewart).
Nichols, G. (1983) *I Is a Long Memoried Woman* (London: Karnac House).
Nicholson, M. (1994) 'Unpopular Gals', *The Vancouver Review*, Spring, p. 22.
O'Farrell, M. (2000) *After You'd Gone* (London: Penguin).
Patterson, M. (2012) 'On "Combative Love": Q and A with Helen Oyeyemi', *Toronto Review of Books*, Issue 3, 17 April, http://www.torontoreviewofbooks.com/2012/04/on-combative-love-q-and-a-with-helen-oyeyemi/
Pearce, P. (1958) *Tom's Midnight Garden* (Oxford: Oxford University Press).
Poe, E. A. [1842] (1966) 'The Pit and the Pendulum', in *Complete Stories and Poems of Edgar Allan Poe* (New York: Doubleday/Dell Publishing Group).
Punter, D. (ed.) (2012) *A New Companion to the Gothic* (2nd edn.) (Oxford: Blackwell).
Rice, A. (1985) *The Vampire Lestat* (New York: Knopf).
Rich, A. [1980] (1994) 'Compulsory Heterosexuality and Lesbian Existence', in *Blood, Bread, and Poetry* (New York: Norton).
rubystar21 (2014) '2113—The Vampires Rule', https://www.wattpad.com/18524350-2113-the-vampires-rule-chapter-1-madeleine
Russ, J. (1993) 'Someone's Trying to Kill Me and I Think It's My Husband', in *The Female Gothic*, J. E. Fleenor (ed.) (Montreal: Eden Press).
Rutledge, G. E. (1999) 'Speaking in Tongues: An Interview with Science Fiction Writer Nalo Hopkinson', *African American Review*, Vol. 33, No. 4.

Sage, L. (ed.) (1994) *Flesh and the Mirror: Essays on the Art of Angela Carter* (London: Virago).
Smith, L. J. (1996) *Night World: Secret Vampire* (New York: Simon & Schuster).
Spivak, G. C. (1988) 'Can the Subaltern Speak?', in *Marxism and the Interpretation of Culture*, C. Nelson and L. Grossberg (eds.) (Basingstoke: Macmillan Education).
Szasz, T. S. (1961) *The Myth of Mental Illness: Foundations of a Theory of Personal Conduct* (New York: Hoeber-Harper).
Tem, M. (1992) *Blood Moon* (London: Women's Press).
Tem, M. (1996) 'Wilding', in *Women Who Run with the Werewolves*, P. Keesey (ed.) (San Francisco: Cleis Press).
Tennant, E. (1992) *Faustine* (London: Faber and Faber).
Tomalin, C. (1989) 'Novel Lacks Plot but Offers Insight on Aging', *The Telegraph*, 19 February.
Townsend Warner, S. [1926] (1993) *Lolly Willowes* (London: Virago).
Townshend, D. (2014) Facebook post, September.
Walker, A. (1983) *In Search of Our Mother's Gardens: Womanist Prose* (New York: Harcourt Brace Jovanovitch).
Wallace, D. and Smith, A. (2009) *The Female Gothic: New Directions* (Basingstoke: Palgrave Macmillan).
Ward-Jouve, N. (1986) *The Street-Cleaner: The Yorkshire Ripper Case on Trial* (London: Marion Boyars).
Waters, S. (2006) *The Night Watch* (London: Virago).
Winterson, J. (1988) *Sexing the Cherry* (London: Bloomsbury).
Wisker, G. (1993) *Creepers: British Horror and Fantasy in the Twentieth Century*, C. Bloom (ed.) (London: Pluto Press).
Wisker, G. (1994) 'Weaving Our Own Web, De-Mythologising/Re-Mythologising and Imagining in the Work of Contemporary Women Writers', in *It's My Party: Reading Twentieth Century Women's Writing* (London: Pluto Press).
Wisker, G. (2002) *Toni Morrison: A Beginner's Guide* (London: Hodder & Stoughton).
Wisker, G. (2003a) *Angela Carter: A Beginner's Guide* (London: Hodder & Stoughton).
Wisker, G. (2005) *Horror Fiction: An Introduction* (New York: Continuum).
Wisker, G. (2006b) 'Postcolonial Gothic', in *Teaching the Gothic*, A. Smith and A. Powell (eds.) (Basingstoke: Palgrave Macmillan).
Wisker, G. (2011) 'Devouring Desires: Lesbian Gothic Horror', in *Queering the Gothic*, W. Hughes (ed.) (Manchester: Manchester University Press).
Wisker, G., Cameron, S. and, Antoniou, M. (2007) *Connotations and Conjunctions: Threshold Concepts, Curriculum Development, and the Cohesion of English Studies* (University of Brighton, Final Report to English Subject Centre, October).

Yarbro, C. Q. (1978–2010) *Count Saint-Germain* novels (New York: Tor Books).
Yeats, W. B. (1939) 'The Circus Animals' Desertion', in *Last Poems and Two Plays* (Shannon: Irish University Press).

Film

Amityville Horror, The (1979) dir. Stuart Rosenberg.
Birds, The (1963) dir. Alfred Hitchcock.
Byzantium (2013) dir. Neil Jordan.
Cabinet of Dr Caligari, The (1920) dir. Robert Wiene.
Carry on Screaming (1966) dir. Gerald Thomas.
Dawn of the Dead (2004) dir. Zack Snyder.
Exorcist, The (1973) dir. William Friedkin.
Girl Walks Home Alone at Night, A (2014) dir. Ana Lily Amirpour.
Godzilla (2014) dir. Gareth Edwards.
Gosford Park (2001) dir. Robert Altman.
I, Frankenstein (2014) dir. Stuart Beattie.
Invasion of the Body Snatchers (1956) dir. Don Siegel.
Invasion of the Body Snatchers (1978) dir. Philip Kaufman.
Loves of Count Iorga, Vampire, The (1970) dir. Bob Kelljan.
My Fair Lady (1964) dir. George Cukor.
Never Let Me Go (2005) dir. Mark Romanek.
Night of the Living Dead, dir. (1969) George A. Romero.
Nightmare on Elm Street, A, (1984) dir. Wes Craven.
Omen, The (1976) dir. Richard Donner.
Pacific Rim (2013) dir. Guillermo del Toro.
Poltergeist (1982) dir. Tobe Hooper.
Psycho (1960) dir. Alfred Hitchcock.
Road, The (2009) dir. John Hillcoat.
Shining, The (2008) dir. Stanley Kubrick.
Transcendence (2014) dir. Wally Pfister.
War of the Worlds, The (1953), dir. Byron Haskin.
War of the Worlds, The (2005), dir. Steven Spielberg.
Woman in Black, The (2012) dir. James Watkins.
Young Frankenstein (1974) dir. Mel Brooks.

Music

Meeropol, A. (1939) *Strange Fruit* (performed by Billie Holiday).

TV

Angela Carter: An Interview (1977), interview with Les Bedford, University of Sheffield.
Buffy the Vampire Slayer (1997–2003) dir. Joss Whedon, the WB and UPN networks.
True Blood (2008–2014) dir. Alan Ball, HBO.
Woman in Black, The (1989) dir. Herbert Wise, ITV.

Theatre

Vampire Story, A (2008) dir. and writer Moira Buffini.
Woman in Black, The (1987) dir. Stephen Mallatratt.

Radio Plays

Carter, A. (1976) *Vampirella*, Radio 3.

Websites

http://www.the-cwwa.org/
http://literature.britishcouncil.org/alice-munro
http://nalohopkinson.com/blog/nalohop
https://www.wattpad.com/18524350-2113-the-vampires-rule-chapter-1-madeleine

Index

A

abuse, 23, 26, 78, 84, 92, 107, 119, 124, 130, 145, 148, 150, 152, 202, 214, 239
  sexual, 47
agency, 17, 23, 35, 39, 40, 44, 46, 50, 55–7, 69, 70, 75–7, 79–84, 90, 102, 118, 125, 130, 135, 136, 147, 155, 158–60, 163, 166, 182, 194, 204, 221, 235, 250
Amirpour, A.L., 3, 203, 204
  A Girl Walks Home Alone at Night, 203
Armitt, L., 18, 22, 23, 50
artifice, 10, 21, 34, 37, 38, 40, 48, 54–6, 58–60, 82, 154, 170, 175, 216, 237, 242
Atwood, M.
  Alias Grace, 28, 74–7, 89
  Bluebeard's Egg, 76
  Cat's Eye, 71, 74–7, 80, 81, 88
  The Handmaid's Tale, 22, 71–3, 75, 76
  Lady Oracle, 22, 74–80, 83, 85, 88

The Robber Bride, 71, 74–7, 80–9, 152
Auerbach, N., 157, 183, 184, 187, 188, 199
Aw, T., 18–19, 127
  The Harmony Silk Factory, 127

B

bigotry, 214, 237
binary divisions, 34, 249
blood, 18, 20, 42, 109, 114, 128, 135, 139, 142, 158, 160–2, 164, 167, 172, 174, 175, 177–9, 182, 184, 193, 196–8, 200, 202
Bluebeard, 22, 28, 48, 50–2, 79, 134–7, 142, 145, 147, 148, 151–3, 155
  and his castle, 28, 43, 50, 133–55
body, 2, 7, 8, 11, 14, 16, 22–4, 41, 44, 64, 78, 96, 98, 101, 102, 105, 107, 110, 112, 114, 127, 129, 131, 134, 136, 138, 142, 144, 146, 148, 149, 153, 159, 168, 176–8, 180, 184, 188, 212–14, 227, 230, 237, 238

Briggs, J., 26, 130, 201, 208, 209–10
Brite, P.Z., 157, 158, 160, 168–73, 178, 181, 184, 187, 188, 203
  Lost Souls, 165, 168, 170–2
Brodber, E., 3, 22, 28, 124, 136–43, 153–5
  Myal, 22, 124, 137–43
Brontë, C., 11, 190, 191, 212, 227
  Jane Eyre, 12, 14, 22, 33, 34, 51, 117, 125, 126, 211, 220, 226
Buffini, M., 184, 188
  Byzantium, 28, 182, 187, 195, 199–204
  A Vampire Story, 28, 182, 187, 195, 199–204
Buffy the Vampire Slayer, 195, 197
Byatt, A.S., 239
  Possession, 239

C

Caribbean
  literature, 137
  myth, 143, 144, 147, 197
carnivalesque, 40, 48, 58–61, 82, 169, 184
Carter, A.
  The Bloody Chamber and Other Stories; 'The Bloody Chamber', 10, 35, 37, 38, 40, 43, 49–54, 136, 152; 'The Company of Wolves', 35, 50, 52, 53; 'The Lady of the House of Love', 39, 42–5, 158, 163, 166, 173; 'Wolf Alice', 52, 53
  Fireworks, 33, 38, 40, 235; 'The Loves of Lady Purple', 39, 42–5, 166, 173
  The Magic Toyshop, 12–14, 35, 38, 40, 45–8, 51, 55
  Nights at the Circus, 34, 35, 38, 40, 41, 46, 54–60

The Sadeian Woman, 4, 36, 38, 49, 51, 59
castles, 42, 43, 51–3, 56, 72, 95, 134, 136, 155, 158, 166, 212
children, 5, 15, 65, 68, 72, 73, 83, 95, 96, 100–2, 106, 139, 141, 142, 145, 146, 148–50, 162, 182, 193, 195, 208, 214–21, 237
circus, 54, 56, 57, 60
civil rights movement, 91, 105
class, 5, 46, 200, 202, 222–8, 243
clothes, 4, 52, 68, 72, 78, 223, 227, 242, 243
colonialism, 12, 18, 92, 117, 119, 126, 130, 134, 138, 140, 154
comic, 5, 40, 59–61, 88, 190
community, 35, 91–5, 101–4, 107, 109, 141–3, 147, 158, 193, 197, 198, 211, 212, 214, 247, 248
Creed, B., 11, 161, 162, 167, 175, 178
  The Monstrous Feminine, 10, 159
curse, 74, 77, 145, 166, 168, 181, 201, 214, 219, 249

D

deceit, 22, 58, 70, 77, 78, 80, 104, 159, 233, 242, 243
defamiliarisation, 2, 19, 26, 37, 68, 73, 80, 122, 152, 209, 240
demonising, 11, 16, 117, 148, 161, 162, 165, 167, 184, 220, 249
demythologising, 33, 46, 133–55
Derrida, J., 92
de Sade, M., 38, 46, 49–50
deviance, 60, 162
dis-ease, 1, 2, 157
disturbance, 2, 14, 83, 209, 210, 240
domestic space, 136, 208

Dracula, 6, 39, 42, 43, 159, 161, 166, 169, 172, 238
Due, T.
  Joplin's Ghost, 91–3, 109–13
  The Living Blood, 195–7
du Maurier, D., 11, 34
  Rebecca, 12–14, 33, 211, 228
dungeons, 83, 247
Dunmore, H., 3, 28
  The Greatcoat, 208, 210, 213, 220–33
duppies, 118, 124, 140, 141, 144, 146, 147
dystopian science fiction, 70

E

education, 57, 98–103, 135, 137–43, 154, 200, 202, 204, 208, 222, 237, 240, 241
entrapment, 7, 38, 43, 46, 50, 56, 63, 65, 71, 76, 77, 79, 82, 136, 150, 158, 211, 212, 222, 224, 225, 232
exorcism, 80, 87, 91, 142
exploration, 3, 4, 21, 27, 33, 36, 53, 60, 63, 71, 88, 89, 91, 152, 176, 181, 187, 188, 190

F

fairytales, 6, 12, 21, 22, 28, 33, 34, 38, 42, 45, 48, 50, 52, 54, 55, 58, 59, 64, 69, 76, 79, 81, 82, 84–9, 125, 134, 144, 149, 151, 152, 166, 192, 226
fallible narrator, 221, 224
family, 2, 9, 15, 16, 18, 21–5, 34, 35, 40, 42, 47, 48, 50, 58, 65, 66, 80, 82, 83, 85, 87, 88, 95, 96, 98, 99, 101–4, 106, 112, 131, 147, 149, 160, 168–70, 173, 176, 187, 188, 191–9, 204, 207, 208, 211–15, 217, 219, 221–7, 229, 233, 237, 241, 245–7
fantastic, 15, 25, 26, 54–6, 58, 60, 78, 97, 143, 176, 192, 227
female
  body, 7, 8, 23, 44
  foreign, 117, 125
  friendship, 70, 76, 86
  objectification, 44
  sexuality, 9, 166
  subjection, 44
feminism
  postcolonial, 153–5
  second wave, 12, 23, 27, 33, 37–9, 66, 80, 153, 190, 232
First World War, 18, 43, 158, 163, 164
folk culture, 136, 137
folklore, 109, 118
  Caribbean, 145, 146
folk tales, 27, 108, 118, 145, 147, 150, 153
  Afro Caribbean, 140, 143, 154
Freud, S., 11, 16, 167, 210
  'The Uncanny', 15, 65, 122, 180

G

gay relationships, 168
gender
  boundaries, 178, 184
  identity, 113, 114
ghost
  ghostings, 6, 13, 14, 91, 92, 97, 101, 108, 110, 114, 117, 123, 133, 151, 207–33
  poltergeist, 98, 103, 224–6
ghost story
  children's, 219, 220
  domestic, 219
  women's, 3, 208, 211–13, 232

Gibert, S. & Gubar, S. *The Mad Woman in the Attic*, 10, 11, 21, 36, 126, 190
Gothic
  African American, 91, 94, 96, 109, 113, 114, 118
  Canadian, 63–90
  critique, 9, 44, 91, 108
  culture, 1, 3, 4, 12, 38, 39, 58, 59, 63, 79, 80, 89, 107, 117–19, 130, 137–40, 143, 147, 161, 169, 171, 172, 174, 179, 194, 204, 229, 237, 243
  diversity, 235–50
  domestic, 207–33
  eighteenth-century, 4, 27
  fantasy, 27, 48, 50, 86, 143, 154
  female, 7, 8, 11, 12, 88
  feminist, 9, 16, 40, 84, 96, 126, 133, 144, 153, 154, 243
  figures, 22, 28, 81, 138, 141, 155, 163, 179, 182, 190, 240
  film, 21
  geographical, 64
  high, 26, 34, 40, 54, 57
  horror, 14–17, 38, 41, 47, 53, 54, 56–8, 107, 109, 143, 177, 178, 183, 194, 213, 214, 229, 236–9
  lesbian, 4, 8, 9, 12, 169, 179–82, 240, 241
  locations, 20, 24, 67, 70, 147
  mindset, 235
  nineteenth-century, 77, 117, 194, 235, 242, 243
  postcolonial, 13, 19, 25, 28, 34, 80, 94, 117–19, 122–4, 130, 131, 133, 134, 136, 138, 143, 147, 153, 155, 236
  queer, 4, 8
  revival of, 4, 20, 208, 236
  romantic, 13, 74–7
  settings, 241
  southern, 170–2, 198
  traditional, 7, 9, 10, 12, 19, 20, 34–6, 39, 43, 69, 76, 78, 79, 88, 94, 211
  travel, 19
  tropes, 6, 20, 73, 106, 123, 196, 240
  twentieth-century, 24, 39, 72, 75, 89
  twenty-first-century, 19, 20, 24, 25, 39, 75, 89
  youth, 172
Gubar, S., 11
  The Mad Woman in the Attic, 10, 21, 36, 126, 190
guilt, 95, 102–5, 110, 112, 137, 150, 159, 162, 211, 220, 230, 233, 236

H
Harris, C.
  Sookie Stackhouse novels, 25, 195, 197, 198
  True Blood, 169, 197, 198
haunting
  cultural, 19, 28, 91–114, 117–31, 212
  domestic space, 131, 136, 208
  family, 95, 96, 98, 99, 101–4, 106
  female body, 7
  haunted house, 17, 19, 92, 93, 96, 103, 104, 136, 148, 150, 155, 227
  postcolonial, 64, 117–31, 136
heredity, 22, 106, 159, 194, 212, 216, 225
Hill, S.
  The Small Hand, 208, 220
  The Woman in Black, 21, 207, 208, 214–20, 233
history

African American, 93, 109, 110, 113, 114
colonial, 22, 28, 117, 120, 130
hidden, 13, 14, 23, 26, 27, 92, 94, 95, 99, 108, 110, 113, 114, 117, 118, 123, 126, 137, 150, 208, 211, 212, 219, 233, 242
imaginative, 118
imperial, 18, 130
memory, 86
postcolonial, 25
revisit, 18–27, 82, 239
rewrite, 117, 238
silenced, 92, 97, 133, 213, 214
Hitchcock, A., 21, 167, 213
Hoglund, J., 5, 235, 236
home, 9, 13–18, 24, 37, 45, 46, 67, 68, 72, 73, 76, 92, 95, 96, 99, 100, 103–8, 135, 148, 149, 151, 155, 159, 178, 182, 191, 192, 198, 200, 201, 203, 208, 211, 212, 216, 220, 222, 223, 226–8, 230, 231, 238, 244
Hopkinson, N.
  'The Glass Bottle Trick', 134, 135, 137, 145, 147, 155
  The New Moon's Arms, 22, 123, 137, 147, 193
  'Precious', 137, 144, 147
  Skin Folk, 22, 135, 144
horror, 1, 5–7, 9, 15–18, 20, 21, 24–7, 38, 41, 42, 44, 47, 50, 53, 54, 58, 73, 89, 91, 95, 96, 98–101, 105, 107, 109, 114, 122, 124, 143, 151, 154, 158, 162–4, 167, 169, 175, 179, 182, 183, 190, 207, 213–15, 217, 226, 229, 235–8
  domestic, 7, 58
houses, 13, 14, 27, 34, 39, 40, 42, 46, 50, 56, 66, 78, 85, 92, 93, 96–8, 101, 103, 104, 106, 125, 127, 128, 130, 134–7, 145, 147–51, 155, 174, 192, 193, 199, 202, 208, 211, 212, 215–18, 220–8, 230, 231, 233, 236, 241–4
hybridity, 151, 175, 196
hypocrisy, 21, 54, 58, 73, 143, 171, 239, 242

I
imperialism, 12, 18, 119, 126, 127, 130, 134, 138, 228, 235
incarceration, 14, 22, 23, 47, 55, 64, 65, 67, 69, 72, 73, 75, 81, 125, 137, 208, 211, 213, 222, 224, 226, 238
inheritance, 9, 12, 20, 61, 101, 125, 126, 158, 173, 175, 178, 191, 194, 197, 199, 212, 215, 216, 241–3
isolation, 64, 65, 68, 74, 149, 192, 215–17

J
James, H.
  The Turn of the Screw, 219, 225
Jancovich, M., 15, 177, 213
Joplin, S., 92, 109–13
Jordan, N., 200, 201
jungle, 127–30

K
Korean War, 91, 105
Kostova, E.
  The Historian, 169, 238, 245
  The Swan Thieves, 239, 245–6
Kristeva, J.
  abjection, 11, 16, 53, 82, 122, 151, 161, 166, 199
  The Powers of Horror, 16, 122
  Strangers to Ourselves, 53, 122

L

land ownership, 158, 173
landscape, 17, 20, 64, 65, 68, 70, 92, 93, 96, 98, 106, 124, 126, 127, 212, 226, 229
language, 4, 14, 26, 34, 37, 51, 53, 54, 60, 70, 72, 82, 85–7, 89, 98–104, 110, 121, 135, 137, 139, 168, 177, 222, 236, 237, 239, 240
lesbian relationships, 3, 168, 176, 181, 184
Lim, C., 3, 28, 117, 127, 130
Little Red Riding Hood, 35, 50, 52
Long Hoeveler, D., 8, 10, 11

M

madness, 95, 101, 149, 211, 226, 242
magic, 54, 55, 58, 63, 79, 97, 103, 126, 128, 129, 142, 143, 147
  realism, 41, 61, 152
Mantel, H., 222, 224
  Eight Months on Ghazzah Street, 238, 243–5
marginalisation, 18, 23, 36, 53, 91, 104, 108, 118, 119, 134, 135, 138, 178, 211, 216, 226
mash-ups, 6, 189–91
memory, 86, 100–5, 112, 123, 124, 127, 140, 149, 221, 229
Meyer, S.
  Twilight, 9, 10, 25, 28, 35, 163, 169, 183, 187, 189, 191–5, 199, 200
mimicry, 136
mirroring, 48, 70, 81, 240
Moers, E., 7, 8
Mootoo, S., 3, 28, 136, 153, 154
  Cereus Blooms at Night, 135, 137, 148–50, 155, 182

Morrison, T.
  Beloved, 22, 25, 91–3, 95–7, 99–104, 112, 113, 212
  Home, 91, 93, 104–8
Mosse, K.
  Labyrinth, 25, 239
  The Winter Ghosts, 25, 208, 211, 213, 239
mothering, 3, 158, 174, 177, 188
Mulvey-Roberts, M., 1
Munford, R., 36
Munro, A., 63–9
  Dear Life, 66; 'To Reach Japan', 67
music, 4, 67, 92, 93, 109–13, 149, 150, 171
myth, 12, 17, 21, 22, 27, 33, 34, 36, 38–40, 42, 45–8, 52, 59, 60, 64, 69, 70, 74–7, 79, 80, 84, 85, 88, 89, 118, 129, 135, 136, 143, 144, 146, 147, 152–5, 160, 162, 163, 165, 166, 169, 175, 183, 184, 191, 194, 196, 197, 249
mythology, 38, 39, 44, 45, 150, 174

N

nation, 3, 5, 95, 141, 203, 237
neighbourliness, 25, 199, 204
neo-Victorianism, 14, 212, 238

O

obsession, 44, 65, 229, 232, 245, 246, 249–50
oppression, 6, 9, 14, 19, 25, 40, 47, 48, 57, 64, 65, 103, 113, 114, 117, 127, 130, 135, 136, 138, 139, 144, 208, 211, 221, 225, 233, 235, 237

Other, 5, 14, 16, 17, 53, 54, 60, 68, 84, 117, 122–6, 129, 130, 133, 135, 144, 158, 166, 167, 169, 172, 180, 183, 196, 222, 237, 238
Otherising, 17, 26, 54, 88, 122, 150, 217, 237
Oyeyemi, H., 3, 28, 136, 154
  Mr Fox, 135, 150–3, 155

P
Palmer, P., 240
  Lesbian Gothic, 8, 11, 179–82, 212
patriarchy, 23, 35, 36, 40, 50, 130, 134, 136, 154, 174, 176, 178, 190, 213
Perkins Gilman, C.
  The Yellow Wallpaper, 19, 22, 226
Poe, E.A., 38, 41, 42, 46, 47, 58–60, 208, 223
politics, 25, 59, 61, 88, 111, 119, 122, 142, 175, 212, 244
  left-wing, 40, 41
pornography, 4, 36, 38, 49, 51, 241
postcolonialism, 1
  places, 18, 28, 121, 131
postmodernism, 26, 238
power, 2, 3, 5, 7, 9, 14, 16, 20, 22, 23, 26–8, 34, 35, 38–42, 44, 46–9, 51, 52, 55–61, 64, 66, 67, 72, 73, 75, 76, 82, 83, 85–7, 93, 99, 104, 107, 109, 117, 119, 120, 122–6, 128, 130, 134–6, 138–45, 148, 152, 153, 155, 159–61, 163, 164, 167, 173–5, 177, 179, 180, 182, 184, 187, 188, 190, 191, 194–8, 202, 203, 207, 211, 213, 216, 222–4, 233, 239–42, 244, 246, 248, 249
Punter, D., 5, 18, 92, 94, 118, 122, 123, 143, 162, 183, 191, 212

The New Companion to the Gothic, 19
puppets, 42, 44–7, 50, 55, 166
purity, 9, 158

Q
queer theory, 1, 179, 180, 184

R
race, 26, 106, 117, 122, 131, 140, 143, 145, 196, 237
racism
  eugenics, 106
  scientific experimentation, 121, 238
rape, 35, 46, 47, 96, 99, 237
Rapunzel, 64, 74–7, 79, 82, 85, 89
recuperation, 18, 19, 96, 147, 155
religion, 20, 24, 26, 122, 140, 142, 154, 172, 192, 243, 248, 249
remythologising, 12, 133–55
repression, 9, 13, 21, 53, 54, 65, 97, 122, 130, 191, 211, 213, 224
return, 4, 6, 9, 19, 21, 39, 67, 73, 77, 79–88, 92, 94, 95, 99–104, 107, 108, 111, 118, 124, 126, 129, 133, 140, 142, 147, 150, 175–8, 181, 182, 187, 189, 190, 207–10, 212–14, 217, 220–2, 228–30, 232, 233, 242, 245
revenants, 4, 13, 93, 117–31, 207–9, 212, 232
revenge tragedy, 58
Rhys, J., 38
  Wide Sargasso Sea, 12–14, 28, 34, 117, 119, 124–6, 239
Rice, A.
  Interview with the Vampire, 165, 173, 176
  Queen of the Damned, 160, 174, 188

romance, 4, 5, 9, 12, 13, 24–7, 33–6, 39, 42, 45, 55, 66, 69, 70, 74, 75, 77–80, 83, 85–9, 124, 125, 160, 163–6, 168, 181, 183, 187, 189–95, 197, 198, 202, 204, 207, 211, 220, 222, 225, 226, 228, 238, 249

romantic fiction, 6, 13, 34, 37, 38, 50, 70, 75, 76, 79, 89, 163, 164, 169, 191–3, 195, 212, 224, 232, 249

romantic love, 7, 43, 77, 158, 160, 163–5, 195, 197, 229, 232, 241

Rushdie, S., 41, 93, 94, 114, 123

S

Saudi Arabia, 243, 244

Second World War, 18, 84, 110, 117, 213, 220, 222, 229, 233, 249

secrets, 4, 19, 23, 72, 82, 88, 104, 106, 125, 142, 146, 148, 150, 182, 192, 193, 207, 209–11, 214, 217, 222, 228, 229, 233, 239–41, 243, 248, 249

self
  identity, 19, 154
  performativity, 154, 169
  split selves, 14, 18, 63–90, 135, 222, 238
  twinning, 54, 82
  violence, 102
  worth, 21, 22, 81, 91, 95, 107, 124, 125, 136, 145, 154, 213

sexism, 25, 102, 108, 117

sexuality
  demonising, 165, 184, 220
  female, 9, 166
  radical, 158
  sado-masochism, 4

shape-shifting, 28, 86, 123, 127–9, 133–55, 190, 199

silencing, 9, 12, 14, 18, 21, 23, 72, 73, 76, 91, 99, 104, 113, 114, 118, 119, 122–4, 126, 134–6, 138, 140, 141, 143–5, 150, 190, 207–9, 212, 217, 233, 237–9

Singapore, 28, 117, 127, 229

slavery, 25, 91, 95, 96, 98–104, 107, 113, 120, 124, 137, 142–4, 148, 155, 173, 181, 212

small towns, 24, 63–6, 69, 192, 195, 198, 204

soucouyants, 118, 124, 138, 144, 149, 155

space, 7, 9, 11, 14, 15, 17–19, 22, 24–8, 36, 39, 43, 54, 55, 57, 65, 68–71, 76, 78, 83, 93, 95, 98, 100, 101, 104–6, 113, 117–19, 121, 124, 127, 130, 131, 135, 136, 140, 141, 147, 148, 150, 151, 168, 171–3, 175, 180, 203, 208, 209, 213, 214, 217, 218, 221, 222, 225, 229–33, 237–41, 244, 246–9

spirit, 13, 14, 18, 39, 117, 128–30, 143, 221, 226, 240, 242
  theft, 137–9, 142, 153, 154

spirituality, 143

Spivak, G.C., 131, 135
  subaltern, 139

Spooner, C., 4, 235, 236

Stoker, B., 19, 38, 159, 216
  Dracula, 6, 43, 159, 160, 162, 164, 177, 245

storytelling, 83, 86, 89, 110, 142, 147
  oral, 123, 129, 138, 140, 149

supernatural, 11, 20, 41, 63, 93, 96, 97, 101, 108, 120, 121, 123, 124, 128–30, 143, 151, 153, 157, 195, 209, 210, 212, 224, 228, 246, 249

superstition, 53, 97, 108, 128, 129, 249

survival, 35, 71–3, 194, 216
survivalist narratives, 63
swarms, 235

T

Tan, S., 28, 117
time, 3, 5, 9, 12, 17, 19–21, 26, 33, 36–9, 41, 44, 48, 50, 55, 57, 61, 63, 72, 73, 78, 80, 87, 92, 95, 97, 101, 106, 109, 111, 124, 126, 140, 152, 157, 162–4, 166, 169, 173–5, 184, 189, 192, 197, 200–2, 204, 207, 211, 212, 217, 219, 223, 225, 227, 230–3, 236, 237, 239, 240, 242, 244–7, 249
transgression, 8, 60, 118, 169, 178, 179, 181, 182, 184
trauma, 25, 92, 100, 102, 104, 124
Tuttle, L., 14, 17, 168, 182, 183, 203
twins, 82, 86, 87, 107, 151, 175, 176, 239
  twinning, 24, 48, 53, 54, 60, 76, 81, 83–5, 151, 240, 242, 250

U

urban narrative, 34

V

vampire
  blood, 20, 42, 158, 161, 162, 177, 179, 182, 184
  escape, 163–5
  family, 168, 176, 192–5
  female, 42, 159, 161, 162, 166, 167, 174, 176, 178, 179, 182, 183, 203
  history, 160–3, 173, 174, 204
  inheritance, 158, 173, 175, 178
  lesbian, 17, 28, 36, 160, 163, 168, 169, 179–82, 191

  radical women's fiction, 159, 160
  romance; romantic fiction, 163, 169; YA fiction, 28, 189–91, 204
  sexual energy, 168
  southern Gothic, 171, 198
  traditional, 159
victim role, 11, 42, 85, 202

W

Warner, M., 83, 87, 137, 138
Waters, S.
  Fingersmith, 23, 212, 239–43
  The Little Stranger, 208, 211, 220–8, 233
Weinstock, J., 108, 130, 131, 210
werecreatures, 6
werewolf, 3, 8, 35, 42, 52, 53, 61, 190, 195
whore, 35, 40, 44–6, 55, 58, 59, 166
wilderness, 64, 71, 75, 89
Winterson, J., 74, 181
  The Daylight Gate, 236, 239, 246–9
witchcraft, 144, 247, 248
witches, 89, 247
women
  artists, 245, 246
  roles, 7, 79
  social position, 219

Y

YA fiction, 28, 189–91, 204
Yahp, B., 3, 28, 117
  The Crocodile Fury, 18, 25, 126–30

Z

zombies, 4, 5, 24, 35, 117, 118, 124, 137–44, 147, 153–5, 157, 190, 191, 235
zombification, 137, 138, 140–2

The manufacturer's authorised representative in the EU is Springer Nature Customer Service Centre GmbH, Europaplatz 3, 69115 Heidelberg, Germany. If you have any concerns regarding our products, please contact ProductSafety@springernature.com

Printed and bound by CPI Group (UK) Ltd, Croydon, CR0 4YY
23/03/2026
02076460-0002